STUDY GUIDE

to accompany

ACCOUNTING PRINCIPLES

6th Edition

VOLUME I / CHAPTERS 1-13

JERRY J. WEYGANDT Ph.D., C.P.A.
Arthur Andersen Alumni Professor of Accounting
University of Wisconsin - Madison
Madison, Wisconsin

DONALD E. KIESO Ph.D., C.P.A.
KPMG Peat Marwick Emeritus Professor of Accountancy
Northern Illinois University
DeKalb, Illinois

PAUL D. KIMMEL Ph.D., C.P.A.
Associate Professor of Accounting
University of Wisconsin - Milwaukee
Milwaukee, Wisconsin

Prepared By
DOUGLAS W. KIESO

JOHN WILEY & SONS, INC.
New York • Chichester • Weinheim • Brisbane • Singapore • Toronto

COVER PHOTO   © James Bareham/Stone.

To order books or for customer service call 1-800-CALL-WILEY (225-5945).

ISBN 0-471-39164-6

Printed in the United States of America

10 9 8 7 6 5 4 3 2 1

Printed and bound by Courier Kendallville, Inc.

CONTENTS

Chapter   1   Accounting in Action

Chapter   2   The Recording Process

Chapter   3   Adjusting the Accounts

Chapter   4   Completion of the Accounting Cycle

Chapter   5   Accounting for Merchandising Operations

Chapter   6   Inventories

Chapter   7   Accounting Information Systems

Chapter   8   Internal Control and Cash

Chapter   9   Accounting for Receivables

Chapter 10   Plant Assets, Natural Resources, and Intangible Assets

Chapter 11   Current Liabilities and Payroll Accounting

Chapter 12   Accounting Principles

Chapter 13   Accounting for Partnerships

(more assets) ↑ my balance sheet.

↓   —sold more   = overstated → I have more than I do

COGS ↓ ↑   — less   understated →   less.

over inv.   inv. ↑
Income : ↓ under

Balance

To The Student

This study guide is provided as a significant aid in your study of *Accounting Principles, 6th Edition* by Jerry J. Weygandt, Donald E. Kieso and Paul D. Kimmel. The material in the study guide is designed to reinforce your understanding of the principles and procedures presented in the textbook. **It is important to recognize that the study guide is a supplement to and not a substitute for the textbook.**

This study guide contains the following materials for each chapter in the textbook: (a) study objectives, (b) a preview of the chapter, (c) a chapter review consisting of 20-30 key points, (d) a demonstration problem, (e) 20 true—false statements, (f) 20 multiple choice questions, (g) a matching question pertaining to key terms, (h) 2-3 exercises, and (i) blank working papers for use in class. At the end of each chapter, answers to questions and exercises are provided in order to enable you to assess your comprehension of the material. Included are solutions explaining why the answer is what it is, so you get immediate feedback as to what, how, or why.

You will realize the maximum benefit from this study guide by following the approach suggested below.
1. Carefully read and study the chapter material in the textbook.
2. Read the chapter preview and review material in the study guide.
3. Answer the questions and exercises for the chapter in the study guide and compare your answers with those provided in the study guide. For any incorrect answers, refer back to the textbook for a discussion of the point you have missed.
4. Solve the end-of-chapter materials in the textbook assigned by your instructor.

The study guide should be helpful in preparing for examinations. The chapter review points and other materials may be used to determine your recall of the information presented in specific chapters. When you have identified topics in need of further study, you can return to the textbook for a complete discussion of the subject matter.

I wish to acknowledge the valuable assistance of the proofer and technical advisor of this study guide, Professor John C. Borke of the University of Wisconsin-Platteville, and our compositor, Mary Ann Benson.

The following supplementary materials are also available from your bookstore, or the publisher, for use with this study guide and with the textbook, *Accounting Principles, 6th Edition.*

Douglas W. Kieso

Student Active Learning Aids

Accounting Principles, Interactive Learning Edition. The Interactive Learning Edition (ILE) combines the full text with interactive learning tools to accommodate the varied learning styles of today's students. This dynamic *ebook* features the text enhanced with a robust search engine, illustrations from the book, and additional media such as animations and videos. The ILE offers an active approach to learning that enables students to take detailed notes in the program's text, highlight important information as they read the text, consult a hypertext glossary by simply rolling over key words in the text, and much more.

Working Papers Volume I: Chapters 1-13 and Volume II: Chapters 14-27. Working papers are partially completed accounting forms for all end-of-chapter exercises, problems, and cases. A convenient resource for organizing and completing homework assignments, they demonstrate how to correctly set up solution formats and are directly tied to textbook assignments.

Electronic Working Papers. Available on a CD-ROM, these Excel-formatted, partially completed accounting forms can be used for all end-of-chapter exercises, problems, and cases.

Problem-Solving Survival Guide Volume I: Chapters 1-13 and Volume II: Chapters 14-27. The Problem-Solving Survival Guide tutorial is designed to improve students' success rates in solving accounting principles homework assignments and exam questions. The Problem-Solving Survival Guide also provides additional insight and tips on how to study accounting. Each chapter includes an overview of key chapter topics and a review of chapter study objectives; purpose statements for each question, case, or exercise and a direct link to study objectives; and tips to alert students to common pitfalls and misconceptions, as well as reminders of concepts and principles to help solve problems. A selection of multiple-choice exercises and cases representative of common exam questions or homework assignments enhances student proficiency, and detailed solutions and explanations assist students in the approach, setup, and completion of problems.

This new edition also features an online companion powered by *eGrade*. This online version includes all of the wonderful resources and tips for solving accounting principles homework assignments and exam questions as the print version, within an interactive Web environment. It provides students with immediate scoring and individualized feedback on their work. The *eGrade* **Student Learning Guide,** automatically bundled with the Problem-Solving Survival Guide, helps students in getting started with the *eGrade* Online Assessment System.

A Reader's Guide to *Accounting Principles:* **Strategies for Successful Reading and Supplemental Glossary.** In this guide, students will learn reading strategies that will increase their comprehension, help them remember information better, and make their experience reading *Accounting Principles* more successful.

Financial Accounting Tutor (FAcT) by *Dan and Rachana Gode.* FAcT is a self-paced CD-ROM tutorial designed to review financial accounting concepts. It uses simple examples that have been carefully crafted to introduce concepts gradually. Throughout, the program emphasizes the logic underlying the accounting process. FAcT uses interactive and graphical tools to enhance the learning process. Intuitive navigation and a powerful search mechanism allow students to easily follow the tutorial from start to finish or skip to the topics they want to complete. The discussions and examples are followed by brief, interactive problems that provide immediate feedback to the student. Built-in tools, such as an online financial calculator, help solve the problems. FAcT is available at a special discounted price when packaged with *Accounting Principles,* Sixth Edition.

Business Extra Web Site at http://www.wiley.com/college/businessextra. The Business Extra Web site gives you instant access to a wealth of current articles dealing with all aspects of financial and managerial accounting. The articles are organized by topic, and discussion questions follow each article. A password card, available for packaging with the text, provides students with registration and access instruction.

WSJ.com at http://www.wiley.com/college/wsjseries. WSJ.com contains articles and activities that put students at the cutting edge of today's business world. *The Journal* offers essential tools for business success, including resources for research and advice on career development. A password card, available for packaging with the text, grants students access to WSJ.com for four months, Business Extra, and a complimentary 10-week subscription to the print edition of *The Wall Street Journal.*

Practice Sets. These practice sets expose students to a real-world simulation of maintaining a complete set of accounting records for a business. Students will find that practice sets reinforce the concepts and procedures learned in each chapter of the textbook, as they integrate the business events, accounting concepts, procedures, and records covered within *Accounting Principles.* Designed to meet a variety of skill levels, particular study objectives, and to be used at various places throughout the course, these practice sets reinforce key concepts and allow students to apply the information they have learned. They are an excellent way to see how these concepts are all brought together to generate the accounting information that is essential in assessing the financial position and operating results of a company. Each of these practice sets has been revised to reflect changes in the text and to modify account information.

Campus Cycle Shop. Business papers add a realistic dimension by enabling students to handle documents—checks, invoices, receipts—that they would encounter in a small company. As students complete this sole proprietorship case, they will become familiar with analyzing and journalizing business transactions. Students can use this practice set after Chapter 4: Completion of the Accounting Cycle.

Heritage Home Furniture. This narrative listing of sole proprietorship business transactions includes the necessary journals, ledgers, and forms for completing the simulation. It reviews and reinforces the transactions emphasized in the Campus Cycle Shop Practice Set, while introducing more complex transactions generally covered in a financial accounting course. Recommended for use after Chapter 11: Current Liabilities and Payroll Accounting.

University Bookstore, Inc. This corporate practice set exposes students to a real-world simulation of maintaining a complete set of accounting records for a business, integrating business events, accounting concepts, and records. Students work with a bond transaction, so the set is recommended for use after Chapter 16: Long-Term Liabilities. The end of the set recommends that students complete a financial analysis of the company, so students will need to complete Chapter 19: Financial Statement Analysis before completing the set. The practice set can be worked either independently or in a group; the set includes few transactions and thus reinforces students' analytical skills and creative problem solving.

Custom Party Associates. This new practice set focuses on a company that specializes in party planning and supplies, which offers students elements of both service and merchandising examples. Custom Party Associates is uniquely set up as both a proprietorship and a corporation offering flexibility in teaching approaches. It requires a bank reconciliation, contains both accounts payable and accounts receivable subsidiary ledgers, focuses on the perpetual inventory system, includes two employee pay periods with the requirement that employee records are maintained, and involves property, plant, and equipment transactions.

General Ledger Software. Available in a Windows stand-alone (Windows 95 or higher) or a network version, the General Ledger Software program allows students to solve selected end-of-chapter text problems, identified by an icon in the margin of the text. GLS is ideal for instructors who want their students to gain a hands-on feel for a computerized accounting system. It has the ability to modify the existing chart of accounts and beginning balances. This increases the instructor's flexibility in assigning alternate problems within the textbook. For the Sixth Edition, GLS has been modified to make it even more user-friendly and easy to use, with little start-up time. A Student Data Disk allows work to be completed both at home and on the school's network.

The General Ledger Software is used to computerize the four practice sets. Students can purchase the GLS alone, packaged with the text, or packaged with one of the practice sets.

Peachtree Complete Accounting Problems and Software. The Peachtree Complete Accounting Problems are selected problems denoted by the Peachtree icon that can be solved using *Peachtree Complete Accounting to Accompany Accounting Principles, Sixth Edition.* A separate student workbook that includes the newly released software is available. The software also allows students to complete the Campus Cycle Shop, Heritage Home Furniture, University Bookstore, Inc., and Custom Party Associates practice sets on a computer. An Instructor's Manual with suggestions for integrating Peachtree into the classroom is also available.

Solving Accounting Principles Problems Using Excel and Lotus 1-2-3. These electronic spreadsheet templates (available in either Excel or Lotus) allow students to complete selected end-of-chapter exercises and problems, identified by the spreadsheet icon in the margin of the text. The manuals, which include the disks, guide students step-by-step from an introduction to computers and Excel or Lotus, to completing preprogrammed spreadsheets, to designing their own spreadsheets. Prepared for students with a range of experience in spreadsheet applications, these templates and tutorials help students develop and hone their computer skills and expose them to software packages often used in real-world business environments.

MAKING YOUR STUDIES PAY

Suggestions for Effective Studying

WANT TO GET BETTER GRADES? READ ON!

Good students have a system to their studying. In the next few pages, we'll give you some guidelines that we think can help improve the way you study—not only for this course, but for any course.

> How to Use a Textbook
> How to Read a Chapter
> How to Take Notes
> How to Use a Study Guide (In General)
> How to Take Tests

If you need more specific help, we suggest that you go to your teacher or your school's career counseling center.

And Good Luck in your College Career!

HOW TO USE A TEXTBOOK

Textbooks often include material designed to help you study. It's worth your while to flip through a textbook to look for:

- **The Preface.** If an author has a point of view, you can find it here, along with notes on how the book is meant to be used.
- **The Table of Contents.** Reading the table of contents will tell you how the book will be developed.
- **Glossary.** The most important terms and ideas for you to know will be in a glossary, either at the end of each chapter or at the end of the book.
- **Appendixes.** Found either after certain chapters or at the end of the book, appendixes contain such things as:
    - * More difficult material.
    - * Statistics or data, such as the present value of money. You may be able to use such data for most of the book.
    - * Answers to selected problems.

HOW TO READ A CHAPTER

Before Class: Skim

Unless you're told to know a chapter completely by class time, it's a good idea just to skim an assigned chapter before class.

- Become familiar with the main ideas so that the lecture will make more sense to you.
- As you skim, ask yourself if you know something about the material.
- Keep any questions you have in mind for the lecture, so that you can listen for the answers.

In particular, look for:

- **Study Objectives.** These are what your teacher will expect you to know—and be able to do or explain—by the end of the chapter.
- **Chapter-Opening Vignettes.** This section is linked to the chapter topic, and gives a general idea of how accounting relates to your day-to-day life.
- **Boldface or *Italic* Terms.** These usually indicate important terms, people, or concepts.
- **Headings.** Read the major headings to see how the material fits together. How are the ideas related to each other? Do they make sense to you?
- **Summary.** A good summary will repeat the general ideas and conclusions of the chapter, but it won't explain them. It usually matches up well with the study objectives and chapter introduction.

After Class: Read

After skimming the chapter and attending class, you are ready to read a chapter in detail.

- **Check for Meaning.** Ask yourself as you read if you understand what the material means.
- **Don't Skip the Tables, Figures, and Illustrations.** These items usually contain important material and may all be on the test.
- **Read the "Sidebars."** These are features that are set off, usually in boxes or by color backgrounds. They can include real-world examples, amusing anecdotes, or additional material. The amusing anecdotes may not come up on the test, but the other kinds of sidebars probably will!
- **Review.** Read the chapter again, especially the parts you had trouble with. Review the study objectives, chapter introduction, summary, and key terms to make sure you understand them.
- **End-of-Chapter Questions.** Do all the end-of-chapter questions, exercises, or problems. For the exercises and problems, make sure you have memorized what equations or rules apply, and why. (Do any practice problems that your teacher gives you, too. These will not only help you but show you what kind of questions might be on the test.) If you have trouble with any:
    * Review the part of the chapter that applies.
    * Look for similar questions.
    * Ask yourself what concept or equation should be applied.
- **Use the Study Guide.** After you've read and studied the chapter, use the study guide to find out what areas you need to review in the text.

HOW TO TAKE NOTES

The ability to take notes is a skill, and one you can learn. First, a few practical tips:

- Arrive in class on time, and don't leave early. You might miss important notes or assignments.

- If you don't have assigned seating, sit close enough to your teachers so that you can hear them and read any overhead transparencies.
- If you don't understand, ask questions.
- Do not read the text during the class—you'll just miss what your teacher is saying. Listen, take notes, and ask questions.

Now, for the note-taking itself:

- **Listen for Ideas.** Don't try to write everything the instructor says. Instead, listen and take notes on the main ideas and any supporting ideas and examples. Make sure you include names, dates, and any new terms. In accounting classes, take down all rules, equations, and theories, as well as every step in a demonstration problem.
- **Use Outlines.** Organize these ideas into outlines. You don't have to use a numbered outline if you don't want to—just indent supporting ideas under the main ones.
- **Abbreviate.** Use any abbreviations you can, whether they're standard or ones you make up. (Leaving out vowels can sometimes help: Lvg out vwls can ...).
- **Leave Space.** Leave enough space in your notes so that you can add material if the instructor goes back to the topic or expands a problem later.

HOW TO USE A STUDY GUIDE (IN GENERAL)

A study guide is devoted to the particular text you're using. It can't replace the text; it can only point out places where you need more work. To make a study guide most effective:

- Use it only after you've read the chapter and reviewed your class notes.
- Ask yourself whether you really understand the chapter's main points and how they relate to one another.
- Go back and reread the sections of your text that deal with any questions you missed. Chances are that a text will not ask the same questions the study guide does, but the text can help you understand the material better. If that doesn't work, ask your instructor for help.
- Remember that a study guide can't cover any extra material that your teacher may have lectured on.

HOW TO TAKE TESTS

Studying for a Test

Studying for tests is a process that starts with the first class and ends only with the last test. All through the semester, it helps to:

- Follow the advice we gave about reading a chapter and taking notes.
- Review your notes:
  - * immediately after class. Clear up anything you can't read and circle important items while the lecture is still fresh in your mind.
  - * periodically during the semester.
  - * before the test.
- Use any videotapes that may be made of lectures.

Now you're ready to do your final studying for this test. Leave as much time as you need, and study under the conditions that are right for you—alone or with a study group, in the library or another quiet place. It helps to schedule several short study sessions rather than to study all at one time.

- **Reread the chapter(s).** Follow this system:
    * Most importantly, look for things you don't remember or don't understand.
    * Reinforce your understanding of the main ideas by rereading the introduction, study objectives, and summary.
    * Read the chapter from beginning to end.
- **Redo the Problems.** Make sure you know what equation to apply or procedure to follow in different situations, and why.
- **Test Yourself.** Cover up something you've just read and try to explain it to yourself—or to a friend—out loud.
- **Use Memory Tricks.** If you're having trouble remembering something—such as a formula or items in a list—try associating it with something you know or by making a sentence up out of the first letters.
- **Study with a Group.** Group study is helpful after you've done all your own studying. You can help each other with problems and by quizzing each other, but you'll probably just distract each other if you try to review a chapter together.

(A Note About Cramming), DON'T! If you cram, you will probably only remember what you've read for a short time, and you'll have trouble knowing how to generalize from it. If you must cram, however, concentrate on the main ideas, the supporting ideas, main headings, boldface or italicized terms, and study objectives.)

Taking a Test

After the following general tips, we'll give you specifics on objective, problem, and essay tests.

- **Before the Test**
    * Make sure you eat well and get enough sleep before the exam.
    * If the instructor doesn't say in class what material will be covered or what kind of test —objective or essay—will be used, ask.
    * Arrive early enough to get settled.
    * Bring everything you need—bluebook, pens, pencils, eraser, calculator—even the book if it's an open-book test.
- **As You Begin the Test**
    * Read the instructions completely. Do you have to answer all of the questions? Do certain questions apply to others? Do some questions count more than others? Will incorrect answers be counted against you?
    * Schedule your time. How many questions are there? Try to estimate how much time to leave for each section. If sections are timed, so that you won't be able to go back to them, make sure you leave enough time to decide which questions to answer.
- **Taking the Test**
    * Read each question completely as you come to it.
    * Answer the easier questions first and go back to the harder ones.
    * Concentrate on questions that count more.
    * Jot notes or equations in the margin if you think it will help.
    * Review your answers, and don't change an answer unless you're sure you were wrong.

- **Dealing with Panic**
  * Relax. Do this by tightening and relaxing one muscle at a time.
  * Breathe deeply.
  * If you don't know an answer, go on to the next question.

Now for some notes on objective, problem, and essay tests.

- **Objective Tests.** (Multiple choice, true/false, matching, and completion or fill-in-the blank.)
  * Watch out for words like always/all/every/none/never. Very few things are always or never so. If a question or answer includes words like these, be careful.
  * If you are uncertain about a multiple choice answer, try to narrow the choices down to two and make an educated guess.
  * Match up the easy ones first on a matching test. This will leave less possibilities for the harder ones.
  * Make educated guesses for other objective questions. (If you really have no idea and wrong answers count against you, leave it blank.)
- **Problem Test**
  * If a formula or equation is quite long, jot it down before you work on the problem.
  * Remember that math builds one equation on another. If you can't remember a particular equation, try to remember how it was derived.
  * Don't despair if you can't figure out what a question is calling for. Try to figure out part of it first. If that doesn't work, go on; sometimes a later question will jog your memory.
  * If your teacher grants some credit for partially correct problems, make sure you include the way you worked out a problem.
  * Make sure you know how your calculator works before the test. And make sure you know how to do the problems without it. Sometimes you can hit the wrong button, so it helps to have a rough idea of what your calculator should be giving you.
- **Essay Test**
  * Write a rough outline before you begin. If that takes too much time, just jot down all the things you want to say and then number them. Organize what you're going to say into groups of related ideas.
  * Make a point in each paragraph. The easiest way is to make the point in the paragraph's first sentence and then to back it up.
  * Use examples, facts, and dates to back up what you are saying.
  * Do what the question asks for. If it asks you to compare two things, for example, go back and forth between them; don't spend all your time on one of them.
  * If you have no idea what to write, try to remember ideas that the teacher stressed in class and see if you can relate the question to those ideas.
  * Check your time. If you're running out, write your last points down without explaining them; your teacher will at least know what you are going to explain.

Chapter 1

ACCOUNTING IN ACTION

The Navigator ✓
- Scan Study Objectives ☐
- Read Preview ☐
- Read Chapter Review ☐
- Work Demonstration Problem ☐
- Answer True-False Statements ☐
- Answer Multiple-Choice Questions ☐
- Match Terms and Definitions ☐
- Solve Exercises ☐

CHAPTER STUDY OBJECTIVES

After studying this chapter, you should be able to:
1. Explain what accounting is.
2. Identify the users and uses of accounting.
3. Understand why ethics is a fundamental business concept.
4. Explain the meaning of generally accepted accounting principles and the cost principle.
5. Explain the meaning of the monetary unit assumption and the economic entity assumption.
6. State the basic accounting equation and explain the meaning of assets, liabilities, and owner's equity.
7. Analyze the effect of business transactions on the basic accounting equation.
8. Understand what the four financial statements are and how they are prepared.

PREVIEW OF CHAPTER 1

The purpose of this chapter is to show you that accounting is the system used to provide useful financial information. The content and organization of the chapter are as follows:

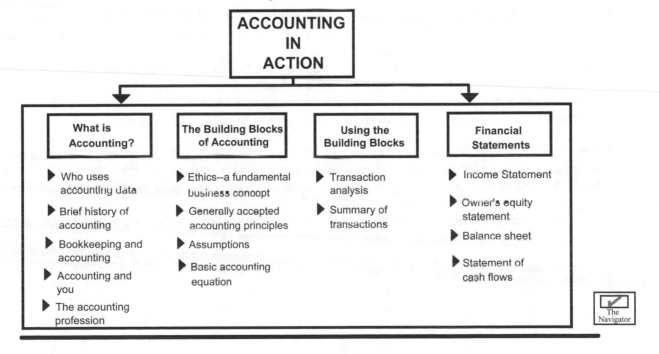

CHAPTER REVIEW

Accounting Defined

1. (S.O. 1) **Accounting** is an information system that identifies, records, and communicates the economic events of an organization to interested users.
    a. The first part of the process, **identifying,** involves selecting those events that are considered evidence of economic activity relevant to a particular business organization.
    b. **Recording** is the keeping of a chronological diary of events, measured in dollars and cents.
    c. **Communication** occurs through the preparation and distribution of accounting reports.

2. The accounting process consists of:

    Identification → Recording → Communication.

3. (S.O. 2) **Internal users** of accounting information are managers who plan, organize, and run a business. These include marketing managers, production supervisors, finance directors, and company officers.

4. **External users** include investors, creditors, taxing authorities, regulatory agencies, labor unions, customers, and economic planners outside the business.

5. **Bookkeeping** is not the same as accounting. Bookkeeping involves only the recording of economic events, while accounting also includes identification, recording, and communication. Bookkeeping is therefore only a part of accounting.

6. Accounting is also divided into financial versus managerial accounting. **Financial accounting** is the field of accounting that provides economic and financial information for investors, creditors, and other external users. **Managerial accounting** provides economic and financial information for managers and other internal users.

7. **Public accounting** provides the services of auditing, taxation, and management consulting.
    a. **Auditing** involves examining financial statements of companies and expressing an opinion as to the fairness of their presentation.
    b. **Taxation** includes providing tax advice and planning, preparing tax returns, and representing clients before governmental agencies.
    c. **Management consulting** involves providing advice for managers on such matters as financial planning and control and the development of computer systems.

8. **Private accounting** involves the employment of accountants within individual companies. The private accountant performs a wide variety of duties such as general accounting, cost accounting, budgeting, accounting information systems, tax accounting, and internal auditing.

9. **Not-for-profit accounting** pertains to not-for-profit organizations such as governmental units, foundations, hospitals, colleges, universities, and charities.

Ethics

10. (S.O. 3) The standards of conduct by which one's actions are judged as right or wrong, honest or dishonest, fair or not fair, are **ethics.** The process of analyzing ethical issues is to recognize that an ethical issue is involved, identify and analyze the principle elements in the situation (especially those harmed or benefited), identify the alternatives and weigh the impact of each alternative on the various stakeholders, then select the most ethical alternative.

GAAP and the Cost Principle

11. (S.O. 4) **Generally accepted accounting principles** (GAAP) are a common set of guidelines (standards) used by accountants in reporting economic events.

12. The **Securities and Exchange Commission** (SEC) is an independent regulatory agency of the United States government. The SEC has the legal power to enforce the form and content of financial statements of corporations that wish to sell securities to the public.

13. The **Financial Accounting Standards Board** (FASB) has been granted the power from the SEC to establish GAAP.

14. Under the **cost principle** assets should be recorded at their cost. Cost is the value exchanged at the time something is acquired.

The Monetary Unit and Economic Entity Assumptions

15. (S.O. 5) The accounting profession has developed certain assumptions that serve as guidelines for the accounting process.
    a. The **monetary unit assumption** requires that only transaction data that can be expressed in terms of money be included in the accounting records.
    b. The **economic entity assumption** requires that the activities of the entity be kept separate and distinct from (1) the activities of its owner and (2) all other economic entities.

Business Enterprises

16. Three types of business enterprises are proprietorships, partnerships, and corporations.
    a. A **proprietorship** is a business owned by one person.
    b. A **partnership** is a business owned by two or more persons associated as partners.
    c. A **corporation** is a business organized as a separate legal entity under state corporation law with ownership divided into transferable shares of stock.

The Accounting Equation

17. (S.O. 6) The **basic accounting equation** is:

$$\text{Assets} = \text{Liabilities} + \text{Owner's Equity.}$$

The accounting equation applies to all economic entities regardless of size, nature of business, or form of business organization.

18. The key components of the basic accounting equation are:
    a. **Assets** are resources owned by a business
    b. **Liabilities** are claims against assets.
    c. **Owner's equity** is the claims of owners.

19. In proprietorships, there are four **subdivisions** of owner's equity:
    a. **Investments by Owner** are the assets put in the business by the owner.
    b. **Revenues** are the gross increases in owner's equity resulting from business activities entered into for the purpose of earning income.
    c. **Drawings** are withdrawals of cash or other assets by the owner for personal use.
    d. **Expenses** are the cost of assets consumed or services used in the process of earning revenue.

20. Revenues and expenses determine if a **net income** or **net loss** occurs as follows:
    a. Revenues > Expenses = Net Income.
    b. Revenues < Expenses = Net Loss.

Transactions

21. (S.O. 7) **Transactions** are the economic events of the enterprise recorded. Transactions may be identified as either external or internal transactions.

22. Each transaction must be analyzed in terms of its effect on the components of the basic accounting equation. The analysis must also identify the specific items affected and the amount of the change in each item.

23. Each transaction has a dual effect on the equation. For example, if an individual asset is increased, there must be a corresponding:
    a. decrease in another asset, or
    b. increase in a specific liability, or
    c. increase in owner's equity.

24. A tabular summary may be prepared to show the cumulative effect of transactions on the basic accounting equation. The summary demonstrates that:
    a. Each transaction must be analyzed in terms of its effect on (1) the three components of the equation and (2) specific types of items within each component.
    b. The two sides of the equation must always be equal.
    c. The causes of each change in the owner's claim on assets must be indicated in the owners' equity column.

The Financial Statements

25. (S.O. 8) Four financial statements are prepared from the summarized accounting data:
    a. An **income statement** presents the revenues and expenses and resulting net income (or net loss) for a specific period of time.
    b. An **owner's equity statement** summarizes the changes in owner's equity for a specific period of time.
    c. A **balance sheet** reports the assets, liabilities, and owner's equity at a specific date.
    d. A **statement of cash flows** summarizes information concerning the cash inflows (receipts) and outflows (payments) for a specific period of time.

26. The financial statements are **interrelated** because:
    a. Net income (or net loss) shown on the income statement is added (subtracted) to (from) the beginning balance of owner's capital in the owner's equity statement.
    b. Owner's capital at the end of the reporting period shown in the owner's equity statement is reported in the balance sheet.
    c. The amount of cash shown on the balance sheet is reported on the statement of cash flows.

27. In the income statement, revenues are listed first, followed by expenses. Then below expenses is the resulting amount of net income (or net loss).

28. The owner's equity statement shows the owner's capital at the beginning of the period, additional investments, net income (or net loss) for the period, owner's drawings, and the owner's capital at the end of the period.

29. In the balance sheet, assets are listed at the top, followed by liabilities and owner's equity.

30. The statement of cash flows reports the sources, uses, and net increase or decrease in cash. Chapter 18 will examine in detail how the statement is prepared.

The Navigator

DEMONSTRATION PROBLEM (S.O. 8)

Prepare a balance sheet for the Morse Soybean Company on December 31, 2002, using the following list of accounts.

Accounts Payable	$4,000
Accounts Receivable	3,500
Cash	6,000
Equipment	7,000
Notes Payable	6,500
J. J. Morse, Capital	?
Salaries Payable	2,000
Supplies	2,500
Automobile	4,500

SOLUTION TO DEMONSTRATION PROBLEM

MORSE SOYBEAN COMPANY
Balance Sheet
December 31, 2002

Assets

Cash	$ 6,000
Accounts Receivable	3,500
Supplies	2,500
Equipment	7,000
Automobile	4,500
Total assets	$23,500

Liabilities and Owner's Equity

Liabilities

Accounts Payable	$ 4,000
Salaries Payable	2,000
Notes Payable	6,500
Total liabilities	12,500

Owner's Equity

J.J. Morse, Capital	11,000
Total liabilities and owner's equity	$23,500

REVIEW QUESTIONS AND EXERCISES

TRUE—FALSE

Indicate whether each of the following is true (T) or false (F) in the space provided.

_____ 1. (S.O. 1) Accounting provides the principal medium for communicating financial information of a business to all interested parties.

_____ 2. (S.O. 1) Identifying is the process of keeping a chronological diary of events measured in dollars and cents.

_____ 3. (S.O. 2) Customers and regulatory agencies are external users of accounting data.

_____ 4. (S.O. 2) Bookkeeping and accounting mean the same thing.

_____ 5. (S.O. 2) Management consulting includes examining the financial statements of companies and expressing an opinion as to the fairness of their presentation.

_____ 6. (S.O. 2) Cost accounting is part of private accounting.

_____ 7. (S.O. 3) Accountants do not have to worry about issues of ethics.

_____ 8. (S.O. 4) GAAP is an acronym for "governmentally approved accounting principles."

_____ 9. (S.O. 4) At the time an asset is acquired, cost and value should be the same.

_____ 10. (S.O. 5) Under the economic entity assumption, it is assumed that the company is separate and distinct from its owner(s).

_____ 11. (S.O. 5) The monetary unit assumption requires that all dollar amounts be rounded to the nearest dollar.

_____ 12. (S.O. 5) Proprietors are liable only for the amount they have invested in the business.

_____ 13. (S.O. 6) An asset may be intangible and represent nonphysical rights.

_____ 14. (S.O. 6) Owner's equity is the ownership claim on total assets.

_____ 15. (S.O. 6) Expenses are the decreases in owner's equity that result from operating the business.

_____ 16. (S.O. 6) If a liability increases, there would either have to be an equal decrease in another liability, a decrease in an asset, or an increase in owner's equity for the basic accounting equation to remain equal.

_____ 17. (S.O. 6) The basic accounting equation is in balance when the creditor and ownership claims against the business equal the assets.

_____ 18. (S.O. 7) External transactions involve economic events between the company and some other enterprise or party.

_____ 19. (S.O. 8) In the owner's equity statement, revenues are listed first, followed by expenses, and net income (or net loss).

_____ 20. (S.O. 8) The balance sheet is often referred to as the operating statement.

The Navigator

MULTIPLE CHOICE

Circle the letter that best answers each of the following statements.

1. (S.O. 1) Which of the following is not part of the accounting process?
    a. Recording.
    b. Identifying.
    c. Financial decision making.
    d. Communicating.

2. (S.O. 2) Internal users of accounting data include:
    a. economic planners.
    b. investors.
    c. customers.
    d. company officers.

3. (S.O. 2) Auditing is:
    a. the examination of financial statements by a CPA in order to express an opinion on their fairness.
    b. a part of accounting that involves only recording of economic events.
    c. an area of accounting that involves such activities as cost accounting, budgeting, and accounting information systems.
    d. conducted by the Securities and Exchange Commission to ensure that registered financial statements are presented fairly.

4. (S.O. 2) The private accountant might be involved in:
    a. internal auditing.
    b. tax accounting.
    c. designing accounting and total information systems.
    d. all of the above.

5. (S.O. 4)   The organization(s) primarily responsible for establishing generally accepted accounting principles is(are) the:

	FASB	**SEC**
a.	no	no
b.	yes	no
c.	no	yes
d.	yes	yes

6. (S.O. 5) The monetary unit assumption:
    a. provides that the unit of measure fluctuates over time.
    b. is unimportant in applying the cost principle.
    c. is only used for financial statements of banks.
    d. requires that only transaction data capable of being expressed in terms of money be included in the accounting records of the economic entity.

7. (S.O. 5) A proprietorship is a business:
    a. owned by one person.
    b. owned by two or more persons.
    c. organized as a separate legal entity under state corporation law.
    d. owned by a governmental agency.

8. (S.O. 6) A net loss will result during a time period when:
    a. assets exceed liabilities.
    b. assets exceed owner's equity.
    c. expenses exceed revenues.
    d. revenues exceed expenses.

9. (S.O. 7)   A company might carry on many activities that do not represent business transactions such as:
    a. borrowing money from the bank.
    b. placing an order for merchandise with a supplier.
    c. using office supplies.
    d. paying wages.

10. (S.O. 7) An example of an internal transaction is the:
    a. payment of monthly rent.
    b. hiring of employees.
    c. sale of pizza puffs to customers.
    d. use of paper, pens, and other office supplies.

11. (S.O. 7) The Relias Uptown Grill receives a bill of $400 from the Erml Advertising Agency. The owner, John Relias, is postponing payment of the bill until a later date. The effect on specific items in the basic accounting equation is:
    a. a decrease in Cash and an increase in Accounts Payable.
    b. a decrease in Cash and an increase in R. Relias, Capital.
    c. an increase in Accounts Payable and a decrease in R. Relias, Capital.
    d. a decrease in Accounts Payable and an increase in R. Relias, Capital.

12.   (S.O. 7)   The Nagy Company is owned by Lynn Nagy.   Jim James, the inventory clerk, indicates that $975 of supplies were used during the period.   The effect on specific items in the basic accounting equation is:
   a.   a decrease in Supplies and a decrease in L. Nagy, Capital.
   b.   a decrease in Cash and an increase in Supplies.
   c.   an increase in Accounts Payable and a decrease in Supplies.
   d.   an increase in Supplies Payable and a decrease in L. Nagy, Capital.

13.   (S.O. 7)   Doug Foerch, owner of the Poindexter Company, withdraws $500 in cash for personal use.   The effect on the specific items in the basic accounting equation is:
   a.   an increase in Accounts Receivable and a decrease in Doug Foerch, Capital.
   b.   an increase in Salary Expense and a decrease in Cash.
   c.   an increase in Doug Foerch, Capital and a decrease in Cash.
   d.   a decrease in Doug Foerch, Capital and a decrease in Cash.

14.   (S.O. 7)   Jeanie Company purchases $600 of equipment from Mundelein Inc. for cash.   The effect on the components of the basic accounting equation of Jeanie Company is:
   a.   an increase in assets and liabilities.
   b.   a decrease in assets and liabilities.
   c.   no change in total assets.
   d.   an increase in assets and a decrease in liabilities.

15.   (S.O. 7)   The Vessely Company has the following at September 17:   assets $13,000; liabilities $8,000; and owner's equity $5,000.   On September 18, Vessely Company receives $500 of cash revenue and earns $200 of revenue on credit.   Mike McEllen, the only worker that day, works 8 hours and receives a wage rate of $10 per hour.   Mike will not get paid until September 21.   No other transactions occur during the day.   At the end of September 18 the new totals are:

	Assets	Liabilities	Owner's Equity
a.	$13,500	$7,880	$5,620
b.	$12,500	$8,000	$4,500
c.	$13,500	$8,120	$5,380
d.	$13,700	$8,080	$5,620

16.   (S.O. 7)   As of December 31, 2002, Morley Company has liabilities of $5,000 and owner's equity of $7,000.   It received revenues of $23,000 during the year ended December 31, 2002.   What are the assets for Morley Company as of December 31, 2002?
   a. $2,000.
   b. $12,000.
   c. $25,000.
   d. $35,000.

17. (S.O. 8) The statement that reports revenues and expenses is the:
   a. income statement.
   b. balance sheet.
   c. owner's equity statement.
   d. statement of cash flows.

18. (S.O. 8) Morreale Beaver Company buys a $12,000 van on credit. The transaction will affect the:
   a. income statement only.
   b. balance sheet only.
   c. income statement and owner's equity statement only.
   d. income statement, owner's equity statement, and balance sheet.

19. (S.O. 8) The financial statement that summarizes the financial position of a company is the:
   a. income statement.
   b. balance sheet.
   c. operating statement.
   d. owner's equity statement.

20. (S.O. 8) Which of the following would not appear on the DeFlippo Company's balance sheet?
   a. Accounts receivable.
   b. M. DeFlippo, Capital.
   c. Utilities expense.
   d. Wages payable.

The Navigator

MATCHING

Match each term with its definition by writing the appropriate letter in the space provided.

Terms

_____ 1. Revenues.

_____ 2. Owner's equity statement.

_____ 3. Owner's equity.

_____ 4. Balance sheet.

_____ 5. Monetary unit assumption.

_____ 6. Income statement.

_____ 7. Economic entity assumption.

_____ 8. Assets.

_____ 9. Accounting.

_____ 10. Transactions.

_____ 11. Expenses.

_____ 12. Liabilities.

_____ 13. Generally accepted accounting principles.

_____ 14. Cost principle.

Definitions

a. Economic events of the enterprise recorded by accountants.

b. An information system that identifies, records, and communicates the economic information of an organization to interested users.

c. The gross increases in owner's equity resulting from business activities entered into for the purpose of earning income.

d. Resources owned by the business.

e. Reports the assets, liabilities, and owner's equity of a business enterprise at a specific date.

f. Presents the revenues and expenses and resulting net income of a company for a specific period of time.

g. Cost of assets consumed or services used in the process of earning revenue.

h. Creditorship claims on total assets.

i. Ownership claim on total assets.

j. Summarizes the changes in owner's equity for a specific period of time.

k. Requires that only transaction data capable of being expressed in terms of money be included in the accounting records.

l. States that the activities of the entity be kept separate and distinct from the activities of its owner and all other economic activities.

m. States that assets should be recorded at their cost.

n. A common set of rules, procedures, and guidelines (standards) used by accountants in reporting economic events.

EXERCISES

EX. 1-1   (S.O. 8) Some amounts are omitted in each of the following financial statements.

INCOME STATEMENT
For the Year Ended December 31, 2002

	Tang Company	June Company	Diana Company
Revenues	$48,000	$ (D)	$82,000
Expenses	(A)	52,000	64,000

OWNER'S EQUITY STATEMENT
For the Year Ended December 31, 2002

	Tang Company	June Company	Diana Company
Capital, January 1	$ (B)	$45,000	$50,000
Net income	15,000	24,000	(G)
Drawings	12,000	(E)	17,000
Capital, December 31	33,000	54,000	(H)

BALANCE SHEET
December 31, 2002

	Tang Company	June Company	Diana Company
Total assets	$75,000	$ (F)	$91,000
Total liabilities	(C)	56,000	40,000
Total owner's equity	33,000	54,000	(I)

Instructions
Determine the missing amounts and indicate your answers in the spaces provided below.

(A)_____   (D)_____   (G)_____

(B)_____   (E)_____   (H)_____

(C)_____   (F)_____   (I)_____

EX. 1-2 (S.O. 7) On March 1, Laurie Fiala opened the Wahoo Beauty Salon. During the first
month, the following selected transactions occurred.
1.   Deposited $5,000 cash in the City Bank in the name of the business.
2.   Paid $800 cash for beauty supplies.
3.   Purchased equipment at a cost of $12,000, paying $2,000 in cash and the balance on
account.
4.   Received $1,200 cash for services rendered.
5.   Paid $500 cash as a salary to a beautician.
6.   Withdrew $400 cash for personal expenses.

Instructions
Prepare a tabular summary of the transactions, using the following column headings: Cash
Supplies, Equipment, Accounts Payable, and L. Fiala, Capital.

Trans-action	Cash	+	Supplies	+	Equipment	=	Accounts Payable	+	L. Fiala Capital
1.									
2.									
3.									
4.									
5.									
6.									

EX. 1-3 (S.O. 8) Selected financial statement items for the Geimer Company are presented
below.
a.   Accounts payable
b.   Service revenue
c.   B. Geimer, Capital, 1/1/02
d.   Rent expense
e.   Supplies
f.   Advertising expense

g.   B. Geimer, Capital 12/31/02
h.   Land
i.   Utilities expense
j.   B. Geimer, Drawing
k.   Net income
l.   Salaries payable

Instructions
Indicate the financial statement(s) in which each item should be reported using the following code
number(s):   (1) Income statement for the year ended December 31, 2002, (2) Owner's equity
statement for the year ended December 31, 2002, and (3) Balance sheet, December 31, 2002.
(**Note:** More than one code number may be required for an item.)

Item	Financial Statement	Item	Financial Statement	Item	Financial Statement
a.		e.		i.	
b.		f.		j.	
c.		g.		k.	
d.		h.		l.	

The Navigator

SOLUTIONS TO REVIEW QUESTIONS AND EXERCISES

TRUE-FALSE

1. (T)
2. (F) **Identifying** is selecting those events that are considered evidence of economic activity relevant to a particular business organization. The process of keeping a chronological diary of events measured in dollars and cents is **recording**.
3. (T)
4. (F) **Bookkeeping** involves only the recording of economic events, while **accounting** encompasses the process of identification and communication along with recording.
5. (F) **Management consulting** provides advice to managers of companies concerning various aspects of a company's operations. Examining the financial statements of companies and expressing an opinion as to the fairness of their presentation is the field of auditing.
6. (T)
7. (F) Accountants have to worry about ethical issues just like everybody else.
8. (F) GAAP is an acronym for "generally accepted accounting principles."
9. (T)
10. (T)
11. (F) The monetary unit assumption requires that only transaction data capable of being expressed in terms of money be included in the accounting records of the economic entity.
12. (F) A proprietor has unlimited liability for the debts incurred by the business. The stockholders of a corporation have limited liability.
13. (T)
14. (T)
15. (T)
16. (F) If a liability increases, there would have to be an equal decrease in another liability, an increase in an asset, or a decrease in owner's equity for the basic accounting equation to remain equal.
17. (T)
18. (T)
19. (F) It is the income statement which has revenues listed first, followed by expenses, and then net income (or net loss).
20. (F) The income statement is often referred to as the operating statement.

MULTIPLE CHOICE

1. (c) **Accounting** is defined as an information system that identifies, records, and communicates economic events of an organization to interested users. The interested users then make the financial decisions based on the information provided.

2. (d) Economic planners, customers, and investors are **external** users of accounting data. Company officers, managers, and employees are **internal** users of accounting data.

3. (a) Auditing is the examination of financial statements by a CPA in order to express an opinion on their fairness. Choice (b) is incorrect because a part of accounting that involves only recording of economic events is bookkeeping. Choice (c) is incorrect because an area of accounting that involves such activities as cost accounting, budgeting, and accounting information systems is private (or managerial) accounting. Choice (d) is incorrect because CPAs perform the actual auditing function, not the SEC.

4. (d) The private accountant might be involved in internal auditing, tax accounting, and designing accounting and information systems, as well as cost accounting, budgeting, and general accounting.

5. (d) Both the FASB and the SEC are the organizations primarily responsible for establishing generally accepted accounting principles.

6. (d) The **monetary unit assumption** requires that only transaction data capable of being expressed in terms of money be included in the accounting records of the economic entity. Choice (a) is false because this assumption assumes that the unit of measure remains sufficiently constant over time. Choice (b) is incorrect because the monetary unit assumption is vital in applying the cost principle. Choice (c) is incorrect because this assumption is used for all types of entities.

7. (a) A proprietorship is a business owned by only one person.

8. (c) A net loss will result when expenses exceed revenues. Net income results when revenues exceed expenses.

9. (b) Borrowing from the bank, using office supplies, and paying wages are all recognized as business transactions, thus causing (a), (c), and (d) to be incorrect. Placing an order for merchandise with a supplier is not recognized as a business transaction even though it may lead to a business transaction when the merchandise is delivered by the supplier.

10. (d) The use of office supplies is an internal transaction because an outside party is not involved when the office supplies are used. Answers (a) and (c) involve outside parties and are, therefore, external transactions. Choice (b) is not a transaction.

11. (c) The transaction is an advertising expense that has been incurred on account. Thus, the transaction decreases owner's equity J. Relias, Capital and increases the liability Accounts Payable.

12. (a) The using up of supplies is an expense. Thus, the transaction decreases the asset Supplies and decreases owner's equity L. Nagy, Capital.

13.   (d)   The withdrawal of cash by an owner for personal use reduces owner's capital. Drawings do not result in either an expense or a receivable.

14.   (c)   The transaction results in an increase in the asset Equipment and an equal decrease in the asset Cash. Therefore, there is no change in total assets.

15.   (d)   The effects of the transactions are summarized below.

	Assets	**=**	**Liabilities**	**+**	**Owner's Equity**
September 17	$13,000		$8,000		$5,000
Cash revenue	+ 500				+ 500
Credit revenue	+ 200				+ 200
Wage expense			+ 80		- 80
September 18	$13,700	=	$8,080	+	$5,620

16.   (b)   The balance sheet equation states: Assets = Liabilities + Owner's Equity. Thus, if liabilities are $5,000 and owner's equity is $7,000, assets must equal $12,000. The revenue is already in the December 31, 2002 totals and therefore is not relevant to the answer.

17.   (a)   The income statement reports revenues and expenses as well as net income. The balance sheet reports assets, liabilities, and owner's equity. The owner's equity statement explains the changes in owner's equity. The statement of cash flows shows cash flows.

18.   (b)   The transaction represents an increase in assets of $12,000 and an increase in liabilities of an equal amount. The transaction causes a change in balance sheet items only.

19.   (b)   The balance sheet reports the financial position of a company. The income statement (or operating statement) presents revenues and expenses. The owner's equity statement explains the changes in owner's equity that have occurred during a given period of time.

20.   (c)   Accounts receivable, M. DeFlippo, Capital, and Wages payable are all balance sheet items causing (a), (b), and (d) to be incorrect. Utilities expense is an item that is reported on the income statement.

MATCHING

1.	c.	6.	f.	11.	g.
2.	j.	7.	l.	12.	h.
3.	i.	8.	d.	13.	n.
4.	e.	9.	b.	14.	m.
5.	k.	10.	a.		

EXERCISES

EX. 1-1
(A) $33,000 (Revenues $48,000 - net income $15,000).
(B) $30,000 (Capital, 12/31 $33,000 + drawings $12,000 - net income $15,000).
(C) $42,000 (Assets $75,000 - owner's equity $33,000)
(D) $76,000 (Expenses $52,000 + net income $24,000)
(E) $15,000 (Capital, 1/1/ $45,000 + net income $24,000 - capital, 12/31 $54,000)
(F) $110,000 (Liabilities $56,000 + owner's equity $54,000)
(G) $18,000 (Revenues $82,000 - expenses $64,000)
(H) $51,000 (Capital, 1/1/ $50,000 + net income $18,000 - drawings $17,000)
(I) $51,000 (Assets $91,000 - liabilities $40,000).

EX. 1-2

Trans-action	Cash	+	Supplies	+	Equipment	=	Accounts Payable	+	L. Fiala Capital	
1.	+$5,000								+$5,000	Investment
2.	- 800		+$800							
	4,200	+	800			=			5,000	
3.	- 2,000				+$12,000		+$10,000			
	2,200	+	800	+	12,000	=	10,000	+	5,000	
4.	+ 1,200								+ 1,200	Service Revenue
	3,400	+	800	+	12,000	=	10,000	+	6,200	
5.	- 500								- 500	Salary Expense
	2,900	+	800	+	12,000	=	10,000	+	5,700	
6.	- 400								- 400	Drawings
	$2,500	+	$800	+	$12,000	=	$10,000	+	$5,300	

EX. 1-3

Item	Financial Statement	Item	Financial Statement	Item	Financial Statement
a.	3	e.	3	i.	1
b.	1	f.	1	j.	2
c.	2	g.	2, 3	k.	1, 2
d.	1	h.	3	l.	3

1																	1
2																	2
3																	3
4																	4
5																	5
6																	6
7																	7
8																	8
9																	9
10																	10
11																	11
12																	12
13																	13
14																	14
15																	15
16																	16
17																	17
18																	18
19																	19
20																	20
21																	21
22																	22
23																	23
24																	24
25																	25
26																	26
27																	27
28																	28
29																	29
30																	30
31																	31
32																	32
33																	33
34																	34
35																	35
36																	36
37																	37
38																	38
39																	39
40																	40

Chapter 2

*T*HE RECORDING PROCESS

The Navigator	✓
■ Scan Study Objectives	☐
■ Read Preview	☐
■ Read Chapter Review	☐
■ Work Demonstration Problem	☐
■ Answer True-False Statements	☐
■ Answer Multiple-Choice Questions	☐
■ Match Terms and Definitions	☐
■ Solve Exercises	☐

CHAPTER STUDY OBJECTIVES

After studying this chapter, you should be able to:
1. Explain what an account is and how it helps in the recording process.
2. Define debits and credits and explain how they are used to record business transactions.
3. Identify the basic steps in the recording process.
4. Explain what a journal is and how it helps in the recording process.
5. Explain what a ledger is and how it helps in the recording process.
6. Explain what posting is and how it helps in the recording process.
7. Prepare a trial balance and explain its purposes.

PREVIEW OF CHAPTER 2

In Chapter 1, we analyzed business transactions in terms of the accounting equation and presented the cumulative effects of these transactions in tabular form. In this chapter, we will introduce and illustrate the basic procedures and records that are used. The organization and content of the chapter are as follows:

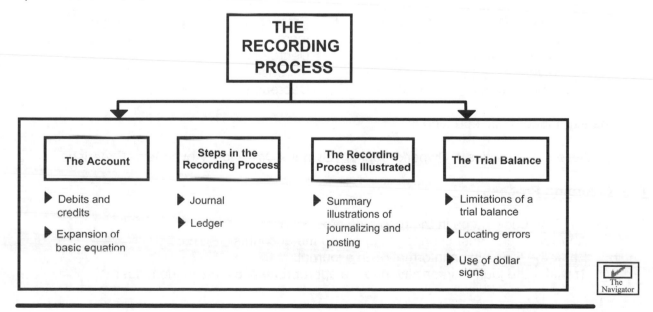

CHAPTER REVIEW

The Account

1. (S.O. 1) An **account** is an individual accounting record of increases and decreases in a specific asset, liability, or owner's equity item.

2. In its simplest form, an account consists of (a) the title of the account, (b) a left or debit side, and (c) a right or credit side. The alignment of these parts resembles the letter T, and therefore the account form is called a **T-account.**

Debits and Credits

3. (S.O. 2) The terms **debit** and **credit** mean left and right, respectively.
    a. The act of entering an amount on the left side of an account is called **debiting** the account and making an entry on the right side is **crediting** the account.
    b. When the debit amounts exceed the credits, an account has a **debit balance;** when the reverse is true, the account has a **credit balance.**

4. In a **double-entry** system, equal debits and credits are made in the accounts for each transaction. Thus, the total debits will always equal the total credits.

5. The effects of debits and credits on **assets** and **liabilities** and the normal balances are:

Accounts	Debits	Credits	Normal Balance
Assets	Increase	Decrease	Debit
Liabilities	Decrease	Increase	Credit

6. Accounts are kept for each of the four subdivisions of owner's equity: capital, drawings, revenues, and expenses.

7. The effects of debits and credits on the owner's equity accounts and the normal balances are:

Accounts	Debits	Credits	Normal Balance
Owner's Capital	Decrease	Increase	Credit
Owner's Drawing	Increase	Decrease	Debit
Revenues	Decrease	Increase	Credit
Expenses	Increase	Decrease	Debit

8. The expanded basic equation is:

Assets = Liabilities + Owner's Capital - Owner's Drawing + Revenues - Expenses

The Recording Process

9. (S.O. 3) The basic steps in the recording process are:
    a. Analyze each transaction for its effect on the accounts.
    b. Enter the transaction information in a journal.
    c. Transfer the journal information to the appropriate accounts in the ledger.

The Journal

10. (S.O. 4) Transactions are initially recorded in a journal.
    a. A journal is referred to as a book of original entry.
    b. A **general journal** is the most basic form of journal.

11. The journal makes several significant contributions to the recording process:
    a. It discloses in one place the complete effect of a transaction.
    b. It provides a chronological record of transactions.
    c. It helps to prevent or locate errors because the debit and credit amounts for each entry can be readily compared.

12. Entering transaction data in the journal is known as **journalizing.** When three or more accounts are required in one journal entry, the entry is known as a **compound entry.**

The Ledger

13. (S.O. 5) The ledger is the entire group of accounts maintained by a company. It keeps in one place all the information about changes in account balances and it is a source of useful data for management.

14. The **standard form of a ledger account** has three money columns and the balance in the account is determined after each transaction.

15. (S.O. 6) **Posting** is the procedure of transferring journal entries to the ledger accounts. The following steps are used in posting:
    a. In the ledger, enter in the appropriate columns of the account(s) debited the date, journal page, and debit amount.
    b. In the reference column of the journal, write the account number to which the debit amount was posted.
    c. Perform the same steps in a. and b. for the credit amount.

The Chart of Accounts

16. A **chart of accounts** is a listing of the accounts and the account numbers which identify their location in the ledger. The numbering system usually starts with the balance sheet accounts and follows with the income statement accounts.

The Basic Steps

17. The basic steps in the recording process are illustrated as follows:

    Transaction   On September 4, Fesmire Inc. pays $3,000 cash to a creditor in full payment of the balance due.

    Basic analysis   The liability Accounts Payable is decreased $3,000, and the asset Cash is decreased $3,000.

    Debit-credit analysis   Debits decrease liabilities: debit Accounts Payable $3,000.
    Credits decrease assets: credit Cash $3,000.

Journal entry	Sept. 4	Accounts Payable	26	3,000	
		Cash	1		3,000
		(Paid creditor in full)			

Posting

Cash	1		Accounts Payable	26
Sept. 4 3,000		Sept. 4 3,000		

The Trial Balance

18.   (S.O. 7) A **trial balance** is a list of accounts and their balances at a given time. The primary purpose of the trial balance is to prove the mathematical equality of the debits and credits after posting.

19.   A trial balance does not prove that all transactions have been recorded or that the ledger is correct because the trial balance may still balance when
   a.   a transaction is not journalized.
   b.   a correct journal entry is not posted.
   c.   an entry is posted twice.
   d.   incorrect accounts are used in journalizing or posting.
   e.   offsetting errors are made in recording the amount of a transaction.

The Navigator

DEMONSTRATION PROBLEM (S.O. 4)

Doug Stein, the owner of Accounting Consultants, had the following transactions occur during the month of January 2002:

Jan. 2 D. Stein begins business with a cash investment of $222,000.

6 Buys an office building for $120,000.

10 Hires Pat Delaney as his assistant.

14 Performs consulting services for Simon, Inc. worth $10,000 but is not paid by J. Simon at this time.

17 Purchases supplies for $500 on credit.

20 Receives a $10,000 check from Simon, Inc.

28 Pays Pat Delaney $2,000 in wages for January.

30 Withdraws $3,000 for personal use to vacation in Jamaica.

Instructions
Prepare the general journal entries for each of these transactions.

SOLUTION TO DEMONSTRATION PROBLEM

	General Journal		J1
Date	**Account Title**	**Debit**	**Credit**
2002			
Jan. 2	Cash	222,000	
	D. Stein, Capital		222,000
	(Investment in business)		
6	Office Building	120,000	
	Cash		120,000
	(Purchase of office building)		
14	Accounts Receivable	10,000	
	Consulting Revenue		10,000
	(Services performed for Simon, Inc.)		
17	Supplies	500	
	Accounts Payable		500
	(Purchase of supplies)		
20	Cash	10,000	
	Accounts Receivable		10,000
28	Wages Expense	2,000	
	Cash		2,000
	(Paid Delaney for his wages earned)		
30	D. Stein, Drawing	3,000	
	Cash		3,000
	(Withdraw cash for personal use)		

REVIEW QUESTIONS AND EXERCISES

TRUE—FALSE

Indicate whether each of the following is true (T) or false (F) in the space provided.

_____ 1. (S.O. 2) In accounting the terms debit and credit mean left and right respectively.

_____ 2. (S.O. 2) The double-entry system is a logical method for recording transactions and results in equal debits and credits for each transaction.

_____ 3. (S.O. 2) Revenue accounts normally have debit balances.

_____ 4. (S.O. 2) The normal balance of an expense is a credit.

_____ 5. (S.O. 2) The expanded basic equation is: Assets = Liabilities + Owner's Capital + Owner's Drawing + Revenues - Expenses.

_____ 6. (S.O. 4) The journal discloses in one place the complete effect of a transaction.

_____ 7. (S.O. 4) The journal provides a chronological record of transactions.

_____ 8. (S.O. 4) Separate journal entries are made for each transaction.

_____ 9. (S.O. 4) The general journal is the most basic form of journal.

_____ 10. (S.O. 5) A ledger is a list of accounts and their balances at a given time.

_____ 11. (S.O. 5) The ledger is merely a bookkeeping device and therefore does not provide much useful data for management.

_____ 12. (S.O. 5) The standard form of ledger account has three money columns for debit, credit, and balance.

_____ 13. (S.O. 6) Posting is the procedure of entering transaction data in the general journal.

_____ 14. (S.O. 6) The chart of accounts is a listing of the accounts and the account numbers which identify their location in the ledger.

_____ 15. (S.O. 6) The purpose of transaction analysis is to first identify the type of account involved and then identify whether a debit or a credit to the account is required.

_____ 16. (S.O. 7) A trial balance lists the accounts and their location in the ledger.

_____ 17. (S.O. 7) The primary purpose of a trial balance is to prove the mathematical equality of the debits and credits after posting.

_____ 18. (S.O. 7) A trial balance is usually prepared daily.

_____ 19. (S.O. 7) A trial balance does not prove that all transactions have been recorded or that the ledger is correct.

_____ 20. (S.O. 7) The trial balance will not balance when incorrect account titles are used in journalizing or posting.

MULTIPLE CHOICE

Circle the letter that best answers each of the following statements.

1. (S.O. 1) An account is an individual accounting record of increases and decreases in specific:
   a. liabilities.
   b. assets.
   c. expenses.
   d. assets, liabilities, and owner's equity items.

2. (S.O. 2) Credits:
   a. increase both assets and liabilities.
   b. decrease both assets and liabilities.
   c. increase assets and decrease liabilities.
   d. decrease assets and increase liabilities.

3. (S.O. 2) An account which is increased by a credit is:
   a. an asset account.
   b. a liability account.
   c. a drawing account.
   d. an expense account.

4. (S.O. 2) Which of the following rules is **incorrect?**
   a. Credits decrease the drawing account.
   b. Debits increase the capital account.
   c. Credits increase revenue accounts.
   d. Debits decrease liability accounts.

5. (S.O. 2) An account which is increased by a debit is a:
   a. liability account.
   b. drawing account.
   c. capital account.
   d. revenue account.

6. (S.O. 2) An account which is increased by a credit is a(n):
   a. drawing account.
   b. revenue account.
   c. expense account.
   d. asset account.

7. (S.O. 3) Which of the following is the correct sequence of steps in the recording process?
   a. Posting, journalizing, analyzing.
   b. Journalizing, analyzing, posting.
   c. Analyzing, posting, journalizing.
   d. Analyzing, journalizing, posting.

8. (S.O. 4) The column in the general journal which is not used during journalizing is the:
   a. date column.
   b. account title column.
   c. reference column.
   d. debit amount column.

9. (S.O. 4) Which of the following is a **false** statement?
   a. The account Revenue from Fees is increased with a credit.
   b. A compound entry is when two or more accounts are required in one journal entry.
   c. Owner's drawing is increased by a debit entry.
   d. All transactions are initially recorded in a journal.

10. (S.O. 4) Which of the following is not considered a significant contribution of the journal to the recording process?
    a. The journal provides a chronological record of all transactions.
    b. The journal provides a means of accumulating in one place all the information about changes in account balances.
    c. The journal discloses in one place the complete effect of a transaction.
    d. The journal helps prevent or locate errors since the debit and credit amounts for each entry can be readily compared.

11. (S.O. 4) McClory Company purchases equipment for $900 and supplies for $300 from Rudnicky Co. for $1,200 cash. The entry for this transaction will include a:
    a. debit to Equipment $900 and a debit to Supplies Expense $300 for Rudnicky.
    b. credit to Cash for Rudnicky.
    c. credit to Accounts Payable for McClory.
    d. debit to Equipment $900 and a debit to Supplies $300 for McClory.

12. (S.O. 4) Laventhol Company sells $300 of equipment to Reiner Company on credit. Reiner will enter the transaction in the journal with a:
    a. debit to Accounts Receivable and a credit to Sales.
    b. debit to Accounts Receivable and a credit to Equipment.
    c. credit to Accounts Payable and a debit to Equipment.
    d. credit to Cash and a debit to Equipment.

13. (S.O. 4) Szykowny Co. buys a machine from Scott Company paying half in cash and putting the balance on account. The journal entry for this transaction by Szykowny will include a:
    a. credit to Accounts Payable and a credit to Cash.
    b. credit to Notes Payable and a credit to Cash.
    c. debit to Supplies and a credit to Cash.
    d. debit to Machinery and a credit to Notes Payable.

14. (S.O. 4) Hrubec Company pays $900 cash for a one-year insurance policy on July 1, 2002. The policy will expire on June 30, 2000. The entry on July 1, 2002 is:
    a. Debit Insurance Expense $900; credit Cash $900.
    b. Debit Prepaid Insurance $900; credit Cash $900.
    c. Debit Insurance Expense $900; credit Accounts Payable $900.
    d. Debit Prepaid Insurance $900; credit Accounts Payable $900.

15. (S.O. 4) Kevin Walsh withdraws $300 cash from his business for personal use. The entry for this transaction will include a debit of $300 to:
    a. Kevin Walsh, Drawing.
    b. Kevin Walsh, Capital.
    c. Owner's Salary Expense.
    d. Salaries Expense.

16. (S.O. 4) Vicki Wagner Dance Studio bills a client for dancing lessons earned during the past week. The journal entry will include a credit to:
    a. Vicki Wagner, Capital.
    b. Unearned Dance Fees.
    c. Dance Fees Earned.
    d. Accounts Receivable.

17. (S.O. 4) Golden Pork Company receives $400 from a customer on October 15 in payment of balance due for services billed on October 1. The entry by Golden Pork Company will include a credit of $400 to:
    a. Notes Receivable.
    b. Service Revenue.
    c. Accounts Receivable.
    d. Unearned Service Revenue.

18. (S.O. 4) On October 3, Mike Baker, a carpenter, received a cash payment for services previously billed to a client. Mike paid his telephone bill, and he also bought equipment on credit. For the three transactions, at least one of the entries will include a:
    a. credit to Mike Baker, Capital.
    b. credit to Notes Payable.
    c. debit to Accounts Receivable.
    d. credit to Accounts Payable.

19. (S.O. 6) The chart of accounts is a:
    a. list of accounts and their balances at a given time.
    b. device used to prove the mathematical accuracy of the ledger.
    c. listing of the accounts and the account numbers which identify their location in the ledger.
    d. required step in the recording process.

20. (S.O. 7) A trial balance will not balance if:
    a. a journal entry is posted twice.
    b. a wrong amount is used in journalizing.
    c. incorrect account titles are used in journalizing.
    d. a journal entry is only partially posted.

The
Navigator

MATCHING

Match each term with its definition by writing the appropriate letter in the space provided.

Terms

_____ 1. Account.

_____ 2. T-account.

_____ 3. Posting.

_____ 4. Trial balance.

_____ 5. Debit.

_____ 6. Credit.

_____ 7. Chart of accounts.

_____ 8. Ledger.

_____ 9. Journalizing.

_____ 10. Journal.

_____ 11. Double-entry system.

Definitions

a. The entire group of accounts maintained by a company.

b. A list of accounts and the account numbers which identify their location in the ledger.

c. An individual accounting record of increases and decreases in a specific asset, liability, or owner's equity item.

d. The right side of an account.

e. The left side of an account.

f. The procedure of transferring journal entries to the ledger accounts.

g. A system that records the dual effect of each transaction in appropriate accounts.

h. The form of an account with a title and a left or debit side and a right or credit side.

i. An accounting record in which transactions are initially recorded in chronological order.

j. The procedure of entering transaction data in the journal.

k. A list of accounts and their balances at a given time.

EXERCISES

EX. 2-1   (S.O. 3) The ledger of the Gilbert Company includes the accounts listed below.

Instructions
For each account indicate (a) whether it is an asset, liability, or owner's equity item, and (b) its normal balance. Use the following format for your answer. The account, Cash, is given as an example.

Account	(a) Type of Account	(b) Normal Balance
Cash	Asset	Debit
Equipment		
Wages Payable		
Telephone Expense		
Notes Receivable		
Commissions Earned		
J. Gilbert, Capital		
Rent Expense		
Supplies		
J. Gilbert, Drawing		
Fees Earned		

EX. 2-2 (S.O. 4) Aristotle Onassis, the ship captain and President of Onassis Ship Lines, had the following transactions occur during the month of February 2002:

Feb. 3 Paid $1,000 to Jean Paul Getty, the ship's bursar, for wages earned in January. These wages were expensed in January.

7 Received $35,000 cash from J.P. Morgan for a cruise taken by J.P. and his family last month. This revenue was properly recorded last month.

11 Purchased equipment from J.D. Rockefeller for $50,000 on credit.

20 Received $25,000 cash from Andrew Carnegie upon completion of a cruise taken by Andrew and his friends this month. (Credit Cruise Revenues)

26 Received $31,000 cash from H.L. Hunt for a cruise to be taken next month.

28 Paid $20,000 cash to Vanderbilt Insurance Company for a 6-month insurance policy to expire August 31.

Instructions
Journalize the transactions in the journal provided below.

	General Journal		J1
Date	Account Title	Debit	Credit
2002			

General Journal			J1
Date	Account Title	Debit	Credit

EX. 2-3 (S.O. 7) The ledger for the Thorson Advertising Agency at October 31, 2002 contains the data listed below. Assume that all accounts have normal balances.

Accounts Receivable	$ 9,500
Accounts Payable	7,500
P. Thorson, Capital	10,500
P. Thorson, Drawing	500
Cash	?
Commissions Earned	7,000
Supplies	600
Rent Expense	900
Salaries Expense	4,060
Unearned Fees	1,200

Instructions
Prepare a trial balance at October 31, 2002.

THORSON ADVERTISING AGENCY
Trial Balance
October 31, 2002

	Debit	Credit

SOLUTIONS TO REVIEW QUESTIONS AND EXERCISES

TRUE-FALSE

1. (T)
2. (T)
3. (F) The normal balance of a revenue account is a credit.
4. (F) The normal balance of an expense account is a debit.
5. (F) The expanded basic equation is:
   Assets = Liabilities + Owner's Capital - Owner's Drawing + Revenues - Expenses.
6. (T)
7. (T)
8. (T)
9. (T)
10. (F) The ledger is the entire group of accounts maintained by a company. It keeps in one place all the information about changes in account balances. The trial balance is a list of accounts and their balances at a given time.
11. (F) The ledger gives management useful information about account balances; e.g., Accounts Receivable can be inspected to ascertain the amounts due from customers.
12. (T)
13. (F) Posting is the procedure of transferring journal entries to the ledger accounts. Journalizing is the procedure of entering transaction data in a journal.
14. (T)
15. (T)
16. (F) The trial balance is a list of accounts and their balances at a given time. The chart of accounts is a listing of accounts and their location in the ledger.
17. (T)
18. (F) A trial balance can be prepared at any point in time, but is customarily prepared at the end of an accounting period.
19. (T)
20. (F) One of the limitations of the trial balance is that it will still balance when incorrect account titles are used in journalizing or posting.

MULTIPLE CHOICE

1. (d) An account is an individual accounting record of increases and decreases in specific asset, liability, and owner's equity items.

2. (d) Credits decrease assets and increase liabilities.

3. (b) An asset account (a), a drawing account (c), and an expense account (d) are all accounts that have normal balances of debits; thus, they are increased by debits.

4. (b) Debits decrease the capital account because the capital account has a credit balance as its normal balance. Choices (a), (c), and (d) are all correct rules concerning increasing or decreasing accounts.

5. (b) A liability account (a), a capital account (c), and a revenue account (d) are all accounts that have a normal balance as a credit; therefore, they are increased by a

credit. The drawing account has a normal balance as a debit and will increase with a debit.

6. (b) A drawing account (a), an expense account (c), and an asset account (d) are all accounts that have a normal balance of debits. A revenue account has a normal balance as a credit and will increase with a credit entry.

7. (d) The basic steps in the recording process are:
   1. Analyze each transaction.
   2. Enter the transaction information in a journal (journalizing).
   3. Post the journal information to the ledger.

8. (c) The date column (a), the account title column (b), and the debit amount column (d) are all used during the journalizing procedure. The reference column is used later when the journal entries are posted to the ledger.

9. (b) A compound entry is when three or more accounts are required in one journal entry. Choices (a), (c), and (d) are all true statements.

10. (b) The ledger—not the journal—provides a means of accumulating in one place all the information about changes in account balances. Answers (a), (c), and (d) are all considered significant contributions by the journal to the recording process.

11. (d) McClory Company will make the following entry:

Equipment	900	
Supplies	300	
Cash		1,200

12. (c) Reiner Co. will make the following entry:

Equipment	300	
Accounts Payable		300

13. (a) The journal entry for this transaction is as follows:

Equipment	XXXX	
Accounts Payable		XXXX
Cash		XXXX

14. (b) The one-year policy will benefit more than one accounting period. Therefore, the entry is:

Prepaid Insurance	900	
Cash		900

15. (a) The withdrawal of cash and other assets by an owner for personal use is a drawing and not an expense. The entry is:

Kevin Walsh, Drawing	300	
Cash		300

16. (c) The transaction is recorded in the journal as follows:

Accounts Receivable	XXXX	
Dance Fees Earned		XXXX

17. (c) The entry by Golden Pork Company is:

Cash...	400	
Accounts Receivable		400

18. (d) The three transactions are recorded in the journal as follows:

Cash...	XXXX	
Accounts Receivable		XXXX
Telephone Expense..	XXXX	
Cash		XXXX
Equipment..	XXXX	
Accounts Payable..		XXXX

19. (c) The chart of accounts is a listing of the accounts and the account numbers which identify their location in the ledger. Both answers (a) and (b) are characteristics of a trial balance. Answer (d) is incorrect because a chart of accounts is not required.

20. (d) The trial balance may still balance even when a journal entry is posted twice (a), a wrong amount is used in journalizing (b), and incorrect account titles are used (c). A journal entry that is only partially posted means that a debit or credit posting is omitted; thus, the trial balance will not balance.

MATCHING

1.	c	5.	e	9.	j		
2.	h	6.	d	10.	i		
3.	f	7.	b	11.	g		
4.	k	8.	a				

EXERCISES

EX. 2-1

Account	(a) Type of Account	(b) Normal Balance
Equipment	Asset	Debit
Wages Payable	Liability	Credit
Telephone Expense	Owner's equity	Debit
Notes Receivable	Asset	Debit
Commissions Earned	Owner's equity	Credit
J. Gilbert, Capital	Owner's equity	Credit
Rent Expense	Owner's equity	Debit
Supplies	Asset	Debit
J. Gilbert, Drawing	Owner's equity	Debit
Fees Earned	Owner's equity	Credit

EX. 2-2

General Journal			J1
Date	**Account Title**	**Debit**	**Credit**
2002			
Feb. 3	Wages Payable	1,000	
	Cash		1,000
	(Paid wages earned in January)		
7	Cash	35,000	
	Accounts Receivable		35,000
	(Received payment from J.P. Morgan)		
11	Equipment	50,000	
	Accounts Payable		50,000
	(Purchased equipment from J.D.		
	Rockefeller on account)		
20	Cash	25,000	
	Cruise Revenues		25,000
26	Cash	31,000	
	Unearned Cruise Revenue		31,000
	(Received advance from H.L. Hunt		
	for future cruise)		
28	Prepaid Insurance	20,000	
	Cash		20,000
	(Paid 6-month policy; effective		
	date March 1)		

EX. 2-3

THORSON ADVERTISING AGENCY
Trial Balance
October 31, 2002

	Debit	Credit
Cash	$10,640	
Accounts Receivable	9,500	
Supplies	600	
Accounts Payable		$ 7,500
Unearned Fees		1,200
P. Thorson, Capital		10,500
P. Thorson, Drawing	500	
Commissions Earned		7,000
Rent Expense	900	
Salaries Expense	4,060	
	$26,200	$26,200

1																				1
2																				2
3																				3
4																				4
5																				5
6																				6
7																				7
8																				8
9																				9
10																				10
11																				11
12																				12
13																				13
14																				14
15																				15
16																				16
17																				17
18																				18
19																				19
20																				20
21																				21
22																				22
23																				23
24																				24
25																				25
26																				26
27																				27
28																				28
29																				29
30																				30
31																				31
32																				32
33																				33
34																				34
35																				35
36																				36
37																				37
38																				38
39																				39
40																				40

Chapter 3

The Navigator ✓
- ■ Scan Study Objectives ☐
- ■ Read Preview ☐
- ■ Read Chapter Review ☐
- ■ Work Demonstration Problem ☐
- ■ Answer True-False Statements ☐
- ■ Answer Multiple-Choice Questions ☐
- ■ Match Terms and Definitions ☐
- ■ Solve Exercises ☐

ADJUSTING THE ACCOUNTS

CHAPTER STUDY OBJECTIVES

After studying this chapter, you should be able to:
1. Explain the time period assumption.
2. Explain the accrual basis of accounting.
3. Explain why adjusting entries are needed.
4. Identify the major types of adjusting entries.
5. Prepare adjusting entries for prepayments.
6. Prepare adjusting entries for accruals.
7. Describe the nature and purpose of an adjusted trial balance.
*8. Prepare adjusting entries for the alternative treatment of prepayments.

*Note: All **asterisked** (*) items relate to material contained in the Appendix to the chapter.

PREVIEW OF CHAPTER 3

In Chapter 2 we examined the recording process through the preparation of the trial balance. Before we will be ready to prepare financial statements from the trial balance, additional steps need to be taken. Before financial statements can be prepared, questions relating to the recognition of revenues and expenses must be answered. With the answers in hand, the relevant account balances can then be adjusted. The organization and content of the chapter are as follows:

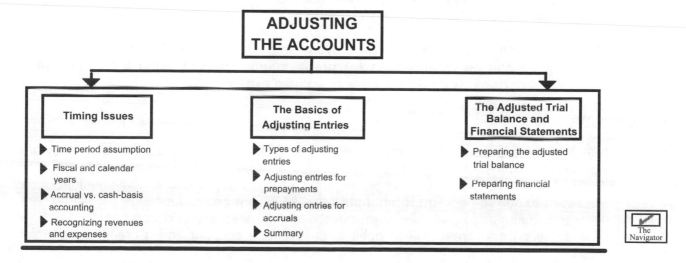

CHAPTER REVIEW

Time-Period Assumption

1. (S.O. 1) The **time period (or periodicity) assumption** assumes that the economic life of a business can be divided into artificial time periods.

2. Accounting time periods are generally a month, a quarter, or a year. The accounting time period of one year in length is usually known as a **fiscal year.**

Accrual Basis of Accounting

3. (S.O. 2) The revenue recognition and matching principles are used under the **accrual basis of accounting.** Under **cash basis accounting,** revenue is recorded only when cash is received and expenses are recorded only when paid.

4. Generally accepted accounting principles require accrual basis accounting rather than cash basis accounting because the cash basis of accounting often leads to misleading financial statements.

Revenue Recognition Principle

5. The **revenue recognition principle** states that revenue should be recognized in the accounting period in which it is earned.

The Matching Principle

6. The **matching principle** dictates that efforts (expenses) be matched with accomplishments (revenues).

Adjusting Entries

7. (S.O. 3) Adjusting entries are made in order for:
    a. Revenues to be recorded in the period in which they are earned, and for expenses to be recognized in the period in which they are incurred.
    b. The revenue recognition and matching principles to be followed.

8. (S.O. 4)   Adjusting entries are required every time financial statements are prepared. Adjusting entries can be classified as (a) **prepayments** (prepaid expenses or unearned revenue) or (b) **accruals** (accrued revenues or accrued expenses).

Prepayments

9. (S.O. 5) Prepaid expenses are expenses paid in cash and recorded as assets before they are used or consumed.
    a. Prepaid expenses expire with the passage of time or through use and consumption.
    b. An **asset-expense account relationship** exists with prepaid expenses.
    c. Prior to adjustment, **assets are overstated** and **expenses are understated.**
    d. The adjusting entry results in a debit to an expense account and a credit to an asset account.
    e. Examples of prepaid expenses include supplies, insurance, and depreciation.

f. To illustrate a prepaid adjusting entry, assume on October 1, Kubitz Company pays $2,400 cash to Sandy Insurance Co. for a one-year insurance policy effective October 1. The adjusting entry at October 31 is:

Insurance Expense ($2,400 X 1/12)	200	
Prepaid Insurance		200

10. **Depreciation** is the process of allocating the cost of an asset to expense over its useful life in a rational and systematic manner.
    a. The purchase of equipment or a building is viewed as a long-term prepayment of services and, therefore, is allocated in the same manner as other prepaid expenses.
    b. Depreciation is an estimate rather than a factual measurement of the cost that has expired.
    c. In recording depreciation, Depreciation Expense is debited and a contra asset account, Accumulated Depreciation, is credited.
    d. In the balance sheet, Accumulated Depreciation is offset against the asset account. The difference between the cost of the asset and its related accumulated depreciation is referred to as the **book value** of the asset.
    e. To illustrate an adjusting entry for depreciation, assume Resch Co. purchases a machine for $6,000 cash on January 1, 2002. Assuming that annual depreciation is $1,200, the adjusting entry at December 31, 2002 is:

Depreciation Expense...	1,200	
Accumulated Depreciation—Machinery		1,200

11. **Unearned revenues** are revenues received and recorded as liabilities before they are earned.
    a. Unearned revenues are subsequently earned by rendering service to a customer.
    b. A **liability-revenue account relationship** exists with unearned revenues.
    c. Prior to adjustment, **liabilities are overstated** and **revenues are understated.**
    d. The adjusting entry results in a debit to a liability account and a credit to a revenue account.
    e. Examples of unearned revenues include rent, magazine subscriptions, and customer deposits for future service.
    f. To illustrate an unearned revenue adjusting entry, assume on October 1, Schoen Co. receives $3,000 cash from a renter in payment of monthly rent for the period October through December. At October 31, the adjusting entry to record the rent earned in October is:

Unearned Rent Revenue...	1,000	
Rent Revenue ($3,000 X 1/3).............................		1,000

Accruals

12. (S.O. 6) **Accrued revenues** are revenues earned but not yet received in cash.
    a. Accrued revenues may accumulate with the passing of time as in the case of interest and rent, or through services performed but not billed or collected.
    b. An **asset-revenue account relationship** exists with accrued revenues.
    c. Prior to adjustment, **both assets and revenues are understated.**
    d. The adjusting entry results in a debit to an asset account and a credit to a revenue account.
    e. To illustrate an accrued revenue adjusting entry, assume in October, Mayer, a dentist, performs $800 of services for patients who are not billed until November. The adjusting entry at October 31 is:

Accounts Receivable..	800	
Dental Fees Earned		800

13. **Accrued expenses** are expenses incurred but not yet paid or recorded.
    a. Accrued expenses result from the same causes as accrued revenues and include interest, rent, taxes, and salaries.
    b. A **liability-expense account relationship** exists with accrued expenses.
    c. Prior to adjustment, both **liabilities and expenses are understated.**
    d. The adjusting entry results in a debit to an expense account and a credit to a liability account.
    e. To illustrate an accrued expense adjusting entry, assume Schwenk Company incurs salaries of $4,000 during the last week of October that will be paid in November. The adjusting entry on October 31 is:

Salaries Expense	4,000	
Salaries Payable		4,000

14. Each adjusting entry affects one balance sheet account and one income statement account.

Adjusted Trial Balance

15. (S.O. 7)   After all adjusting entries have been journalized and posted an **adjusted trial balance** is prepared. This trial balance shows the balances of all accounts, including those that have been adjusted, at the end of the accounting period.

16. The **purpose** of an adjusted trial balance is to prove the equality of the total debit balances and the total credit balances in the ledger after all adjustments have been made.

17. The accounts in the adjusted trial balance contain all data that are needed for the preparation of financial statements.

Alternative Treatment

*18. (S.O. 8)   Under the alternative treatment, at the time an expense is prepaid, an expense account is debited, and when unearned revenues are received a revenue account is credited.

*19. The alternative treatment of prepaid expenses and unearned revenues has the same effect on the financial statements as the procedures described in the chapter.

*20. When a prepaid expense is initially debited to an expense account,
    a. No adjusting entry will be required if the prepayment is fully expired or consumed before the next financial statement date.
    b. If the prepayment is not fully expired or consumed, an adjusting entry is required.
    c. Prior to adjustment an **expense account is overstated** and an **asset account is understated.**
    d. The adjusting entry results in a debit (increase) to an asset account and a credit (decrease) to an expense account.
    e. To illustrate the adjusting entry, assume Gonzalez Company purchases $1,200 of supplies and debits Office Supplies Expense. At the next financial statement date, $300 of supplies are on hand. The adjusting entry is:

Office Supplies	300	
Office Supplies Expense		300

*21. When an unearned revenue is initially credited to a revenue account, the procedures are similar to those described above for prepaid expenses. In this case, however,
    a. Prior to adjustment, a **revenue account is overstated** and a **liability account is understated.**
    b. The adjusting entry results in a debit to a revenue account and a credit to a liability account.

DEMONSTRATION PROBLEM (S.O. 5 and 6)

At December 31, 2002, the unadjusted trial balance of Kari Thresher Company shows the following balances for selected accounts:

Supplies	$ 8,500
Prepaid Insurance	12,000
Equipment	40,000
Accumulated Depreciation	16,000
Unearned Fees	15,000
Notes Payable	50,000
Fees Earned	40,000

Analysis reveals the following additional data pertaining to these accounts:
1. Supplies on hand at December 31, 2002, $3,000.
2. Insurance began on July 1, 2002 for a one-year policy.
3. The equipment was purchased January 1, 2000. Annual depreciation is $8,000.
4. $12,000 of the unearned fees have been earned.
5. The note is dated July 1, 2002, payable in 2004 and bears interest at 10% per year.
6. Services rendered other customers but not billed at December 31, 2002 totaled $3,500.
7. Salaries of $2,500 were unpaid at December 31, 2002.

Instructions
Prepare the adjusting entries for the year ending December 31, 2002.

The
Navigator

SOLUTION TO DEMONSTRATION PROBLEM

General Journal

J1

Date	Account Title	Debit	Credit
2002 Dec. 31	Supplies Expense	5,500	
	Supplies		5,500
	($8,500 - $3,000)		
31	Insurance Expense	6,000	
	Prepaid Insurance		6,000
	($12,000 X 6/12)		
31	Depreciation Expense	8,000	
	Accumulated Depreciation		8,000
31	Unearned Fees	12,000	
	Fees Earned		12,000
31	Interest Expense	2,500	
	Interest Payable		2,500
	($50,000 X 10% X 6/12)		
31	Accounts Receivable	3,500	
	Fees Earned		3,500
31	Salaries Expense	2,500	
	Salaries Payable		2,500

REVIEW QUESTIONS AND EXERCISES

TRUE—FALSE

Indicate whether each of the following is true (T) or false (F) in the space provided.

_____ 1. (S.O. 1) The time-period assumption assumes that the economic life of a business can be divided into artificial time periods.

_____ 2. (S.O. 1) A calendar year and a fiscal year must be the same.

_____ 3. (S.O. 2) The revenue recognition principle states that revenue should be recognized in the accounting period cash is received.

_____ 4. (S.O. 2) The matching principle requires that expenses be matched with revenues.

_____ 5. (S.O. 3) Adjusting entries are journalized throughout the accounting period.

_____ 6. (S.O. 3) In general, adjusting entries are required each time financial statements are prepared.

_____ 7. (S.O. 3) In general, adjusting entries are necessary even if the records are free of errors.

_____ 8. (S.O. 3) Every adjusting entry affects one balance sheet account and one income statement account.

_____ 9. (S.O. 3) Adjusting entries are journalized but need not be posted.

_____ 10. (S.O. 5) Prepaid expenses are expenses paid in cash and recorded in an asset account before they are used or consumed.

_____ 11. (S.O. 5) Depreciation is a process of valuation.

_____ 12. (S.O. 5) The Accumulated Depreciation account is a contra asset account that is reported on the balance sheet.

_____ 13. (S.O. 5) The difference between the cost of an asset and its related accumulated depreciation is referred to as the asset's book value.

_____ 14. (S.O. 5) Revenues received in advance of the accounting period in which they are earned are liabilities.

_____ 15. (S.O. 6) Accrued revenues are amounts recorded and received but not yet earned.

_____ 16. (S.O. 6) Prior to an adjustment for accrued revenues, assets and revenues are both understated.

_____ 17. (S.O. 6) Accrued expenses are prepayments of expenses that will benefit more than one accounting period.

_____ 18. (S.O. 6) An adjusting entry for accrued expenses results in a debit to an expense account and a credit to a liability account.

_____ 19. (S.O. 7) An adjusted trial balance should be prepared before the adjusting entries are made.

_____ 20. (S.O. 7) The accounts in the adjusted trial balance contain all data that are needed for the preparation of financial statements.

_____ *21. (S.O. 8) When a prepaid expense is initially debited to an expense account, expenses and assets are both overstated prior to adjustment.

_____ *22. (S.O. 8) When an unearned revenue is initially credited to a revenue account, the adjusting entry will result in a debit to a revenue account and a credit to a liability account.

The Navigator

MULTIPLE CHOICE

Circle the letter that best answers each of the following statements.

1. (S.O. 2) Which of the following statements concerning the accrual basis of accounting is **incorrect?**
   a. The accrual basis of accounting follows the revenue recognition principle.
   b. The accrual basis of accounting is the method required by generally accepted accounting principles.
   c. The accrual basis of accounting recognizes expenses when they are paid.
   d. The accrual basis of accounting follows the matching principle.

2. (S.O. 2) The revenue recognition principle recognizes that:
   a. revenue should be recognized in the accounting period in which it is earned.
   b. the economic life of a business can be divided into artificial time periods.
   c. expenses should be matched with revenues.
   d. the fiscal year should correspond with the calendar year.

3. (S.O. 2) The matching principle dictates that:
   a. each debit be matched with an equal credit.
   b. revenue should be recognized in the accounting period in which it is earned.
   c. expenses should be matched with revenues.
   d. the fiscal year should match the calendar year.

4. (S.O. 5) For prepaid expense adjusting entries:
   a. an expense-liability account relationship exists.
   b. prior to adjustment, expenses are overstated and assets are understated.
   c. the adjusting entry results in a debit to an expense account and a credit to an asset account.
   d. none of the above.

5.   (S.O. 5)   The beginning balance of Supplies for Lu Inc. was $900.   During the year additional supplies were purchased for $450.   At the end of the year an inventory count indicates $700 of supplies on hand.   The adjusting entry at December 31, is:

a.	Supplies..	650	
	Supplies Expense		650
b.	Supplies..	450	
	Supplies Expense		450
c.	Supplies Expense..	250	
	Supplies		250
d.	Supplies Expense......,...	650	
	Supplies		650

6.   (S.O. 5) Demaet Cruise Lines purchased a five-year insurance policy for its ships on April 1, 2002 for $100,000.   Assuming that April 1 is the effective date of the policy, the adjusting entry on December 31, 2002 is:

a.	Prepaid Insurance..	15,000	
	Insurance Expense		15,000
b.	Insurance Expense...	15,000	
	Prepaid Insurance..		15,000
c.	Insurance Expense...	20,000	
	Prepaid Insurance..		20,000
d.	Insurance Expense...	5,000	
	Prepaid Insurance..		5,000

7.   (S.O. 5) Cost less accumulated depreciation for a plant asset is often called:
    a.   book value.
    b.   market value.
    c.   original value.
    d.   none of the above.

8.   (S.O. 5) Accumulated depreciation plus book value will equal the asset's:
    a.   cost.
    b.   market value.
    c.   depreciable cost.
    d.   none of the above.

9.   (S.O. 5) Tamara Company purchased a machine on January 1, 2002. Annual depreciation is $800. At December 31, 2004, the balance in the accumulated depreciation account, after adjustment, should be:
    a. $800.
    b. $1,600.
    c. $2,400.
    d. $3,200.

10.   (S.O. 5) For unearned revenue adjusting entries, the **incorrect** statement is:
    a.   a liability-revenue account relationship exists.
    b.   prior to adjustment, revenues are overstated and liabilities are understated.
    c.   the adjusting entry results in a debit to a liability account and a credit to a revenue account.
    d.   if the adjustment is not made, revenues will be understated.

11. (S.O. 5) On May 1, 2002, Maricel Advertising Company received $3,000 from Kathy Siska for advertising services to be completed April 30, 2003. At December 31, 2002, $2,000 of the fees have been earned. The adjusting entry on December 31, 2002 by Maricel will include a:
    a. $1,000 credit to Unearned Fees.
    b. $1,000 debit to Fees Earned.
    c. $2,000 credit to Unearned Fees.
    d. $2,000 debit to Unearned Fees.

12. (S.O. 5) The account Unearned Revenues is a(n):
    a. revenue account.
    b. contra revenue account.
    c. liability account.
    d. asset account.

13. (S.O. 6) For accrued revenue adjusting entries,
    a. an asset-revenue account relationship exists.
    b. prior to adjustment, assets and revenues are both overstated.
    c. the adjusting entry results in a debit to a revenue account and a credit to an asset account.
    d. none of the above.

14. (S.O. 6) On June 30, Wian Marketing Services is preparing its financial statements. $600 of fees were earned in June that were not billed to clients prior to June 30. The adjusting entry at June 30 is:
    a. Unearned Fees 600
          Fees Earned 600
    b. Accounts Receivable 600
          Fees Earned 600
    c. Fees Earned 600
          Accounts Receivable 600
    d. Fees Earned 600
          Unearned Fees 600

15. (S.O. 6) For accrued expense adjusting entries, the **incorrect** statement is:
    a. a liability-expense account relationship exists.
    b. prior to adjustment, both expenses and liabilities are understated.
    c. if the adjusting entry is not made, expenses will be overstated in the income statement.
    d. the adjusting entry results in a debit to an expense account and a credit to a liability account.

16. (S.O. 6) Gardner Company purchased a truck from Kutner Co. by issuing a 6-month 10% note payable for $30,000 on November 1. On December 31, the accrued expense adjusting entry is:
    a. No entry is required.
    b. Interest Expense 3,000
          Interest Payable 3,000
    c. Interest Expense 6,000
          Interest Payable 6,000
    d. Interest Expense 500
          Interest Payable 500

17. (S.O. 6) Cathy Cline, an employee of the Wheeler Company, will not receive her paycheck until April 2. Based on services performed from March 15 to March 30 her salary was $800. The adjusting entry for Wheeler Company on March 31 is:

    a.   Salaries Expense...   800
           Salaries Payable..   800
    b.   No entry is required.
    c.   Salaries Expense...   800
           Cash   800
    d.   Salaries Payable...   800
           Cash   800

18. (S.O. 7) Financial statements are prepared directly from the:
    a.   general journal.
    b.   ledger.
    c.   trial balance.
    d.   adjusted trial balance.

*19. (S.O. 8) On January 2, Van Alstyne Food Services pays $3,000 cash for office supplies. Office Supplies Expense is debited because the supplies are expected to be used before financial statements are prepared on June 30. At June 30, there are $300 of office supplies on hand. The adjusting entry is:

    a.   Office Supplies..   300
           Office Supplies Expense...   300
    b.   Office Supplies..   2,700
           Office Supplies Expense...   2,700
    c.   Office Supplies Expense......................................   2,700
           Office Supplies...   2,700
    d.   Office Supplies Expense......................................   300
           Office Supplies...   300

*20. (S.O. 8) On May 1, Walsh Inc. credited Fees Earned when $4,000 cash was received for future services. On June 30, the next date financial statements are prepared, $600 of the services have not been rendered. The June 30 adjusting entry will include a:
    a.   credit to Fees Earned of $600.
    b.   debit to Fees Earned of $600.
    c.   debit to Unearned Fees of $3,400.
    d.   credit to Unearned Fees of $3,400.

MATCHING

Match each term with its definition by writing the appropriate letter in the space provided.

Terms

_____ 1. Depreciation.

_____ 2. Time-period assumption.

_____ 3. Matching principle.

_____ 4. Revenue recognition principle.

_____ 5. Fiscal years.

_____ 6. Contra asset account.

_____ 7. Adjusted trial balance.

_____ 8. Prepaid expenses.

_____ 9. Unearned revenues.

_____ 10. Adjusting entries.

_____ 11. Accrued revenues.

_____ 12. Accrued expenses.

_____ 13. Accrual basis of accounting.

_____ 14. Cash basis of accounting.

Definitions

a. An account that is offset against an asset account in the balance sheet.

b. Expenses paid in cash and recorded in an asset account before they are used or consumed.

c. Revenues earned but not yet received or recorded at the statement date.

d. Accounting periods that are one year in length.

e. The principle that efforts (expenses) be matched with accomplishments (revenues).

f. An accounting basis in which events that change a company's financial statements are recorded in the periods in which the events occur.

g. Expenses incurred but not yet paid or recorded at the statement date.

h. A list of accounts and their balances after all adjustments have been made.

i. The assumption that the economic life of a business can be divided into artificial time periods.

j. Revenue is recorded only when cash is received and expense is recorded only when cash is paid.

k. The process of allocating the cost of an asset to expense over its useful life in a rational and systematic manner.

l. Revenues received and recorded as liabilities before they are earned.

m. Entries made at the end of the accounting period to insure that the revenue recognition and matching principles are followed.

n. The principle that revenue be recognized in the accounting period in which it is earned.

The Navigator

EXERCISES

EX. 3-1 (S.O. 5 and 6) McDaniels Painting Company is at the end of its fiscal year December 31, 2002 and needs to record its adjusting entries. Adjustment data are as follows:

a.   Four months ago, Judy Bernstein made a $8,000 prepayment for the painting of her house. McDaniels recorded the original entry as Unearned Revenue. At December 31, one-fourth of the painting of the house remains to be done.

b.   McDaniels purchased a truck from Donnelly Vehicles on January 1, 2001 at a cost of $20,000. Annual depreciation is $4,000. Depreciation was correctly recorded for 2001.

c.   An employee, Pam Travis had earned wages of $500 for the last week in December. She will not be paid until January 5.

d.   McDaniels purchased a $24,000, four-year insurance policy from Heinsen Insurance four months ago. The effective date of the policy was September 1, 2002.

e.   McDaniels began painting Peggy Thompson's clubhouse in November at a price of $32,000. McDaniels determines that $20,000 of the revenue has been earned at December 31. Thompson has not made any payment to McDaniels, and McDaniels has not billed Thompson for services rendered.

Instructions
Prepare the adjusting entries at December 31, 2002.

	General Journal		J1
Date	**Account Title**	**Debit**	**Credit**
2002			

General Journal			J
Date	Account Title	Debit	Credit

EX. 3-2 (S.O. 7) The adjusted trial balance of the Susan Dey Company at November 30, 2002, is as follows:

SUSAN DEY COMPANY
Adjusted Trial Balance
November 30, 2002

	Debit	Credit
Cash	$ 7,250	
Accounts Receivable	17,000	
Supplies	500	
Prepaid Insurance	2,500	
Land	12,000	
Equipment	40,000	
Accumulated Depreciation		$ 16,000
Notes Payable		7,500
Accounts Payable		5,950
Interest Payable		350
Unearned Fees		7,500
Salaries Payable		5,000
S. Dey, Capital		38,000
Fees Earned		19,700
Salaries Expense	11,500	
Supplies Expense	400	
Rent Expense	2,000	
Insurance Expense	2,500	
Depreciation Expense	4,000	
Interest Expense	350	
	$100,000	$100,000

Instructions

(a) Prepare an income statement and an owner's equity statement for the year ended November 30, 2002.

(b) Prepare a balance sheet at November 30, 2002.

(a)

SUSAN DEY COMPANY
Income Statement
For the Year Ended November 30, 2002

_____

_____

_____

_____

_____

_____

_____

_____

_____

_____

SUSAN DEY COMPANY
Owner's Equity Statement
For the Year Ended November 30, 2002

_____

_____

_____

_____

_____

_____

(b)

SUSAN DEY
Balance Sheet
November 30, 2002

The
Navigator

SOLUTIONS TO REVIEW QUESTIONS AND EXERCISES

TRUE-FALSE

1. (T)
2. (F)   The calendar year begins January 1 and ends December 31. Fiscal years usually begin with the first day of any month and end on the last day of a month, twelve months later. Of course, the fiscal year could coincide with the calendar year.
3. (F)   The revenue recognition principle states that revenue should be recognized in the accounting period in which it is earned. Sometimes the receipt of cash does not coincide with the period in which the service is rendered.
4. (T)
5. (F)   Adjusting entries are only prepared at the end of an accounting period.
6. (T)
7. (T)
8. (T)
9. (F)   Adjusting entries must be both journalized and posted.
10. (T)
11. (F)   Depreciation is the process of allocating the cost of an asset to expense over its useful life in a rational and systematic manner.
12. (T)
13. (T)
14. (T)
15. (F)   Accrued revenues are revenues earned but not yet received in cash.
16. (T)
17. (F)   Accrued expenses are expenses incurred but not yet paid or recorded.
18. (T)
19. (F)   The adjusted trial balance can only be prepared after the adjusting entries are made.
20. (T)
*21. (F)   Prior to adjustment, expenses are overstated and assets are understated.
*22. (T)

MULTIPLE CHOICE

1. (c)   The accrual basis of accounting recognizes expenses when they are incurred. Choices (a), (b), and (d) are all correct statements concerning the accrual basis of accounting.

2. (a)   Choice (b) is the time-period assumption. Choice (c) is the matching principle. Answer (d) pertains to the time-period assumption. Also, the fiscal year does not have to correspond with the calendar year.

3. (c)   Choice (a) is the dual effect of the double-entry system discussed in Chapter 2. Choice (b) is the revenue recognition principle. Choice (d) is an incorrect statement because the fiscal year does not necessarily have to be the calendar year.

4. (c)   Answer (a) is incorrect because an asset-expense account relationship exists. Answer (b) is incorrect because prior to adjustment, assets are overstated and expenses are understated.

5. (d) The total cost of supplies is $1,350 ($900 + $450). Since the ending inventory is $700, the supplies expense for the period is $650 ($1,350 - $700).

6. (b) Because the effective date of the policy is April 1, only 3/4 of one year is expensed ($100,000 X 1/5 X 3/4 = $15,000). Insurance Expense is debited and Prepaid Insurance is credited because the $100,000 payment was debited to Prepaid Insurance.

7. (a) The market value (b) is the current exchange value of the asset. The original value (c) would refer to the cost.

8. (a) Cost less the related accumulated depreciation is equal to book value; therefore, changing the equation, accumulated depreciation plus book value equals the cost of the asset.

9. (c) The balance should be the accumulated depreciation for three years ($2,400 ($800 X 3).

10. (b) Prior to adjustment liabilities are overstated and revenues are understated. The other answer choices are correct.

11. (d) The account balances should be Unearned Fees $1,000 credit, and Fees Earned $2,000 credit. Thus, the adjusting entry is:

    Unearned Fees.. 2,000
         Fees Earned...   2,000

12. (c) Unearned Revenue is the receipt of cash or an asset before the service has been performed. The obligation to perform this service is indicated in the records by crediting a liability account.

13. (a) Answer (b) is incorrect because prior to adjustment both assets and revenues are understated. Answer (c) is incorrect because an asset account is debited and a revenue account is credited.

14. (b) The amount owed by the clients is a receivable that is debited to an asset account. The services concerning this receivable have been performed and thus, earned; therefore, a revenue account is credited.

15. (c) In an accrued expense adjusting entry, expenses are understated prior to adjustment (b). Therefore, if the adjusting entry is not made, expenses will be understated.

16. (d) The accrued interest is $500 ($30,000 X 10% X 2/12).

17. (a) The accrued expense is recognized by debiting Salaries Expense and crediting Salaries Payable.

18.   (d)   The adjusted trial balance is prepared after all adjusting entries have been posted. Accordingly, the financial statements can be prepared directly from it.

*19.   (a)   At June 30, $300 of office supplies is on hand, which is the balance that should be in the asset account, Office Supplies. Since the unadjusted balance in this account is zero, Office Supplies must be debited for $300. Given the inventory on hand, office supplies expense for the period is $2,700 ($3,000 - $300). The unadjusted balance in Office Supplies Expense is $3,000. Therefore, this account must be credited for $300.

*20.   (b)   At June 30, $600 of the $4,000 of future services have not been rendered and $3,400 has been earned ($4,000 - $600). Prior to adjustment, the balances are Unearned Fees $0 and Fees Earned $4,000. Thus, the adjusting entry is a debit to Fees Earned $600 and a credit to Unearned Fees $600.

MATCHING

1.	k	5.	d	9.	l	13.	f
2.	i	6.	a	10.	m	14.	j
3.	e	7.	h	11.	c		
4.	n	8.	b	12.	g		

EX. 3-1

Date	Account Title	Debit	Credit
	General Journal		**J1**
2002			
	Adjusting Entries		
	a.		
Dec. 31	Unearned Revenue	6,000	
	Painting Revenue		6,000
	(To record revenue earned, $8,000 X		
	3/4)		
	b.		
31	Depreciation Expense	4,000	
	Accumulated Depreciation		4,000
	(To record annual depreciation)		
	c.		
31	Wages Expense	500	
	Wages Payable		500
	(To record accrued wages)		
	d.		
31	Insurance Expense	2,000	
	Prepaid Insurance		2,000
	(To record insurance expired;		
	$24,000 X 4/48)		
	e.		
31	Accounts Receivable	20,000	
	Painting Revenue		20,000
	(To accrued revenue earned)		

EX. 3-2

(a)

SUSAN DEY
Income Statement
For the Year Ended November 30, 2002

Revenues		
Fees earned		$19,700
Expenses		
Salaries expense	$11,500	
Depreciation expense	4,000	
Insurance expense	2,500	
Rent expense	2,000	
Supplies expense	400	
Interest expense	350	
Total expense		20,750
Net loss		$ 1,050

SUSAN DEY
Owner's Equity Statement
For the Year Ended November 30, 2002

S. Dey, Capital, December 1, 2001	$38,000
Less: Net loss	1,050
S. Dey, Capital, November 30, 2002	$36,950

(b)

SUSAN DEY
Balance Sheet
November 30, 2002

Assets

Cash		$ 7,250
Accounts receivable		17,000
Supplies		500
Prepaid insurance		2,500
Land		12,000
Equipment	$40,000	
Less: Accumulated depreciation	16,000	24,000
Total assets		$63,250

Liabilities and Owner's Equity

Liabilities	
Notes payable	$ 7,500
Accounts payable	5,950
Interest payable	350
Unearned fees	7,500
Salaries payable	5,000
Total liabilities	26,300
Owner's Equity	
S. Dey, Capital	36,950
Total liabilities and owner's equity	$63,250

	1	2	3	4	5	6	7	8	
1									1
2									2
3									3
4									4
5									5
6									6
7									7
8									8
9									9
10									10
11									11
12									12
13									13
14									14
15									15
16									16
17									17
18									18
19									19
20									20
21									21
22									22
23									23
24									24
25									25
26									26
27									27
28									28
29									29
30									30
31									31
32									32
33									33
34									34
35									35
36									36
37									37
38									38
39									39
40									40

Chapter 4

COMPLETION OF THE ACCOUNTING CYCLE

The Navigator ✓
- ■ Scan Study Objectives ☐
- ■ Read Preview ☐
- ■ Read Chapter Review ☐
- ■ Work Demonstration Problem ☐
- ■ Answer True-False Statements ☐
- ■ Answer Multiple-Choice Questions ☐
- ■ Match Terms and Definitions ☐
- ■ Solve Exercises ☐

CHAPTER STUDY OBJECTIVES

After studying this chapter, you should be able to:
1. Prepare a work sheet.
2. Explain the process of closing the books.
3. Describe the content and purpose of a post-closing trial balance.
4. State the required steps in the accounting cycle.
5. Explain the approaches to preparing correcting entries.
6. Identify the sections of a classified balance sheet.
*7. Prepare reversing entries.

Note: All **asterisked** (*) items relate to material contained in the Appendix to the chapter.

PREVIEW OF CHAPTER 4

In this chapter we will explain the role of the work sheet in accounting as well as the remaining steps in the accounting cycle, most especially, the closing process. Then we will consider (1) correcting entries and (2) classified balance sheets. The organization and content of the chapter are as follows:

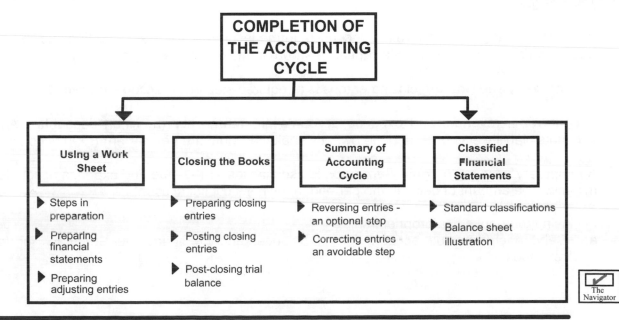

CHAPTER REVIEW

Preparing a Worksheet

1. (S.O. 1) The **steps** in preparing a work sheet are:
   a. Prepare a trial balance on the work sheet.
   b. Enter the adjustments in the adjustments columns.
   c. Enter adjusted balances in the adjusted trial balance columns.
   d. Extend adjusted trial balance amounts to appropriate financial statement columns.
   e. Total the statement columns, compute the net income (or loss), and complete the work sheet.

2. A **work sheet** is a multiple-column form that may be used in the adjustment process and in preparing financial statements. The **basic form** of a work sheet consists of the following columns:

Account Titles	Trial Balance		Adjustments		Adjusted Trial Balance		Income Statement		Balance Sheet	
	Dr.	Cr.	Dr.	Cr.	Dr.	Cr.	Dr.	Cr.	Dr.	Cr.

3. For each account in the work sheet, the amount in the **adjusted trial balance columns** is equal to the account balance that will appear in the ledger after the adjusting entries have been journalized and posted.

4. After the work sheet has been completed the **statement columns** contain all data that are required for the preparation of financial statements. The income statement is prepared from the income statement columns, and the owner's equity statement and balance sheet are prepared from the balance sheet columns.

5. Using a work sheet accountants can prepare financial statements **before** adjusting entries are journalized and posted.

6. A work sheet is not a journal and it cannot be used as a **basis** for posting to ledger accounts.

Closing Entries

7. (S.O. 2) **Closing entries** formally recognize in the ledger the transfer of net income (or loss) and owner's drawings to owner's capital as shown in the owner's equity statement.

8. **Journalizing and posting** closing entries is a required step in the accounting cycle.

9. The drawing, revenue, and expense accounts are **temporary** (nominal) accounts. Asset accounts, liability accounts, and the owner's capital account are **permanent** (real) accounts.

10. A temporary account, **Income Summary,** is used in closing revenue and expense accounts to minimize the amount of detail in the permanent owner's capital account.

11. In closing the books of a proprietorship:
    a. Debit each revenue account for its balance, and credit Income Summary for total revenues.

b.   Debit Income Summary for total expenses, and credit each expense account for its balance.

c.   Debit Income Summary, and credit Owner's Capital for the amount of net income; conversely, credit Income Summary and debit Owner's Capital if a net loss exists.

d.   Debit Owner's Capital for the balance in the Owner's Drawing account and credit Owner's Drawing for the same amount.

Post-Closing Trial Balance

12.   (S.O. 3)   After all closing entries have been journalized and posted, a **post-closing trial balance** is prepared.   The purpose of this trial balance is to prove the equality of the **permanent account balances** that are carried forward into the next accounting period.

Steps in the Accounting Cycle

13.   (S.O. 4)   The required steps in the accounting cycle are:
a.   Analyze business transactions.
b.   Journalize the transactions.
c.   Post to ledger accounts.
d.   Prepare a trial balance.
e.   Journalize and post adjusting entries: Prepayments/Accruals.
f.   Prepare an adjusted trial balance.
g.   Prepare financial statements: Income statement, Owner's equity statement, Balance sheet.
h.   Journalize and post closing entries.
i.   Prepare a post-closing trial balance.

14.   A **reversing entry** is the exact opposite of an adjusting entry.   The preparation of reversing entries is an optional bookkeeping procedure that is not a required step in the accounting cycle.

Correcting Entries

15.   (S.O. 5)   Errors that occur in recording transactions should be corrected as soon as they are discovered by preparing **correcting entries.**   Correcting entries:
a.   are unnecessary if the records are free of errors.
b.   are journalized and posted whenever an error is discovered.
c.   may involve any combination of balance sheet and income statement accounts.

16.   To determine the correcting entry, it is useful to compare the incorrect entry with the correct entry, and then make a correcting entry.   Another approach is to reverse the incorrect entry and then prepare the correct entry.

Classified Balance Sheet

17.   (S.O. 6)   Financial statements become more useful when the elements are classified into significant subgroups.   A **classified balance sheet** generally has the following standard classifications:

	Liabilities and
Assets	**Owner's Equity**
Current assets	Current liabilities
Long-term investments	Long-term liabilities
Property, plant, and	Owner's equity
equipment	
Intangible assets	

Assets

18. **Current assets** are cash and other resources that are reasonably expected to be realized in cash or sold or consumed in the business within one year of the balance sheet date or the company's operating cycle, whichever is longer. Current assets are listed in the order of their liquidity.

19. The **operating cycle** of a company is the average time that is required to go from cash to cash in producing revenues.

20. **Long-term investments** are resources that can be realized in cash but the conversion into cash is not expected within one year or the operating cycle, whichever is longer.

21. Tangible resources of a relatively permanent nature that are used in the business and not intended for sale are classified as **property, plant, and equipment.**

22. **Intangible assets** are noncurrent resources that do not have physical substance, such as patents and copyrights.

Liabilities

23. **Current liabilities** are obligations that are reasonably expected to be paid from existing current assets or through the creation of other current liabilities within one year or the operating cycle, whichever is longer.

24. Obligations expected to be paid after one year are classified as **long-term liabilities (or long-term debt).**

Owner's Equity

25. The content of the owner's equity section varies with the form of business organization. In a proprietorship, there is a single owner's equity account, called (Owner's Name), Capital. In a partnership, there are separate capital accounts for each partner. For a corporation, owners' equity is called stockholders' equity and it consists of two accounts: Capital Stock and Retained Earnings.

Form of Balance Sheet

26. A balance sheet is most often presented in **report form** with the assets shown above the liabilities and owner's equity. It may also be presented in **account form** with the assets section placed on the left and the liabilities and owner's equity section on the right.

Reversing Entries

*27. (S.O. 7) A reversing entry is made at the beginning of the next accounting period. The **purpose** of reversing entries is to simplify the recording of a subsequent transaction related to an adjusting entry.

*28. Reversing entries are most often used to reverse two types of adjusting entries: **accrued revenues** and **accrued expenses.**

DEMONSTRATION PROBLEM (S.O. 1, 2, and 6)

Gardin Company's December 31, 2002 trial balance is as follows:

GARDIN COMPANY
December 31, 2002
Trial Balance

	Debit	Credit
Cash	$16,000	
Accounts Receivable	4,500	
Prepaid Insurance	2,500	
Supplies	3,000	
Equipment	41,500	
Accounts Payable		$ 5,500
Unearned Revenue		1,500
Notes Payable		28,000
Laz Gardin, Capital		24,000
Laz Gardin, Drawing	2,500	
Revenue		16,000
Salaries Expense	3,700	
Utilities Expense	400	
Marketing Expense	900	
Totals	$75,000	$75,000

Gardin Company needs to make the year-end adjusting entries concerning the following data:
1. Insurance expires at the rate of $100 per month.
2. There are $2,400 of supplies on hand at December 31.
3. Monthly depreciation is $200 on the equipment.
4. Interest of $2,800 has accrued on the Notes Payable.
5. Unearned revenue amounted to $700 on December 31.
6. Accrued salaries are $3,200.

Instructions
(a) Prepare a work sheet.
(b) Prepare a classified balance sheet assuming $20,000 of the notes payable are long term.
(c) Journalize the closing entries.

SOLUTION TO DEMONSTRATION PROBLEM

(a)

GARDIN COMPANY
Work Sheet
For the Year Ended Dec. 31, 2002

Account Titles	Trial Balance Dr.	Trial Balance Cr.	Adjustments Dr.	Adjustments Cr.	Adjusted Trial Balance Dr.	Adjusted Trial Balance Cr.	Income Statement Dr.	Income Statement Cr.	Balance Sheet Dr.	Balance Sheet Cr.
Cash	16,000				16,000				16,000	
Accounts Receivable	4,500				4,500				4,500	
Prepaid Insurance	2,500			(a) 1,200	1,300				1,300	
Supplies	3,000			(b) 600	2,400				2,400	
Equipment	41,500				41,500				41,500	
Accounts Payable		5,500				5,500				5,500
Unearned Revenue		1,500	(e) 800			700				700
Notes Payable		28,000				28,000				28,000
Laz Gardin, Capital		24,000				24,000				24,000
Laz Gardin, Drawing	2,500				2,500				2,500	
Revenue		16,000		(e) 800		16,800		16,800		
Salaries Expense	3,700		(f) 3,200		6,900		6,900			
Utilities Expense	400				400		400			
Marketing Expense	900				900		900			
Totals	75,000	75,000								
Insurance Expense			(a) 1,200		1,200		1,200			
Supplies Expense			(b) 600		600		600			
Depreciation Expense			(c) 2,400		2,400		2,400			
Accumulated Depr.—Equip.				(c) 2,400		2,400				2,400
Interest Expense			(d) 2,800		2,800		2,800			
Interest Payable				(d) 2,800		2,800				2,800
Salaries Payable				(f) 3,200		3,200				3,200
Totals			11,000	11,000	83,400	83,400	15,200	16,800	68,200	66,600
Net Income							1,600			1,600
Totals							16,800	16,800	68,200	68,200

(b)
GARDIN COMPANY
Balance Sheet
December 31, 2002

Assets

Current assets		
Cash		$16,000
Accounts Receivable		4,500
Prepaid Insurance		1,300
Supplies..		2,400
Total current assets		24,200
Property, plant, and equipment		
Equipment	$41,500	
Less: Accumulated depreciation—equipment	2,400	39,100
Total assets		$63,300

Liabilities and Owner's Equity

Current liabilities		
Notes payable..		$ 8,000
Accounts payable		5,500
Salaries Payable..		3,200
Interest Payable...		2,800
Unearned Revenue		700
Total current liabilities		20,200
Long-term liabilities		
Notes Payable		20,000
Total liabilities		40,200
Owner's equity		
Laz Gardin, Capital..		23,100*
Total liabilities and owner's equity		$63,300

*Laz Gardin, Capital, $24,000 less drawings $2,500 and plus net income $1,600.

(c)

Dec.	31	Revenue	16,800	
		Income Summary...		16,800
		(To close revenue account)		
	31	Income Summary...	15,200	
		Salaries Expense		6,900
		Utilities Expense		400
		Marketing Expense		900
		Insurance Expense		1,200
		Supplies Expense		600
		Depreciation Expense..		2,400
		Interest Expense		2,800
		(To close expense account)		

Dec.	31	Income Summary...	1,600	
		Laz Gardin, Capital		1,600
		(To close net income to capital)		
	31	Laz Gardin, Capital..	2,500	
		Laz Gardin, Drawing		2,500
		(To close drawings to capital)		

REVIEW QUESTIONS AND EXERCISES

TRUE—FALSE

Indicate whether each of the following is true (T) or false (F) in the space provided.

_T___ 1. (S.O. 1) A work sheet is not a permanent accounting record.

_F___ 2. (S.O. 1) If total debits exceed total credits in the income statement columns on a work sheet, net income has resulted.

_T___ 3. (S.O. 1) After a work sheet has been completed, the statement columns contain all data that are required for the preparation of financial statements.

_F___ 4. (S.O. 1) A work sheet is not a journal, but it can be used as a basis for posting to ledger accounts.

_T___ 5. (S.O. 2) All balance sheet accounts are considered to be permanent or real accounts.

_T___ 6. (S.O. 2) After the closing entries are posted, all nominal accounts will have zero balances.

_T___ 7. (S.O. 2) The journalizing and posting of closing entries is a required step in the accounting cycle.

_T___ 8. (S.O. 2) To close net income to owner's capital, Income Summary is debited and Owner's Capital is credited.

_T___ 9. (S.O. 2) Revenue accounts are closed by debiting the individual revenue accounts and crediting Income Summary for total revenues.

_F___ 10. (S.O. 2) In one closing entry, Owner's Drawing is credited and Income Summary is debited.

_F___ 11. (S.O. 2) Income Summary is used in preparing both adjusting and closing entries. *Ö Summary only*

_F___ 12. (S.O. 3) The post-closing trial balance will contain only owner's equity statement accounts and balance sheet accounts. *only*

_T___ 13. (S.O. 3) The preparation of reversing entries is an optional step in the accounting cycle.

_F___ 14. (S.O. 5) Correcting entries are only made at the end of an accounting period.

_F_ 15. (S.O. 6) The operating cycle of a company is the average time required to collect the receivables resulting from producing revenues.

_T_ 16. (S.O. 6) Current assets are listed in the order of liquidity.

_T_ 17. (S.O. 6) Long-term investments are resources that are not expected to be converted into cash within one year or the operating cycle, whichever is longer.

_F_ 18. (S.O. 6) Property, plant, and equipment are tangible assets that are reported at ~~market value~~ in the balance sheet. *cost less accumulated depreciation*

_T_ 19. (S.O. 6) Current liabilities must be expected to be payable out of existing current assets or through the creation of other current liabilities.

_T_ 20. (S.O. 6) The relationship of current assets and current liabilities is important in evaluating a company's liquidity.

The Navigator

MULTIPLE CHOICE

Circle the letter that best answers each of the following statements.

1. (S.O. 1) The following is **not** a column heading in a work sheet:
   a. Trial Balance.
   b. Income Statement.
   c. Post-Closing Trial Balance.
   d. Adjusted Trial Balance.

2. (S.O. 1) The steps in the preparation of a work sheet do **not** include:
   a. analyzing documentary evidence.
   b. preparing a trial balance on the work sheet.
   c. entering the adjustments in the adjustment columns.
   d. entering adjusted balances in the adjusted trial balance columns.

3. (S.O. 1) Which of the following account balances is extended to the income statement columns on a work sheet?
   a. Prepaid Insurance.
   b. Unearned Revenue.
   c. Depreciation Expense.
   d. Accumulated Depreciation.

4. (S.O. 1) The work sheet is:
   a. used as a basis for posting to the ledger account.
   b. never computerized. *frequently*
   c. part of the ledger.
   d. essentially a working tool of the accountant.

5. (S.O. 2) Balance sheet accounts are considered to be:
   a. temporary owner's equity accounts.
   b. permanent accounts.
   c. capital accounts.
   d. nominal accounts.

6. (S.O. 2) The owner's drawing account is a(n):
   a. expense account.
   b. revenue account.
   c. permanent account.
   d. temporary account.

7. (S.O. 2) Income Summary has a credit balance of $12,000 in J. Spencer, Co. after closing revenues and expenses. The entry to close Income Summary is:
   a. credit Income Summary $12,000, debit J. Spencer, Capital $12,000.
   b. credit Income Summary $12,000, debit J. Spencer, Drawing $12,000.
   c. debit Income Summary $12,000, credit J. Spencer, Drawing $12,000.
   d. debit Income Summary $12,000, credit J. Spencer, Capital $12,000.

8. (S.O. 3) The account that will appear on the post-closing trial balance is:
   a. Fees Earned.
   b. Accumulated Depreciation.
   c. Depreciation Expense.
   d. Drawing.

9. (S.O. 3) The number of accounts appearing in the trial balance will normally be:
   a. less than the number of accounts in the post-closing trial balance.
   b. equal to the number of accounts in the adjusted trial balance.
   c. more than the number of accounts in the post-closing trial balance.
   d. more than the number of accounts in the adjusted trial balance.

10. (S.O. 3) The post-closing trial balance contains only:
    a. income statement accounts.
    b. balance sheet accounts.
    c. balance sheet and income statement accounts.
    d. income statement, balance sheet, and owner's equity statement accounts.

11. (S.O. 4) One of the following statements concerning the accounting cycle is incorrect. The incorrect statement is:
    a. The accounting cycle includes journalizing transactions and posting to ledger accounts.
    b. The accounting cycle includes only one optional step.
    c. The steps in the accounting cycle are performed in sequence.
    d. The steps in the accounting cycle are repeated in each accounting period.

12. (S.O. 5) On September 23, the Polar Company received a $350 check from Mike Moluf for services to be performed in the future. The bookkeeper for Polar Company incorrectly debited Cash for $350 and credited Accounts Receivable for $350. The amounts have been posted to the ledger. To correct this entry, the bookkeeper should:
   a. debit Cash $350 and credit Unearned Fees $350.
   b. debit Accounts Receivable $350 and credit Unearned Fees $350.
   c. debit Accounts Receivable $350 and credit Cash $350.
   d. debit Accounts Receivable $350 and credit Fees Earned $350.

13. (S.O. 5) On June 19, the Pinkowski Company bought office supplies on account from the Ewell Company for $550. Pinkowski Company incorrectly debited Office Equipment for $500 and credited Accounts Payable for $500. The entries have been posted to the ledger. The correcting entry should be:

a.	Office Supplies..	550	
	Accounts Payable...		550
b.	Office Supplies..	550	
	Accounts Payable...		500
	Office Equipment..		50
c.	Office Supplies..	550	
	Office Equipment..		550
d.	Office Supplies..	550	
	Office Equipment..		500
	Accounts Payable...		50

14. (S.O. 6) Which of the following accounts is not classified under the current asset section of the balance sheet?
   a. Prepaid Expenses.
   b. Supplies.
   c. Equipment.
   d. Cash.

15. (S.O. 6) One of the following statements about current assets is correct. The correct statement is:
   a. The time period for current assets is within one year after the balance sheet date or the company's operating cycle, whichever is longer.
   b. The time period for current assets is within one year after the balance sheet date or the company's operating cycle, whichever is shorter.
   c. The operating cycle is the average time to collect accounts receivable in the process of earning revenue.
   d. Current assets are listed in the balance sheet in the order of magnitude.

16. (S.O. 6) Long-term investments are:
   a. reported in the balance sheet after property, plant, and equipment.
   b. resources that are not expected to be realized in cash within one year or operating cycle, whichever is longer.
   c. resources that are intended for use or consumption.
   d. resources that may include rights and privileges granted by governmental authority.

17. (S.O. 6) Which of the following statements is **incorrect?** Property, plant and equipment:
   a. includes tangible resources that are held for use and not for sale.
   b. is reported in the balance sheet at cost less accumulated depreciation.
   c. includes long-lived, non-physical resources such as patents and copyrights.
   d. includes land, buildings, equipment, and machinery.

18. (S.O. 6) Current liabilities:
   a. must reasonably be expected to be paid from existing current assets or through the creation of other current liabilities.
   b. are listed in the balance sheet in order of their expected maturity.
   c. must reasonably be expected to be paid within one year or the operating cycle, whichever is shorter.
   d. should not include long-term debt that is expected to be paid within the next year.

*19. (S.O. 7) Malikowski Company had accrued salaries between September 15 and September 30 of $6,000 that will be paid on October 5. The appropriate adjusting entry was made at the year end, September 30. If a reversing entry is made on October 1, the entry would be:
   a. debit Salaries Payable $6,000 and credit Salaries Expense $6,000.
   b. credit Salaries Payable $6,000 and debit Salaries Expense $6,000.
   c. debit Salaries Payable $6,000 and credit Income Summary $6,000.
   d. credit Salaries Payable $6,000 and debit Income Summary $6,000.

*20. (S.O. 7) On November 1, 2002, Nillson Company issued a $12,000, 10% three-month note payable to Barshinger Bank. At the year end, Nillson made the appropriate adjusting and reversing entries. On February 1, 2003, Nillson paid Barshinger Bank the amount of the note payable plus the appropriate interest. The entry on February 1, 2003 is:

a.	Notes Payable	12,000	
	Cash		12,000
b.	Notes Payable	12,000	
	Interest Expense	300	
	Cash		12,300
c.	Notes Payable	12,000	
	Interest Payable	200	
	Interest Expense	100	
	Cash		12,300
d.	Notes Payable	12,000	
	Interest Payable	300	
	Cash		12,300

The
Navigator

MATCHING

Match each term with its definition by writing the appropriate letter in the space provided.

Terms	Definitions

Terms

___h___ 1. Reversing entry.

___i___ 2. Operating cycle.

___l___ 3. Income summary.

___j___ 4. Work sheet.

___o___ 5. Property, plant, and equipment.

___n___ 6. Current liabilities.

___d___ 7. Intangible assets.

___k___ 8. Classified balance sheet.

___m___ 9. Long-term liabilities.

___b___ 10. Current assets.

___c___ 11. Liquidity. *мягкое состояние*

___f___ 12. Closing entries.

___g___ 13. Long-term investments.

___a___ 14. Post-closing trial balance.

___e___ 15. Correcting entries.

Definitions

a. A listing of the accounts and their balances after closing entries have been journalized and posted.

b. Cash and other assets that are reasonably expected to be realized in cash or sold or consumed in the business within one year of the balance sheet date or the company's operating cycle, whichever is longer.

c. The ability of a company to meet obligations expected to come due in the next year or operating cycle.

d. Noncurrent resources that do not have physical substance.

e. Entries made when errors are discovered.

f. Entries at the end of the accounting period that transfer each nominal account to the permanent owner's equity account.

g. Resources that can be realized in cash but conversion is not expected within one year or the operating cycle, whichever is longer.

h. The exact reverse of an adjusting entry.

i. The average time that is required to go from cash to cash in producing revenues.

j. A multiple-column form that may be used in the adjustment process and in preparing financial statements.

k. A balance sheet that contains significant subgroups.

l. An account that is used when making closing entries so excessive detail does not occur in the permanent owner's equity account.

m. Obligations expected to be paid after one year.

n. Obligations that are reasonably expected to be paid from existing current assets or through the creation of other current liabilities.

o. Tangible resources of a relatively permanent nature that are being used in the business and not intended for sale.

The Navigator

EXERCISES

EX. 4-1 (S.O. 1, 2, and 3) King Oliver began Jazz Company on January 1, 2002. At December 31, 2002, the company had the following adjustment data.

    a.   Inventory clerk, Count Basie, determined that $4,000 of supplies were on hand.

    b.   The insurance was obtained through the Dizzy Gillespie Insurance Agency; during the year $3,000 of the insurance had expired.

    c.   The equipment was purchased from Miles Davis on January 1, 2002 and it is depreciated at a rate of $1,000 per year.

    d.   Unearned fees of $450 were earned as a result of the Duke Ellington concert on December 4.

    e.   Fees earned from the Ella Fitzgerald performance on December 31 totaling $2,250 have not been billed.

    f.   The note payable was a loan from Louis Armstrong; interest of $300 has accrued at December 31.

    g.   A salary of $850 earned by Jimmy Dorsey in December has not been recorded or paid.

Instructions

(a)   Enter the adjustments in the adjustment columns of the work sheet that follows and complete the work sheet (use 10-column paper).

(b)   Prepare the closing entries at December 31.

(c)   Prepare a post-closing trial balance at December 31.

(a)

JAZZ COMPANY
Work Sheet
For the Year Ended Dec. 31, 2002

Account Titles	Trial Balance Dr.	Trial Balance Cr.	Adjustments Dr.	Adjustments Cr.	Adjusted Trial Balance Dr.	Adjusted Trial Balance Cr.	Income Statement Dr.	Income Statement Cr.	Balance Sheet Dr.	Balance Sheet Cr.
Cash	6,000									
Fees Receivable	7,850									
Supplies	6,000									
Prepaid Insurance	9,000									
Equipment	10,000									
Note Payable		9,750								
Unearned Fees		3,100								
K. Oliver, Capital		12,000								
Fees Earned		22,000								
Salaries Expense	8,000									
Totals	46,850	46,850								
Supplies Expense										
Insurance Expense										
Accumulated Depreciation										
Depreciation Expense										
Interest Expense										
Interest Payable										
Salaries Payable										
Totals										
Net Income										
Totals										

(b)

	General Journal		J1
Date	Account Title	Debit	Credit

(c)

JAZZ COMPANY
Post-Closing Trial Balance
December 31, 2002

	Debit	Credit

SOLUTIONS TO REVIEW QUESTIONS AND EXERCISES

TRUE-FALSE

1. (T)
2. (F)   If total debits exceed total credits a net loss has occurred.
3. (T)
4. (F)   Since a work sheet is not a journal, it cannot be used as a basis for posting to ledger accounts.
5. (T)
6. (T)
7. (T)
8. (T)
9. (T)
10. (F)   Owner's Drawing is credited and Owner's Capital is debited.
11. (F)   Income Summary is only used in preparing closing entries.
12. (F)   The post-closing trial balance will contain only balance sheet accounts.
13. (T)
14. (F)   Correcting entries are made whenever an error is discovered.
15. (F)   The operating cycle is the average time required to go from cash to cash in producing revenues.
16. (T)
17. (T)
18. (F)   Property, plant, and equipment are reported at cost less accumulated depreciation.
19. (T)
20. (T)

MULTIPLE CHOICE

1. (c)   The trial balance (a), income statement (b), and adjusted trial balance (d), are all columns on the work sheet. A post-closing trial balance is not presented on the work sheet.

2. (a)   The preparation of a work sheet involves the following steps:
    1. Prepare a trial balance on the work sheet.
    2. Enter the adjustments in the adjustment columns.
    3. Enter adjusted balances in the adjusted trial balance columns.
    4. Extend adjusted trial balance amounts to appropriate financial statement columns.
    5. Total the statement columns, compute the net income (or loss), and complete the work sheet.

3. (c)   Prepaid Insurance (a), Unearned Revenue (b), and Accumulated Depreciation (d) are all account balances that are extended to the balance sheet columns. Depreciation Expense is transferred to the income statement columns.

4.   (d)   The work sheet is not used as a basis for posting to the ledger. The work sheet is frequently computerized using a spreadsheet software program (like Lotus 1-2-3). The work sheet is not part of the ledger.

5.   (b)   The drawing, revenue, and expense accounts are considered to be temporary owner's equity accounts (a) or nominal accounts (d). At the end of an accounting period, these accounts are transferred to the capital account. Not all balance sheet accounts are capital accounts (c), but all are permanent accounts.

6.   (d)   The drawing account is not an expense account (a) or a revenue account (b). It is also not a permanent account (c) because it is transferred to the capital account.

7.   (d)   A credit balance in Income Summary indicates the company has earned net income. The closing entry results in a debit to Income Summary and a credit to the owner's capital account.

8.   (b)   Fees Earned, Depreciation Expense, and Drawing are temporary accounts that are closed annually.

9.   (c)   The post-closing trial balance would have the least number of accounts because it would only have the real accounts. The trial balance would have both the real and nominal accounts. The adjusted trial balance would probably have more accounts than the trial balance, because it would have the same real and nominal accounts plus any new accounts resulting from any adjustments.

10.   (b)   The post-closing trial balance contains only balance sheet accounts because income statement accounts are nominal accounts and are closed out.

11.   (b)   The accounting cycle contains two optional steps: (1) use of a work sheet and (2) preparing reversing entries. Each of the other statements about the accounting cycle is true.

12.   (b)   The correct entry in this case was Cash (Dr) $350 and Unearned Fees (Cr) $350. A comparison with the incorrect entry shows that both Accounts Receivable and Unearned Fees are understated by $350. The correcting entry, therefore, is (b).

13.   (d)   The error has caused three accounts to be incorrect. Office Equipment is overstated by $500. Office Supplies is understated by $550, and Accounts Payable is understated by $50. The correcting entry is therefore (d).

14.   (c)   Prepaid Expenses, Supplies, and Cash are current assets. Equipment would be classified as Property, Plant, and Equipment

15.   (a)   The time period for current assets is within one year or the operating cycle, whichever is longer, not shorter as in (b). Choice (c) is incorrect because the operating cycle is the average time to go from cash to cash in producing revenues. Choice (d) is incorrect because current assets are listed in order of liquidity.

16.   (b)   Long-term investments are not expected to be realized in cash within the next year or operating cycle, whichever is longer. Choice (a) is incorrect because long-term investments are reported between current assets and property, plant, and equipment. Choice (c) is incorrect because long-term investments are not expected to be used or consumed. Choice (d) is a correct statement for intangible assets.

17.   (c)   Long-lived, non-physical resources are intangible assets.   Each of the other statements is true.

18.   (a)   This answer choice correctly states the expected source of payment.   Choice (b) is incorrect because current liabilities are not listed in order of maturity.   Choice (c) is incorrect because the time period is one year or the operating cycle, whichever is longer.   Choice (d) is incorrect because current maturities of long-term debt should be reported under current liabilities.

*19.   (a)   First, the adjusting entry should be determined.   For this transaction the following adjusting entry would be made:

   Salaries Expense   6,000
      Salaries Payable   6,000

   Then, to make the reversing entry, the above adjusting entry is reversed, both amount and account titles.

   Salaries Payable   6,000
      Salaries Expense   6,000

*20.   (b)   On December, 31, 2002 an adjusting entry was made to accrue $200 ($12,000 X 10% X 2/12) of interest by debiting Interest Expense for $200 and crediting Interest Payable for $200.   By reversing the entry after the closing entries are made, the balance in the Interest Payable account will be zero, and Interest Expense will have a credit balance of $200.   Therefore, by making the entry in (b), which includes a debit to Interest Expense of $300, the correct amount of interest, $100 ($300 - $200) for January will be shown in Interest Expense.

MATCHING

1. h	5. o	9. m	13. g
2. i	6. n	10. b	14. a
3. l	7. d	11. c	15. e
4. j	8. k	12. f	

EXERCISES

EX. 4-1

(a)

JAZZ COMPANY
Work Sheet
For the Year Ended Dec. 31, 2002

Account Titles	Trial Balance Dr.	Trial Balance Cr.	Adjustments Dr.	Adjustments Cr.	Adjusted Trial Balance Dr.	Adjusted Trial Balance Cr.	Income Statement Dr.	Income Statement Cr.	Balance Sheet Dr.	Balance Sheet Cr.
Cash	6,000				6,000				6,000	
Fees Receivable	7,850		(e) 2,250		10,100				10,100	
Supplies	6,000			(a) 2,000	4,000				4,000	
Prepaid Insurance	9,000			(b) 3,000	6,000				6,000	
Equipment	10,000				10,000				10,000	
Note Payable		9,750				9,750				9,750
Unearned Fees		3,100	(d) 450			2,650				2,650
K. Oliver, Capital		12,000				12,000				12,000
Fees Earned		22,000		(d) 450 (e) 2,250		24,700		24,700		
Salaries Expense	8,000		(g) 850		8,850		8,850			
Totals	46,850	46,850								
Supplies Expense			(a) 2,000		2,000		2,000			
Insurance Expense			(b) 3,000		3,000		3,000			
Accumulated Depreciation				(c) 1,000		1,000				1,000
Depreciation Expense			(c) 1,000		1,000		1,000			
Interest Expense			(f) 300		300		300			
Interest Payable				(f) 300		300				300
Salaries Payable				(g) 850		850				850
Totals			9,850	9,850	51,250	51,250	15,150	24,700	36,100	26,550
Net Income							9,550			9,550
Totals							24,700	24,700	36,100	36,100

(b)

General Journal			J1
Date	Account Title	Debit	Credit
2002			
	Closing entries		
	(1)		
Dec. 31	Fees Earned	24,700	
	Income Summary		24,700
	(2)		
31	Income Summary	15,150	
	Salaries Expense		8,850
	Supplies Expense		2,000
	Insurance Expense		3,000
	Depreciation Expense		1,000
	Interest Expense		300
	(To close expense accounts)		
	(3)		
31	Income Summary	9,550	
	K. Oliver, Capital		9,550
	(To close net income to capital)		

(c)

JAZZ COMPANY
Post-Closing Trial Balance
December 31, 2002

	Debit	Credit
Cash	$ 6,000	
Fees Receivable	10,100	
Supplies	4,000	
Prepaid Insurance	6,000	
Equipment	10,000	
Accumulated Depreciation		$ 1,000
Note Payable		9,750
Unearned Fees		2,650
Salaries Payable		850
Interest Payable		300
K. Oliver, Capital ($12,000 + $9,550)		21,550
	$36,100	$36,100

1																				1
2																				2
3																				3
4																				4
5																				5
6																				6
7																				7
8																				8
9																				9
10																				10
11																				11
12																				12
13																				13
14																				14
15																				15
16																				16
17																				17
18																				18
19																				19
20																				20
21																				21
22																				22
23																				23
24																				24
25																				25
26																				26
27																				27
28																				28
29																				29
30																				30
31																				31
32																				32
33																				33
34																				34
35																				35
36																				36
37																				37
38																				38
39																				39
40																				40

1											1
2											2
3											3
4											4
5											5
6											6
7											7
8											8
9											9
10											10
11											11
12											12
13											13
14											14
15											15
16											16
17											17
18											18
19											19
20											20
21											21
22											22
23											23
24											24
25											25
26											26
27											27
28											28
29											29
30											30
31											31
32											32
33											33
34											34
35											35
36											36
37											37
38											38
39											39
40											40

Chapter 5

ACCOUNTING FOR MERCHANDISING OPERATIONS

The Navigator	✓
■ *Scan Study Objectives*	☐
■ *Read Preview*	☐
■ *Read Chapter Review*	☐
■ *Work Demonstration Problem*	☐
■ *Answer True-False Statements*	☐
■ *Answer Multiple-Choice Questions*	☐
■ *Match Terms and Definitions*	☐
■ *Solve Exercises*	☐

CHAPTER STUDY OBJECTIVES

After studying this chapter, you should be able to:
1. Identify the differences between a service enterprise and a merchandiser.
2. Explain the entries for purchases under a perpetual inventory system.
3. Explain the entries for sales revenues under a perpetual inventory system.
4. Explain the steps in the accounting cycle for a merchandiser.
5. Distinguish between a multiple-step and a single-step income statement.
6. Explain the computation and importance of gross profit.

PREVIEW OF CHAPTER 5

The steps in the accounting cycle for a merchandising company are the same as the steps for a service enterprise. However, merchandising companies use additional accounts and entries which are required in recording merchandising transactions. The content and organization of this chapter are as follows:

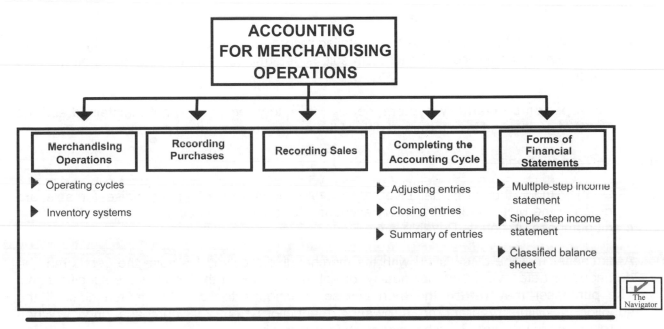

CHAPTER REVIEW

Measuring Net Income

1. (S.O. 1) A merchandiser is an enterprise that buys and sells goods to earn a profit. Merchandisers that purchase and sell directly to consumers are **retailers,** and those that sell to retailers are known as **wholesalers.**

2. The primary source of revenue for a merchandiser is **sales revenue.** Expenses are divided into two categories: (1) cost of goods sold and (2) operating expenses.

3. Sales less cost of goods sold is called the gross profit (or gross margin) on sales. For example, if sales are $5,000 and cost of goods sold is $3,000, gross profit is $2,000.

Sales
—COGS
Gross Profit,

4. After gross profit is calculated, operating expenses are deducted to determine net income (or loss).

5. **Operating expenses** are expenses incurred in the process of earning sales revenue.

Operating Cycles

6. The operating cycle of a merchandiser is as follows:

Inventory Systems

7. A merchandiser may use either a perpetual or a periodic inventory system in determining cost of goods sold.

    a. In a **perpetual inventory system,** detailed records of the cost of each inventory item are maintained and the cost of each item sold is determined from the records when the sale occurs.

    b. In a **periodic inventory system,** detailed inventory records are not maintained and the cost of goods sold is determined only at the end of an accounting period.

Purchase Transactions

8. (S.O. 2) Under the perpetual inventory system, purchases of merchandise for sale are recorded in the Merchandise Inventory account. For a cash purchase, Cash is credited; for a credit purchase, Accounts Payable is credited.

9. A purchaser may be dissatisfied with the merchandise received because the goods may be damaged or defective, of inferior quality, or not in accord with the purchaser's specifications. The purchaser may **return** the merchandise, or choose to keep the merchandise if the supplier is willing to grant an **allowance** (deduction) from the purchase price. When merchandise is returned, Merchandise Inventory is credited.

10. When the credit terms of a purchase on account permits the purchaser to claim a cash discount for the prompt payment of a balance due, this is called a **purchase discount.** If a purchase discount has terms 3/10, n/30, then a 3% discount is taken on the invoice price (less any returns or allowances) if payment is made within 10 days. If payment is not made within 10 days, then there is no purchase discount, and the net amount of the bill is due within 30 days.

11. When an invoice is paid within the discount period, the amount of the discount is credited to Merchandise Inventory. When an invoice is not paid within the discount period, then the usual entry is made with a debit to Accounts Payable and a credit to Cash.

12. **FOB shipping point** means that goods are placed free on board the carrier by the seller, and the buyer must pay the freight costs. **FOB destination** means that goods are placed free on board at the buyer's place of business, and the seller pays the freight.

13. When the buyer pays the freight, Merchandise Inventory is debited. When the seller pays the freight, Delivery Expense or Freight-out is debited. This account is classified as an operating expense by the seller.

Sales Transactions

14. (S.O. 3) In accordance with the **revenue recognition principle,** sales revenues are recorded when earned. Typically sales revenues are earned when the goods are transferred from the seller to the buyer.

15. All sales transactions should be supported by a **business document**. Cash register tapes provide evidence of cash sales; sales invoices provide support for credit sales.

16. A sale on credit is recorded as follows:

Accounts Receivable..	XXXX	
Sales..		XXXX
Cost of Goods Sold	XXXX	
Merchandise Inventory		XXXX

After the cash payment is received by the seller, the following entry is recorded:

Cash	XXXX	
Accounts Receivable..		XXXX

A cash sale is recorded by a debit to Cash and a credit to Sales, and a debit to Cost of Goods Sold and a credit to Merchandise Inventory.

Sales Returns and Allowances

17. A **sales return** results when a customer is dissatisfied with merchandise and is allowed to return the goods to the seller for credit or for a cash refund. A **sales allowance** results when a customer is dissatisfied with merchandise and the seller is willing to grant an allowance (deduction) from the selling price.

18. To give the customer a sales return or allowance, the seller normally prepares a business document known as a **credit memorandum** to inform the customer that a credit has been made to the customer's account receivable. The seller makes the following entry if the sale had been a credit sale (the second entry is made only if the goods are returned):

    Sales Returns and Allowances XXXX
        Accounts Receivable XXXX

    Merchandise Inventory XXXX
        Cost of Goods Sold XXXX

    For a sales return or allowance on a cash sale, a cash refund is made and Cash is credited instead of Accounts Receivable. The second entry is the same as above.

19. Sales Returns and Allowances is a **contra revenue account** and the normal balance of the account is a debit.

Sales Discounts

20. A **sales discount** is the offer of a cash discount to a customer for the prompt payment of a balance due. If a credit sale has terms 2/10, n/30, then a 2% discount is taken on the invoice price (less any returns or allowances) if payment is made within 10 days. If payment is not made within 10 days, then there is no sales discount, and the net amount of the bill, without discount, is due within 30 days. Sales Discounts is a **contra revenue account** and the normal balance of this account is a debit.

21. Both Sales Returns and Allowances and Sales Discounts are subtracted from Sales in the income statement to arrive at **net sales.**

SALES
- R+A
- Sales discounts
Net sales

The Accounting Cycle

22. (S.O. 4) Each of the required steps in the accounting cycle applies to a merchandiser.

Adjusting Entries and Closing Entries

23. A merchandiser generally has the same types of adjusting entries as a service company but a merchandiser using a perpetual inventory system will require an additional adjustment to reflect the difference between a physical count of the inventory and the accounting records. In addition, like a service company, a merchandiser makes closing entries to and from Income Summary.

Multiple-Step vs. Single-Step Income Statement

24. (S.O. 5) A **multiple-step income statement** shows numerous steps in determining net income. It shows two steps: (1) cost of goods sold is subtracted from net sales for determining gross profit and (2) operating expenses are deducted from gross profit to determine net income. In addition, there may be nonoperating sections for:

   a. Revenues and expenses that result form secondary or auxiliary operations, and

   b. Gains and losses that are unrelated to the company's operations.

Gross Profit and Operating Expenses

25. (S.O. 6) **Gross profit** is net sales less cost of goods sold. The gross profit rate is expressed as a percentage by dividing the amount of gross profit by net sales. Operating expenses are the third component in measuring net income for a merchandising company.

26. Nonoperating sections are reported in the income statement after income from operations and are classified as (a) Other revenues and gains and (b) Other expenses and losses.

27. A multiple-step income statement may also subdivide operating expenses into two functional groupings: (a) selling expenses, and (b) administrative expenses.

28. The income statement is referred to as a **single-step income statement** when all data are classified under two categories: (a) Revenues and (b) Expenses, and only one step is required in determining net income or net loss.

Classified Balance Sheet

29. A merchandiser generally has the same type of balance sheet as a service company except merchandise inventory is reported as a current asset.

The
Navigator

DEMONSTRATION PROBLEM (S.O. 2)

Presented below is the following information for Jennifer Company for 2002:

1.   On November 4, purchased merchandise from A. Mobley Company for $20,000 terms 2/10, net/30, FOB shipping point.
2.   On November 5, paid freight cost of $800 on merchandise purchased from A. Mobley.
3.   On November 6, purchased equipment on account for $15,000.
4.   On November 7, returned damaged merchandise to A. Mobley Company and was granted a $4,000 allowance.
5.   On November 13, paid the amount due to A. Mobley Company in full.

Instructions
(a)   Prepare the journal entries to record these transactions on the books of Jennifer Company under a perpetual inventory system.
(b)   Assume that Jennifer Company paid the balance due to A. Mobley Company on November 23 instead of November 13. Prepare the journal entry to record this payment.

SOLUTION TO DEMONSTRATION PROBLEM

(a)

Nov.	4	Merchandise Inventory	20,000	
		Accounts Payable		20,000
Nov.	5	Merchandise Inventory	800	
		Cash		800
Nov.	6	Equipment	15,000	
		Accounts Payable		15,000
Nov.	7	Accounts Payable	4,000	
		Merchandise Inventory		4,000
Nov.	13	Accounts Payable	16,000	
		Cash		15,680
		Merchandise Inventory		320

(b)

Nov.	23	Accounts Payable	16,000	
		Cash		16,000

REVIEW QUESTIONS AND EXERCISES

TRUE—FALSE

Indicate whether each of the following is true (T) or false (F) in the space provided.

_____ 1. (S.O. 1) Merchandisers that sell to wholesalers are known as retailers.

_____ 2. (S.O. 1) Merchandise inventory is reported as a long-term asset on the balance sheet.

_____ 3. (S.O. 1) In a perpetual inventory system no attempt is made to keep detailed inventory records of the goods on hand throughout the period.

_____ 4. (S.O. 1) Under a perpetual inventory system, inventory shrinkage and lost or stolen goods are more readily determined.

_____ 5. (S.O. 2) Under the perpetual inventory system, purchases of merchandise for sale are recorded by a credit to the Merchandise Inventory account.

_____ 6. (S.O. 2) A purchase return is where the purchaser chooses to keep the merchandise if the supplier is willing to grant an allowance (deduction) from the purchase price.

_____ 7. (S.O. 2) The terms 2/10, n/30 state that a 2% discount is available if the invoice is paid within the first 10 days of the next month.

_____ 8. (S.O. 2) When the terms are FOB shipping point, the seller pays the freight costs from the seller's location.

_____ 9. (S.O. 3) Gross profit is computed by subtracting cost of goods sold from net sales.

_____ 10. (S.O. 3) Sales should be recorded in accordance with the matching principle.

_____ 11. (S.O. 3) To record a sale, an asset account is debited and the revenue account Sales is credited.

_____ 12. (S.O. 3) Upon approval of the customer's request for a sales return or allowance, the seller normally prepares a business document known as a credit memorandum.

_____ 13. (S.O. 3) Sales Returns and Allowances is a contra expense account.

_____ 14. (S.O. 3) A sales discount is the offer of a cash discount to a customer for the prompt payment of a balance due.

_____ 15. (S.O. 3) Sales returns and allowances and sales discounts are subtracted from sales in reporting net sales in the income statement.

_____ 16. (S.O. 4) A merchandiser using a perpetual inventory system will usually need to make an adjusting entry to ensure that the recorded inventory agrees with physical inventory count.

_____ 17. (S.O. 5) When a company has other revenues and gains, sales revenue less cost of goods sold and operating expenses equals net income (or loss).

_____ 18. (S.O. 5) If a merchandising company sells land at more than its cost, the gain should be reported in the sales revenue section of the income statement.

_____ 19. (S.O. 5) The single-step statement is so named because only one step, subtracting total expenses from total revenues, is required in determining net income or net loss.

_____ 20. (S.O. 6) The major difference between the balance sheets of a service company and a merchandising company is inventory.

MULTIPLE CHOICE

Circle the letter that best answers each of the following statements.

1. (S.O. 1) A merchandiser sells goods to:

	Retailers	**Consumers**
a.	yes	yes
b.	yes	no
c.	no	yes
d.	no	no

2. (S.O. 1) Brent Company has sales revenue of $13,000, cost of goods sold of $8,000 and operating expenses of $3,000 for the year ended December 31. Brent's gross profit is:
    a. $10,000.
    b. $ 5,000.
    c. $ 2,000.
    d. $ 0.

3. (S.O. 1) For the year ended 2000, Degas Co. has the following amounts: Sales Revenue $350,000; Gross Profit $120,000; and Operating Expenses $90,000. What are the amounts of Cost of Goods Sold and Net Income (Loss)?
    a. $260,000 and $140,000.
    b. $230,000 and $30,000.
    c. $230,000 and $140,000.
    d. $130,000 and $90,000.

4. (S.O. 1) Which of the following is **not** associated with a perpetual inventory system?
    a. Detailed records of the cost of each inventory purchase and sale are maintained.
    b. The system is usually more expensive.
    c. Shrinkage and lost or stolen goods are more readily determined.
    d. The cost of goods sold is determined only at the end of the accounting period.

5. (S.O. 2)   Monet Company made a purchase of merchandise on credit from Claude Corporation on August 3, for $3,000, terms 2/10, n/45. On August 10, Monet makes the appropriate payment to Claude. The entry on August 10 for Monet Company is:

    a.   Accounts Payable   3,000
            Cash...   3,000
    b.   Accounts Payable   2,940
            Cash...   2,940
    c.   Accounts Payable   3,000
            Purchase Returns and Allowances   60
            Cash...   2,940
    d.   Accounts Payable   3,000
            Merchandise Inventory...   60
            Cash...   2,940

6. (S.O. 2) On August 28, Renoir Company purchased merchandise from Sisley Company for $2,375 on credit. Under the perpetual system, the entry by Renoir Company is:

    a.   Merchandise Inventory...   2,375
            Accounts Payable   2,375
    b.   Accounts Payable   2,375
            Merchandise Inventory...   2,375
    c.   Cash   2,375
            Accounts Payable   2,375
    d.   Sales...   2,375
            Accounts Payable   2,375

7. (S.O. 2) Cezanne Co. returned defective goods costing $5,000 to the Bazille Company on March 19, for credit. The goods were purchased March 10, on credit, terms 3/10, n/30. The entry by Cezanne Co. on March 19, in receiving full credit is:

    a.   Accounts Payable   5,000
            Merchandise Inventory...   150
            Cash...   4,850
    b.   Accounts Payable   5,000
            Merchandise Inventory...   150
            Cash...   5,150
    c.   Accounts Payable   5,000
            Purchase Discounts   150
            Merchandise Inventory...   4,850
    d.   Accounts Payable   5,000
            Merchandise Inventory...   5,000

8. (S.O. 2) Seurat Company made a purchase of merchandise on credit from Van Gogh Company on August 3, for $6,000, terms 3/10, n/30. On August 17, Seurat makes the appropriate payment to Van Gogh. The entry on August 17 for Seurat Company is:

a.	Accounts Payable	6,000	
	Cash		6,000
b.	Accounts Payable	5,820	
	Cash		5,820
c.	Accounts Payable	6,000	
	Purchase Returns and Allowances		180
	Cash		5,820
d.	Accounts Payable	6,000	
	Merchandise Inventory		180
	Cash		5,820

9. (S.O. 2) Caillebotte Company purchased inventory from Pissaro Company. The shipping costs were $400 and the terms of the shipment were FOB shipping point. Caillebotte would have the following entry regarding the shipping charges:

a.	There is no entry on Caillebotte's books for this transaction.		
b.	Freight Expense	400	
	Cash		400
c.	Freight-out	400	
	Cash		400
d.	Merchandise Inventory	400	
	Cash		400

10. (S.O. 3) Every credit sale should be supported by a:

	Cash Register Tape	**Sales Invoice**
a.	yes	yes
b.	yes	no
c.	no	yes
d.	no	no

11. (S.O. 3) El Greco Co. made a credit sale to Rubens Company when terms were n/30. Upon payment by Rubens, El Greco Co. should debit Cash and credit:
   a. Sales.
   b. Accounts Receivable and Sales Discounts.
   c. Accounts Receivable.
   d. None of the above.

12. (S.O. 3) On October 2, 2002, DaVinchi Company has cash sales of $3,200 from merchandise having a cost of $2,500. The entries to record the day's cash sales will include:
   a. a $2,500 debit to Cost of Goods Sold.
   b. a $3,200 credit to Cash.
   c. a $2,500 debit to Merchandise Inventory.
   d. a $2,500 debit to Accounts Receivable.

13. (S.O. 3) On October 4, 2002 Terry Corporation had credit sales transactions of $2,500 from merchandising having cost $1,900. The entries to record the day's credit transactions include:
    a. a debit of $2,500 to Merchandise Inventory.
    b. a credit of $2,500 to Sales.
    c. a debit of $1,900 to Merchandise Inventory.
    d. a credit of $1,900 to Cost of Goods Sold.

14. (S.O. 3) A customer, Zurbaran, is dissatisfied with merchandise purchased for $2,000 cash from the Rembrandt Company. Rembrandt Company gives Zurbaran a cash refund of $2,000. The journal entry by Rembrandt Company for the refund will include a:
    a. debit to Sales Returns and Allowances.
    b. credit to Accounts Receivable.
    c. debit to Accounts Receivable.
    d. credit to Sales Returns and Allowances.

15. (S.O. 3) On July 9, Goya Company sells goods on credit to Ed Manet for $3,500, terms 1/10, n/60. Goya receives payment on July 18. The entry by Goya on July 18 is:

    a. Cash 3,500
        Accounts Receivable 3,500
    b. Cash 3,500
        Sales Discounts 35
        Accounts Receivable 3,465
    c. Cash 3,465
        Sales Discounts 35
        Accounts Receivable 3,500
    d. Cash 3,535
        Sales Discounts 35
        Accounts Receivable 3,500

16. (S.O. 3) Which of the following are contra revenue accounts?

	Sales Returns and Allowances	Sales Discounts	Freight-out
a.	yes	yes	no
b.	yes	no	yes
c.	no	yes	yes
d.	yes	no	no

17. (S.O. 4) In the Clark Company, sales were $320,000, sales returns and allowances were $20,000 and cost of goods sold was $180,000. The gross profit rate was:
    a. 60%.
    b. 40%.
    c. 37.5%.
    d. 56.3%.

18. (S.O. 4) When the physical count of BIM company inventory had a cost of $2,700 at year end and the unadjusted balance in Merchandise Inventory was $2,500, BIM will have to make the following entry:

a. Cost of Goods Sold... 200
        Merchandise Inventory.. 200
b. Merchandise Inventory 200
        Cost of Goods Sold... 200
c. Income Summary... 200
        Merchandise Inventory.. 200
d. Cost of Goods Sold... 2,500
        Merchandise Inventory.. 2,500

19. (S.O. 6) The nonoperating sections of the income statement will include a section entitled other:

a. revenues and losses.
b. revenues and gains.
c. expenses and gains.
d. expenses and casualty losses.

20. (S.O. 6) In the balance sheet, ending merchandise inventory is reported:

a. in current assets immediately following accounts receivable.
b. in current assets immediately following prepaid expenses.
c. in current assets immediately following cash.
d. under property, plant, and equipment.

The
Navigator

MATCHING

Match each term with its definition by writing the appropriate letter in the space provided.

Terms

_____ 1. Net sales.

_____ 2. Periodic inventory system.

_____ 3. Perpetual inventory system.

_____ 4. Multiple-step income statement.

_____ 5. Gross profit.

_____ 6. Income from operations.

_____ 7. Other revenues and gains.

_____ 8. Single-step income statement.

_____ 9. FOB shipping point.

_____ 10. Contra revenue account.

_____ 11. Sales discount.

_____ 12. Other expenses and losses.

_____ 13. FOB destination.

_____ 14. Cost of goods sold.

Definitions

a. A system in which detailed inventory records are not maintained and the cost of goods sold is determined only at the end of an accounting period through the taking of physical inventory.

b. Goods are placed free on board at the buyer's place of business, and the seller must pay the freight costs.

c. A detailed inventory system in which the cost of each inventory item is maintained and the records continuously show the inventory that should be on hand.

d. Net sales less cost of goods sold.

e. A nonoperating section of the income statement that shows expenses pertaining to auxiliary operations and losses unrelated to the company's operations.

f. A nonoperating section of the income statement that shows revenues from auxiliary operations and gains unrelated to the company's operations.

g. Sales less sales returns and allowances and sales discounts.

h. Cost of goods available for sale less ending merchandise inventory.

i. An income statement in which numerous steps are involved before net income or net loss is reported.

j. An income statement that shows only one step in determining net income or net loss.

k. An account that is offset against a revenue account on the income statement.

l. Net sales less cost of goods sold and operating expenses.

m. A reduction given by a seller from prompt payment of a credit sale.

n. Goods are placed free on board the carrier by the seller, and the buyer must pay the freight costs.

EXERCISES

EX. 5-1 (S.O. 2 and 3) During the month of October, 2002, the American Fiction Merchandising Company had the following transactions:

Oct.   2   Sold $5,000 of goods that originally cost $4,200 to Jim Michener for cash.

10   Sold goods to Irving Stone for $2,500 on credit, terms 2/10, n/30. The goods originally cost $1,700.

12   Gave a cash refund of $2,500 to Jim Michener because half of the goods purchased on October 2 were defective. The goods were not returned.

15   Purchased $8,000 of merchandise from L'Amour Company on credit, terms 2/10, n/30.

17   Received cash from Irving Stone in full payment of the sale on October 10, less the sales discount.

21   Received an allowance from L'Amour Company of $1,000 because the goods purchased on October 15 did not meet specifications.

24   Paid L'Amour Company the amount due less the purchase discount.

Instructions
Journalize the transactions. (Omit explanations.)

	General Journal		J1
Date	Account Title	Debit	Credit

General Journal			J1
Date	Account Title	Debit	Credit

EX. 5-2 (S.O. 7) On December 31, 2002, the adjusted trial balance of the Mailer Company was as follows:

	Debits		**Credits**
Cash	$ 3,500	Accumulated Depreciation	$ 12,000
Accounts Receivable	13,000	Accounts Payable	16,250
Merchandise Inventory	40,500	N. Mailer, Capital	66,500
Equipment	70,000	Sales	505,000
N. Mailer, Drawing	15,000	Interest Revenue	10,900
Sales Returns and Allowances	13,850		
Sales Discounts	7,750		
Cost of Goods Sold	277,850		
Freight-out	6,000		
Advertising Expense	9,500		
Sales Commissions Expense	35,000		
Office Salaries	83,000		
Utilities Expense	23,000		
Interest Expense	8,700		
Depreciation Expense	4,000		

Other data:
Utilities expense and depreciation expense are both 40% selling and 60% administrative.

Instructions
Prepare a multiple-step income statement for the year ended December 31, 2002.

MAILER COMPANY
Income Statement
For the Year Ended December 31, 2002

MAILER COMPANY
Income Statement
For the Year Ended December 31, 2002
(continued)

The
Navigator

SOLUTIONS TO REVIEW QUESTIONS AND EXERCISES

TRUE-FALSE

1. (F) Merchandisers that sell to retailers are known as wholesalers; retailers are merchandising companies that purchase and sell directly to consumers.
2. (F) Merchandise inventory is reported as a current asset on the balance sheet.
3. (F) In a perpetual inventory system detailed records of the cost of each inventory purchase and sale are maintained and continuously (perpetually) show the inventory that should be on hand for every item.
4. (T)
5. (F) Under a perpetual inventory system, purchases of merchandise for sale are recorded by a debit to the Merchandise Inventory account.
6. (F) A purchase return is where the purchaser returns the goods to the supplier for credit if the sale was made on credit, or for a cash refund if the purchase was originally for cash.
7. (F) The terms 2/10, n/30 state that a 2% discount is available if the invoice is paid within 10 days of the invoice date otherwise the net balance, without cash discount, is due 30 days from the invoice date.
8. (F) When the terms are FOB shipping point, the buyer pays the freight costs; when the terms are FOB destination, the seller pays the freight costs.
9. (T)
10. (F) Sales should be recorded in accordance with the revenue recognition principle.
11. (T)
12. (T)
13. (F) Sales Returns and Allowances is a contra revenue account. It is subtracted from Sales in the computation of Net Sales.
14. (T)
15. (T)
16. (T)
17. (F) The difference between the amounts is income (loss) from operations, not net income (or loss).
18. (F)   If a merchandising company sells land at more than its cost, the gain should be reported in the other revenues and gains section.
19. (T)
20. (T)

MULTIPLE CHOICE

1. (a) A merchandiser sells goods to both retailers and consumers.

2. (b) The gross profit is equal to sales revenue minus cost of goods sold ($13,000 - $8,000 = $5,000).

3. (b) Cost of Goods Sold equals Sales Revenue less Gross Profit ($350,000 - $120,000 = $230,000) and Net Income equals Gross Profit less Operating Expenses ($120,000 - $90,000 = $30,000).

4.   (d)   Under a periodic inventory system, the cost of goods sold is determined only at the end of the accounting period. In a perpetual inventory system, the cost of goods sold is determined and recorded each time a sale occurs. Answers (a), (b), and (c) are all associated with perpetual inventory systems.

5.   (d)   Because the payment was within 10 days, Monet was allowed a purchase discount of $60 ($3,000 X 2%). Thus, credits are needed to Cash $2,940 and Merchandise Inventory $60.

6.   (a)   The purchase of inventory on credit results in a debit to Merchandise Inventory and a credit to Accounts Payable.

7.   (d)   A purchase discount is not involved because a payment was never made. The credit of $5,000 is recorded by debiting Accounts Payable, $5,000 and crediting Merchandise Inventory $5,000.

8.   (a)   Because Seurat failed to make the payment with the time period of 10 days, the full payment must be made on August 17. Therefore, Accounts Payable is debited for $6,000 and Cash is credited for $6,000.

9.   (d)   The terms FOB shipping point mean that goods are placed free on board the carrier by the seller, and the buyer pays the freight costs. When the purchaser directly incurs the freight costs, the account Merchandise Inventory is debited.

10.   (c)   Cash register tapes support cash sales, and sales invoices support credit sales.

11.   (c)   The entry for a receipt of a balance due from a credit sale when terms were n/30 is debit Cash and credit Accounts Receivable.

12.   (a)   The entries to record the day's cash sales are as follows:

Cash	3,200	
Sales		3,200
Cost of Goods Sold	2,500	
Merchandise Inventory		2,500

13.   (b)   The credit transactions by Terry Corporation would be as follows:

Accounts Receivable	2,500	
Sales		2,500
Cost of Goods Sold	1,900	
Merchandise Inventory		1,900

14.   (a)   The entry for the cash refund is debit Sales Returns and Allowances $2,000 and credit Cash $2,000.

15.   (c)   The payment was made within the discount period. Therefore, Cash is debited for $3,465, Sales Discount is debited for $35 ($3,500 X 1%), and the Accounts Receivable account is credited for $3,500.

16. (a) Both Sales Returns and Allowances and Sales Discounts are contra revenue accounts. Freight-out is a selling expense.

17. (b) The gross profit rate is computed by dividing gross profit by net sales. Gross profit is $120,000 [($320,000 - $20,000) - $180,000], and net sales are $300,000; $120,000 ÷ $300,000 = 40%.

18. (b) The account Merchandise Inventory for BIM should be adjusted to reflect the physical count and therefore Merchandise Inventory is increased by $200 ($2,700 - 2,500) with a debit, and Cost of Goods Sold is credited for $200.

19. (b) The nonoperating sections are either entitled (1) Other revenues and gains or (2) Other expenses and losses. Answer (d) is incorrect because other types of losses besides casualty losses can be recorded in this section.

20. (a) Ending inventory is reported in current assets immediately following accounts receivable.

MATCHING

1.	g	6.	l	11.	m
2.	a	7.	f	12.	e
3.	c	8.	j	13.	b
4.	i	9.	n	14.	h
5.	d	10.	k		

EXERCISES

EX. 5-1

	General Journal		J1
Date	**Account Title**	**Debit**	**Credit**
2002 Oct. 2	Cash	5,000	
	Sales		5,000
	Cost of Goods Sold	4,200	
	Merchandise Inventory		4,200
10	Accounts Receivable	2,500	
	Sales		2,500
	Cost of Goods Sold	1,700	
	Merchandise Inventory		1,700
12	Sales Returns and Allowances	2,500	
	Cash		2,500
15	Merchandise Inventory	8,000	
	Accounts Payable		8,000
17	Cash	2,450	
	Sales Discounts ($2,500 X 2%)	50	
	Accounts Receivable		2,500
21	Accounts Payable	1,000	
	Merchandise Inventory		1,000

General Journal			J1
Date	Account Title	Debit	Credit
Oct. 24	Accounts Payable	7,000	
	Merchandise Inventory [($8,000 − $1,000) X 2%]		140
	Cash		6,860

EX. 5-2

MAILER COMPANY
Income Statement
For the Year Ended December 31, 2002

Sales revenues			
Sales			$505,000
Less: Sales returns and allowances		$ 13,850	
Sales discounts		7,750	21,600
Net sales			483,400
Cost of goods sold			277,850
Gross profit			205,550
Operating expenses			
Selling expenses			
Sales commissions expense	35,000		
Advertising expense	9,500		
Utilities expense ($23,000 X 40%)	9,200		
Freight-out	6,000		
Depreciation expense ($4,000 X 40%)	1,600		
Total selling expenses		61,300	
Administrative expenses			
Office salaries	83,000		
Utilities expense ($23,000 X 60%)	13,800		
Depreciation (4,000 X 60%)	2,400		
Total administrative expenses		99,200	
Total operating expenses			160,500
Income from operations			45,050
Other revenues and gains			
Interest revenue		10,900	
Other expenses and losses			
Interest expense		8,700	2,200
Net income			$ 47,250

	1	2	3	4	5	6	7	
1								1
2								2
3								3
4								4
5								5
6								6
7								7
8								8
9								9
10								10
11								11
12								12
13								13
14								14
15								15
16								16
17								17
18								18
19								19
20								20
21								21
22								22
23								23
24								24
25								25
26								26
27								27
28								28
29								29
30								30
31								31
32								32
33								33
34								34
35								35
36								36
37								37
38								38
39								39
40								40

	1	2	3	4	5	6	7	8	
1									1
2									2
3									3
4									4
5									5
6									6
7									7
8									8
9									9
10									10
11									11
12									12
13									13
14									14
15									15
16									16
17									17
18									18
19									19
20									20
21									21
22									22
23									23
24									24
25									25
26									26
27									27
28									28
29									29
30									30
31									31
32									32
33									33
34									34
35									35
36									36
37									37
38									38
39									39
40									40

	1																1
2																	2
3																	3
4																	4
5																	5
6																	6
7																	7
8																	8
9																	9
10																	10
11																	11
12																	12
13																	13
14																	14
15																	15
16																	16
17																	17
18																	18
19																	19
20																	20
21																	21
22																	22
23																	23
24																	24
25																	25
26																	26
27																	27
28																	28
29																	29
30																	30
31																	31
32																	32
33																	33
34																	34
35																	35
36																	36
37																	37
38																	38
39																	39
40																	40

Chapter **6**

	The Navigator	✓
■	*Scan Study Objectives*	☐
■	*Read Preview*	☐
■	*Read Chapter Review*	☐
■	*Work Demonstration Problem*	☐
■	*Answer True-False Statements*	☐
■	*Answer Multiple-Choice Questions*	☐
■	*Match Terms and Definitions*	☐
■	*Solve Exercises*	☐

INVENTORIES

CHAPTER STUDY OBJECTIVES

After studying this chapter, you should be able to:
1. Describe the steps in determining inventory quantities.
2. Prepare the entries for purchases and sales of inventory under a periodic inventory system.
3. Determine cost of goods sold under a periodic inventory system.
4. Identify the unique features of the income statement for a merchandiser using a periodic inventory system.
5. Explain the basis of accounting for inventories and describe the inventory cost flow methods.
6. Explain the financial statement and tax effects of each of the inventory cost flow methods.
7. Explain the lower of cost or market basis of accounting for inventories.
8. Indicate the effects of inventory errors on the financial statements.
9. Compute and interpret inventory turnover.
*10. Describe the two methods of estimating inventories
*11. Apply the inventory cost flow methods to perpetual inventory records.

*Note: All **asterisked** (*) items relate to material contained in the Appendix to the chapter.

PREVIEW OF CHAPTER 6

In this chapter we will explain the procedures for determining the cost of inventory on hand at the balance sheet date. In addition, we will discuss differences in periodic and perpetual inventory systems and the effects of inventory errors on a company's financial statements. The content and organization of this chapter are as follows:

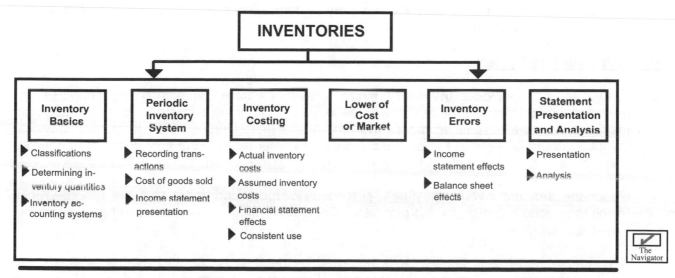

CHAPTER REVIEW

Classifying Inventory

1. (S.O. 1) **Merchandise inventory** has two common characteristics: (a) it is owned by the company and (b) it is in a form ready for sale in the ordinary course of business.

2. A manufacturer's inventory is usually classified into three categories:
    a. **Finished goods** that are completed and ready for sale.
    b. **Work in process** that is in various stages of production but not yet completed.
    c. **Raw materials** that are on hand waiting to be used in production.

Determination of Inventory Quantities

3. The determination of inventory quantities involves (a) taking a physical inventory of goods on hand and (b) determining the ownership of goods.

4. Taking a physical inventory involves counting, weighing or measuring each kind of inventory on hand. Internal control procedures should be followed in taking the inventory in order to minimize errors.

5. For goods in transit, **legal title** is determined by the terms of sale. When the terms are:
    a. **FOB (free on board) shipping point,** ownership of the goods passes to the buyer when the public carrier accepts the goods from the seller.
    b. **FOB destination,** legal title to the goods remains with the seller until the goods reach the buyer.

6. Under a consignment arrangement, the holder of the goods (called the consignee) does not own the goods. Ownership remains with the shipper of the goods (consignor) until the goods are actually sold to a customer. Consigned goods should be included in the consignor's inventory—not the consignee's inventory.

Inventory Accounting Systems

7. One of two basic systems of accounting for inventories may be used: (1) the perpetual inventory system, or (2) the periodic inventory system. This chapter discusses and illustrates the periodic inventory system.

Periodic Inventory System

8. (S.O. 2) In a **periodic inventory system** revenues from the sale of merchandise are recorded when sales are made in the same way as in a perpetual system. But, no attempt is made on the date of sale to record the cost of the merchandise sold. Instead, a physical inventory count is taken at the end of the period to determine (1) the cost of the merchandise then on hand and (2) the cost of the goods sold during the period.

9. Under the periodic inventory system, purchases of merchandise for sale are recorded in a Purchases account. For a cash purchase, Cash is credited; for a credit purchase, Accounts Payable is credited.

10. A purchase return and allowance is recorded by debiting Accounts Payable or Cash and crediting the account Purchase Returns and Allowances. Purchase Returns and Allowances is a temporary account whose normal balance is a credit.

11. If payment is made within a discount period, the amount of the discount is credited to the account Purchases Discounts. When an invoice is not paid within the discount period, then the usual entry is made with a debit to Accounts Payable and a credit to Cash.

12. The recording of sales transactions is the same as Chapter 5, except at the time of the sale no entry is made to record the cost of the merchandise sold.

Cost of Goods Sold

13. (S.O. 3) To determine the **cost of goods sold** under a periodic inventory system, three steps are required: (1) Record purchases of merchandise; (2) Determine the cost of goods purchased; and (3) Determine the cost of goods on hand at the beginning and end of the accounting period.

Cost of Goods Purchased

14. In determining cost of goods purchased, (a) contra purchase accounts are subtracted from purchases to produce **net purchases,** and (b) freight-in is then added to net purchases.

Cost of Inventory

15. **Cost of inventory on hand** under the periodic inventory method is obtained from a physical inventory. Taking a physical inventory involves:
     a.   Counting the units on hand for each item of inventory.
     b.   Applying unit costs to the total units on hand for each item.
     c.   Totaling the costs for each item of inventory, to determine the total cost of goods on hand.

Cost of Goods Sold

16. **Cost of goods sold** is determined by two steps:
     a.   The cost of goods purchased is added to the cost of goods on hand at the beginning of the period to obtain the cost of goods available for sale.
     b.   The cost of goods on hand at the end of the period is subtracted from **the cost of goods available for sale.**

17. The income statement for retailers and wholesalers under a periodic inventory system will generally contain more detail listing the above calculations.

Inventory Costing

18. (S.O. 5) Inventoriable costs may be regarded as a pool of costs that consist of two elements: (a) the cost of the beginning inventory and (b) the cost of the goods purchased during the year.
     a.   The sum of these two equals the cost of goods available for sale.
     b.   Under a periodic inventory system, the costs assignable to the ending inventory are determined first.
     c.   Ending inventory is then subtracted from cost of goods available for sale to determine cost of goods sold.

Specific Identification

19. The **specific identification method** tracks the actual physical flow of the goods so that the cost of the specific unit sold is charged to the cost of goods sold.
    a. This method is possible when a company sells a limited variety of high unit-cost items that can be clearly identified from the time of purchase through the time of sale.
    b. This method may enable management to manipulate net income.

20. The allocation of inventoriable costs may be made under any of the following assumptions as to the **flow of costs** (a) first-in, first-out (FIFO), (b) last-in, first-out (LIFO), or (c) average cost.

FIFO

21. The **FIFO method** assumes that the costs of the earliest goods purchased are the first to be sold.
    a. This method often parallels the actual physical flow of the merchandise.
    b. Under this method, the ending inventory is based on the latest units purchased.

LIFO

22. The **LIFO method** assumes that the costs of the latest units purchased are the first to be sold.
    a. This method seldom coincides with the actual physical flow of inventory.
    b. Under this method, all goods purchased during the period are assumed to be available for the first sale, regardless of the date of purchase.
    c. The ending inventory is found by taking the unit cost of the oldest goods and working forward until all units of inventory are costed.

Average Cost

23. The **average cost method** assumes that the goods available for sale are identical.
    a. Under this method, the cost of goods available for sale is allocated on the basis of **weighted-average unit** cost.
    b. The formula for determining the weighted average unit cost is: Cost of goods available for sale divided by total units available for sale.

Financial Statement Effects

24. (S.O. 6) In periods of rising prices, FIFO produces a higher net income, LIFO the lowest, and average cost falls in the middle. The reverse is true when prices are falling.

25. Companies adopt different inventory costing methods because of:
    a. Balance sheet effects: the inventory costs are closer to current costs under FIFO than under LIFO.
    b. Income statement effects: in addition to the effects on net income in (24) above, LIFO enables the company to avoid reporting paper or phantom profit as economic gain.
    c. Tax effects: in a period of inflation LIFO results in the lowest income taxes.

Lower of Cost of Market

26.   (S.O. 7) When the value of inventory is lower than its cost, the inventory is written down to its market value. This is known as the **lower of cost or market (LCM) method.**

27.   Market is measured by the **current replacement cost** of the goods, not selling price.

Effects of Inventory Errors

28.   (S.O. 8) The effects of **inventory errors** on the current year's income statement are:

Inventory Error	Cost of Goods Sold	Net Income
Beginning inventory understated	Understated	Overstated
Beginning inventory overstated	Overstated	Understated
Ending inventory understated	Overstated	Understated
Ending inventory overstated	Understated	Overstated

29.   The effects of ending inventory errors on the balance sheet are:

Ending Inventory	Assets	Liabilities	Owner's Equity
Overstated	Overstated	None	Overstated
Understated	Understated	None	Understated

30.   In the financial statements:
   a.   Inventory is usually classified as a current asset after receivables in the balance sheet, and cost of goods sold is subtracted from sales in the income statement.
   b.   There should be disclosure of (1) the major inventory classifications, (2) the basis of accounting, and (3) the costing method.

Inventory Turnover Ratio

31.   (S.O. 9) The **inventory turnover ratio** measures the number of times on average the inventory is sold during the period.

$$\text{Cost of Goods Sold} \div \text{Average Inventory} = \text{Inventory Turnover}$$

Estimating Inventories

*32. (S.O. 10) Inventories may have to be estimated when (a) management wants monthly or quarterly financial statements or (b) a fire or other type of casualty makes it impossible to take a physical inventory.

Gross Profit Method

*33. The **gross profit method** is widely used to estimate the ending inventory. Two steps are involved in using this method.
   a.   The estimated cost of goods sold is determined by subtracting the estimated gross profit from net sales.
   b.   The estimated cost of goods sold is subtracted from cost of goods available for sale to determine the estimated cost of the ending inventory.

Retail Inventory Method

*34. The **retail inventory method** is used by retail companies to estimate the cost of the inventory. The steps in using this method are:

a.

$$\begin{array}{ccc}\text{Goods Available} & \text{Net} & \text{Ending Inventory} \\ \text{for Sale at Retail} & - \;\text{Sales}\; = & \text{at Retail}\end{array}$$

b.

$$\begin{array}{ccc}\text{Goods Available} & \text{Goods Available} & \text{Cost to} \\ \text{for Sale at Cost} & \div \;\text{for Sale at Retail}\; = & \text{Retail Ratio}\end{array}$$

c.

$$\begin{array}{ccc}\text{Ending} & \text{Cost to} & \text{Estimated Cost} \\ \text{Inventory} \;\text{X}\; & \text{Retail} \;=\; & \text{of Ending} \\ \text{at Retail} & \text{Ratio} & \text{Inventory}\end{array}$$

*Applying Perpetual Inventory

*35. (S.O. 11) Each of the inventory cost flow methods may be used in a perpetual inventory system.
   a. Under FIFO, the cost of the earliest goods on hand prior to each sale is charged to cost of goods sold.
   b. When the **moving average method** is used, a new average is computed after each purchase by dividing the cost of goods available for sale by the units on hand.
   c. Under the LIFO method, the most recent purchase prior to sale is allocated to the units sold.

DEMONSTRATION PROBLEM No. 1 (S.O. 3)

The following information is given for Jennifer Company for 2002:

Purchases	$28,500
Purchase Discounts	2,400
Merchandise Inventory, 1/1/02	7,500
Freight-in	700
Purchase Returns and Allowances	1,500
Merchandise Inventory, 12/31/02	10,600

Instructions
Prepare the cost of goods sold section of the income statement for Jennifer Company.

SOLUTION TO DEMONSTRATION PROBLEM No. 1

Cost of goods sold			
Merchandise Inventory, 1/1/02			$ 7,500
Purchases		$28,500	
Less: Purchase returns and allowances	$1,500		
Purchase discounts	2,400	3,900	
Net Purchases		24,600	
Add: Freight-in		700	
Cost of goods purchased			25,300
Cost of goods available for sale			32,800
Merchandise Inventory, 12/31/02			10,600
Cost of goods sold			$22,200

---

*DEMONSTRATION PROBLEM No. 2 (S.O. 10)

The inventory of Edison Company was destroyed by fire on October 1, 2002. From an examination of the accounting records, the following data for the prior months of the year 2002 were obtained: Sales $462,000, Sales Returns and Allowances $8,500, Purchases $73,000, Freight-in $5,600, and Purchase Returns and Allowances $7,200.

Instructions
Determine the merchandise lost by fire, assuming a beginning inventory of $252,000 and a gross profit rate of 35% on net sales.

SOLUTION TO DEMONSTRATION PROBLEM No. 2

Sales	$462,000	
Sales Returns and Allowances	8,500	
Net sales		$453,500
Less: Estimated gross profit (35% X $453,500)		158,725
Estimated cost of goods sold		$294,775
Beginning inventory		$252,000
Purchases	$73,000	
Add: Freight-in	5,600	
Less: Purchases returns and allowances	(7,200)	
Cost of goods purchased		71,400
Cost of goods available for sale		323,400
Less: Estimated cost of goods sold		294,775
Estimated cost of ending inventory		$ 28,625

REVIEW QUESTIONS AND EXERCISES

TRUE—FALSE

Indicate whether each of the following is true (T) or false (F) in the space provided.

_____ 1. (S.O. 1) Merchandise inventory has two common characteristics: (a) it is owned by the company and (b) it is on hand waiting to be used in production.

_____ 2. (S.O. 1) Finished goods are a classification of inventory in a manufacturing enterprise that are completed and ready for sale.

_____ 3. (S.O. 1) The determination of inventory quantities involves taking a physical inventory and determining the ownership of goods.

_____ 4. (S.O. 1) Under the terms FOB destination, ownership of the goods passes to the buyer when the public carrier accepts the goods from the seller.

_____ 5. (S.O. 2) Net purchases is determined by subtracting purchase returns and allowances and purchase discounts from purchases.

_____ 6. (S.O. 3) In determining the cost of goods purchased, Freight-out is added to purchases.

_____ 7. (S.O. 3) Ending merchandise inventory is subtracted from the cost of goods available for sale in determining the cost of goods sold.

_____ 8. (S.O. 3) The cost of ending inventory is added to the cost of goods available for sale to determine cost of goods sold.

_____ 9. (S.O. 5) The primary basis of accounting for inventories is market value.

_____ 10. (S.O. 5) The pool of inventory costs consists of the beginning inventory plus the cost of goods purchased.

_____ 11. (S.O. 5) The inventory method of specific identification is appropriate for costly, easily distinguishable items such as pianos, automobiles, fur coats, and antiques.

_____ 12. (S.O. 5) Under the FIFO method, the costs of the earliest units purchased are the first charged to cost of goods sold.

_____ 13. (S.O. 6) In a period of falling prices, the LIFO method results in a lower cost of goods sold than the FIFO method.

_____ 14. (S.O. 6) In a period of rising prices, the FIFO method reports the highest net income, LIFO the lowest, and average cost falls in the middle.

_____ 15. (S.O. 7) Under the lower of cost or market basis, market is defined as selling price.

_____ 16. (S.O. 7) The lower of cost or market basis is an example of the accounting concept of conservatism.

_____ 17. (S.O. 7) The lower of cost or market basis must be applied to each individual item of inventory.

_____ 18. (S.O. 8) If beginning inventory is overstated, net income will be overstated in the same year.

_____ 19. (S.O. 8) Inventories are reported in the current asset section of the balance sheet immediately below receivables.

_____ *20. (S.O. 10) The gross profit method is based on the assumption that the rate of gross profit remains constant from one year to the next.

_____ *21. (S.O. 10) In the retail method, the cost to retail ratio is applied to the goods available for sale at retail to determine the estimated cost of the inventory.

_____ *22. (S.O. 11) In a perpetual inventory system, the cost of goods sold under the FIFO method is based on the cost of the latest goods on hand during the period.

_____ *23. (S.O. 11) Under the LIFO method, the cost of the most recent purchase prior to sale is allocated to the units sold in a perpetual inventory system.

The Navigator

MULTIPLE CHOICE

Circle the letter that best answers each of the following statements.

1. (S.O. 1) Inventory items on an assembly line in various stages of production are classified as:
   a. Finished goods.
   b. Work in process.
   c. Raw materials.
   d. Merchandise inventory.

2. (S.O. 1) L. Pasteur Company's inventory at December 31, 2002, was $300,000 based on a physical count of goods made on December 31. The following items were in transit:

   * Goods costing $5,000 were shipped FOB shipping point on December 29, 2002 to a customer and received by the customer on January 3, 2003.

   * Goods costing $10,000 were shipped FOB destination on December 30, 2002 to a customer and received by the customer on January 4, 2003.

   What amount should L. Pasteur report as inventory on its December 31, 2002 balance sheet?
   a. $290,000.
   b. $305,000.
   c. $310,000.
   d. $315,000.

3. (S.O. 2) Which of the following is true concerning Freight-in?
   a. Freight-in is subtracted from net purchases in determining cost of goods purchased.
   b. Freight-in is added to net purchases in determining cost of goods purchased.
   c. Freight-in is a selling expense.
   d. Freight-in is an administrative expense.

4. (S.O. 3) On December 31, Degas Co. has the following account balances: Purchases $307,000; Purchase Returns and Allowances $34,000; Purchase Discounts $26,000; and Freight-in $18,000. The cost of goods purchased for Degas Co. is:
   a. $265,000.
   b. $281,000.
   c. $349,000.
   d. $229,000.

5. (S.O. 3) On December 31, Seurat Company has the following amounts in the determination of cost of goods purchased; Purchases $60,000; Freight-in $10,000; Net purchases $48,000; Purchase returns and allowances $7,000; and Cost of goods purchased $58,000. What is the amount of purchase discounts?
   a. $2,000.
   b. $3,000.
   c. $5,000.
   d. $15,000.

6. (S.O. 3) On December 31, Van Gogh Company has the following data: Cost of goods purchased $184,500; Beginning Inventory $19,000, Ending inventory $25,000, and Sales $300,000. The cost of goods sold for Van Gogh Corporation is:
   a. $121,500.
   b. $190,500.
   c. $178,500.
   d. $109,500.

7. (S.O. 3) Caillebotte Company has the following amounts in the determination of cost of goods sold: Cost of Goods Purchased $76,000; Ending Inventory $34,000; Cost of Goods Sold $82,000. The dollar amount of beginning inventory is:
   a. $28,000.
   b. $40,000.
   c. $42,000.
   d. $48,000.

8. (S.O. 5) Rudolf Diesel Company's inventory records show the following data:

	Units	Unit Cost
Inventory, January 1	10,000	$9.00
Purchases: June 18	9,000	8.00
November 8	6,000	7.00

A physical inventory on December 31 shows 8,000 units on hand. Under the FIFO method, the December 31 inventory is:
   a. $56,000.
   b. $58,000.
   c. $64,000.
   d. $72,000.

9. (S.O. 5) Fermat Company had 300 units of inventory on hand at January 1 costing $32 each. Purchases during the month of January were as follows:

	Units	Unit Cost
Jan. 15	400	$33
23	550	34
29	100	35

A physical count on January 31 shows 450 units on hand. The cost of the inventory at January 31 under the LIFO method is:
a. $15,400.
b. $14,900.
c. $14,550.
d. $14,400.

Items 10 and 11 are based on the following data:

Sig Freud Bookstore had 200 electric pencil sharpeners on hand at January 1, costing $18 each. Purchases and sales of electric pencil sharpeners during the month of January were as follows:

Date	Purchases	Sales
Jan. 14		150@ $28
17	100 @ $20	
25	100 @ $22	
29		100 @ $32

Sig Freud does not maintain perpetual inventory records. According to a physical count, 150 electric pencil sharpeners were on hand at January 31.

10. (S.O. 5) The cost of the inventory at January 31, under the FIFO method is:
a. $400.
b. $2,700.
c. $3,100.
d. $3,200.

11. (S.O. 5) The cost of the inventory at January 31, under the LIFO method is:
a. $400.
b. $2,700.
c. $3,100.
d. $3,200.

12.   (S.O. 5) Ampere Company recorded the following data:

Date	Units Received	Units Sold	Units On Hand	Unit Cost
1/1 Inventory			400	$1.00
1/8 Purchased	600		1,000	1.10
1/12 Sold		800	200	

The weighted average unit cost of the inventory at January 31 is:
a. $1.00.
b. $1.05.
c. $1.06.
d. $1.10.

13.   (S.O. 6) In a period of rising prices, FIFO will have a
a.   lower net income than LIFO.
b.   lower cost of goods sold than LIFO.
c.   lower income tax expense than LIFO.
d.   lower net purchases than LIFO.

14.   (S.O. 6) In a period of inflation, the use of the LIFO method will result in:
a.   a more realistic inventory value than FIFO.
b.   a better matching of costs and revenues than FIFO.
c.   higher income taxes than FIFO.
d.   higher net income than FIFO.

15.   (S.O. 8) On December 31, 2002, Cavendish, Inc. overstated its ending inventory by $4,000. Assuming no correcting entry was made, the effects on the following **2003** income statement items are:

	Net Income	Sales	Cost of Goods Sold
a.	overstated	no effect	understated
b.	understated	no effect	overstated
c.	overstated	overstated	understated
d.	understated	no effect	understated

16.   (S.O. 8) Euler Company made an inventory count on December 31, 2002. During the count, one of the clerks made the error of counting an inventory item twice. For the balance sheet at December 31, 2002, the effects of this error are:

	Assets	Liabilities	Owner's Equity
a.	overstated	understated	overstated
b.	understated	no effect	understated
c.	overstated	no effect	overstated
d.	overstated	overstated	understated

*17. (S.O. 10) Doppler Company wishes to prepare an income statement for the month of March when its records show Net Sales, $300,000; Beginning Inventory, $59,000; and Cost of Goods Purchased, $155,000. The company realizes a 30% gross profit rate. The estimated cost of the ending inventory at March 31 under the gross profit method is:
a. $4,000.
b. $55,000.
c. $63,000.
d. $72,000.

*18. (S.O. 10) Oppenheimer Company's records indicate the following information for the year:

Merchandise inventory, 1/1	$ 550,000
Purchases	2,250,000
Net Sales	3,000,000

On December 31, a physical inventory determined that ending inventory of $600,000 was in the warehouse. Oppenheimer's gross profit on sales has remained constant at 30%. Oppenheimer suspects some of the inventory may have been taken by some new employees. At December 31, what is the estimated cost of missing inventory?
a. $100,000.
b. $200,000.
c. $300,000.
d. $700,000.

Items 19 and 20 are based on the following data: On December 31, Gottlieb Retailers has the following information under the retail inventory method.

	Cost	Retail
Beginning inventory	$40,500	$ 57,000
Cost of goods purchased	57,000	73,000
Goods available for sale	$97,500	130,000
Sales (net)		72,000
Ending inventory at retail		$ 58,000

*19. (S.O. 10) The cost to retail ratio is:
a. 71%.
b. 78%.
c. 75%.
d. 80%.

*20. (S.O. 10) The estimated cost of the ending inventory is:
a. $41,210.
b. $45,286.
c. $43,500.
d. $22,500.

Items *21-*23 relate to the perpetual inventory system of the Zollmer Company. During May, the following purchases and sales were made for Product X298. There was no beginning inventory.

		Purchases			**Sales**
May	3	20 units @ $20	May	15	25 units
	14	20 units @ $22		24	10 units
	21	10 units @ $25			

*21.   (S.O. 11) Under the FIFO method, the cost of goods sold for each sale is:

		May 15	**May 24**
	a.	$500	$200
	b.	550	220
	c.	510	220
	d.	625	250

*22.   (S.O. 11) Under the LIFO method, the cost of goods sold for each sale is:

		May 15	**May 24**
	a.	$540	$250
	b.	625	220
	c.	500	200
	d.	550	250

*23.   (S.O. 11) Under the average cost method, the cost of goods sold for each sale is:

		May 15	**May 24**
	a.	$575	$235
	b.	525	226
	c.	550	240
	d.	525	218

The
Navigator

MATCHING

Match each term with its definition by writing the appropriate letter in the space provided.

<table>
<tr><td colspan="2" align="center">**Terms**</td><td colspan="2" align="center">**Definitions**</td></tr>
<tr>
<td>_____ 1.</td><td>Inventoriable costs.</td>
<td>a.</td><td>An inventory system in which the accounting records continuously show the inventory that should be on hand at any point in time.</td>
</tr>
<tr>
<td>_____ 2.</td><td>Perpetual inventory system.</td>
<td>b.</td><td>The inventory costing method that tracks the actual physical flow of the goods available for sale.</td>
</tr>
<tr>
<td>_____ 3.</td><td>Specific identification method.</td>
<td>c.</td><td>The inventory costing method which assumes that the latest units purchased are the first to be allocated to cost of goods sold.</td>
</tr>
<tr>
<td>_____ 4.</td><td>First-in, first-out method (FIFO).</td>
<td>d.</td><td>The inventory costing method which assumes that the earliest goods acquired are the first to be recognized as cost of goods sold.</td>
</tr>
<tr>
<td>_____ 5.</td><td>Last-in, first-out method (LIFO).</td>
<td>e.</td><td>The inventory costing method which assumes that the goods available for sale are homogeneous.</td>
</tr>
<tr>
<td>_____ 6.</td><td>Average cost method.</td>
<td>f.</td><td>A method used to estimate the cost of the ending inventory in which the estimated cost of goods sold is subtracted from the cost of goods available for sale.</td>
</tr>
<tr>
<td>_____ 7.</td><td>Retail inventory method.</td>
<td>g.</td><td>A pool of costs that consists of the cost of the beginning inventory and the cost of goods purchased during the period.</td>
</tr>
<tr>
<td>_____ 8.</td><td>Gross profit method.</td>
<td>h.</td><td>The sum of the beginning merchandise inventory plus the cost of goods purchased.</td>
</tr>
<tr>
<td>_____ 9.</td><td>Lower of cost or market basis.</td>
<td>i.</td><td>A method used to estimate the cost of the ending inventory by using a cost to retail ratio.</td>
</tr>
<tr>
<td>_____ 10.</td><td>Cost of goods available for sale.</td>
<td>j.</td><td>A method of valuing inventory that recognizes the decline in the value when the current purchase price (market) is less than cost.</td>
</tr>
</table>

EXERCISES

EX. 6-1 (S.O.4) On December 31, 2002, the adjusted trial balance of the Mailer Company was as follows:

	Debits		**Credits**
Cash	$ 3,500	Accumulated Depreciation	$ 12,000
Accounts Receivable	13,000	Accounts Payable	16,250
Merchandise Inventory	42,000	N. Mailer, Capital	66,500
Equipment	70,000	Sales	505,000
N. Mailer, Drawing	15,000	Purchase Returns and Allow-	
Sales Returns and Allowances	13,850	ances	14,350
Sales Discounts	7,750	Purchase Discounts	22,000
Purchases	300,000	Interest Revenue	10,900
Freight-in	12,700		
Freight-out	6,000		
Advertising Expense	9,500		
Sales Commissions Expense	35,000		
Office Salaries	83,000		
Utilities Expense	23,000		
Interest Expense	8,700		
Depreciation Expense	4,000		

Other data:
1. Merchandise inventory December 31, 2002 is $40,500.
2. Utilities expense and depreciation expense are both 40% selling and 60% administrative.

Instructions
Prepare a multiple-step income statement for the year ended December 31, 2002.

MAILER COMPANY
Income Statement
For the Year Ended December 31, 2002

MAILER COMPANY
Income Statement
For the Year Ended December 31, 2002
(continued)

EX. 6-2   (S.O. 5) On January 1, Fermi Company had a beginning inventory of 200 units that cost $30 each. The following purchases were made during the year.

May	5	240 units at $28
Aug.	8	350 units at $31
Nov.	29	300 units at $33

Fermi Company uses a periodic inventory system. The count of the ending inventory was 500 units at December 31.

Instructions

Compute the cost of the ending inventory and the cost of goods sold for Fermi Company for the year ended December 31 for each of the following methods: (a) FIFO, (b) LIFO, and (c) average cost (round to two decimals)

<u>**Pool of Costs**</u>
<u>**Cost of Goods Available for Sale**</u>

Date	Units	Unit Cost	Total Cost

<u>**FIFO Method**</u>

Ending Inventory:

Date	Units	Unit Cost	Total Cost

FIFO Method (continued)

Cost of goods sold:

Date	Units	Unit Cost	Total Cost

LIFO Method

Ending Inventory:

Date	Units	Unit Cost	Total Cost

Cost of goods sold:

_____

_____

Average Cost Method

Weighted average unit cost:

_____

Ending Inventory:

_____

_____

Cost of goods sold:

_____

_____

***EX. 6-3** (S.O. 10) The records of A.G. Bell Company show the following data for the month of October:

Net sales	$230,000
Inventory at cost, October 1	122,500
Inventory at retail, October 1	175,000
Goods purchased at cost	149,600
Goods purchased at retail	220,000

Instructions
(a) Using the retail inventory method, compute the estimated cost of the inventory at October 31. (Round to two decimals.)
(b) Assuming a gross profit rate of 30%, compute the estimated cost of the inventory at October 31 using the gross profit method.

(a)

(b)

SOLUTIONS TO REVIEW QUESTIONS AND EXERCISES

TRUE-FALSE

1. (F) Merchandise inventory has two common characteristics: (1) it is owned by the company and (2) it is in a form ready for sale to customers in the ordinary course of business.

2. (T)
3. (T)
4. (F) Under the terms, FOB destination, legal title to the goods remains with the seller until the goods are delivered to the buyer by the transportation company.

5. (T)
6. (F) Freight-in is added to net purchases; Freight-out is a selling expense.
7. (T)
8. (F) The cost of ending inventory is subtracted from the cost of goods available for sale to determine the cost of goods sold.

9. (F) The primary basis of accounting for inventories is cost.
10. (T)
11. (T)
12. (T)
13. (T)
14. (T)
15. (F) Under the lower of cost or market basis, market is defined as current replacement cost, not selling price.

16. (T)
17. (F) This basis may also be applied to major categories of inventory or to total inventory.
18. (F) If beginning inventory is overstated, net income will be understated in the same year.
19. (T)
*20. (T)
*21. (F) The cost to retail ratio is applied to the ending inventory at retail.
*22. (F) The cost of goods sold is based on the earliest goods on hand prior to the sale.
*23. (T)

MULTIPLE CHOICE

1. (b) Finished Goods (a) are inventory that is completed and ready for sale. Raw Materials (c) are inventory that is on hand waiting to be used in production. Merchandise inventory (d) does not apply to a manufacturing company.

2. (c) The company should add the cost of the goods ($10,000) that are in transit with the terms FOB destination. The goods were not included in the physical count because they were in transit on December 31. They should be included in inventory because legal title to these goods remains with the seller until these goods are delivered to the buyer by the transportation company.

3. (b)   Freight-in is a temporary account whose normal balance is a debit; therefore, it is added to purchases in determining the cost of goods purchased.

4. (a)   The cost of goods purchased is computed as follows:

Purchases		$307,000
Less: Purchase returns and allowances........	$34,000	
Purchase discounts.............................	26,000	60,000
Net purchases		247,000
Add: Freight-in..		18,000
Cost of goods purchases................................		$265,000

5. (c)   Purchase discounts is determined as follows:

Purchases	$60,000
Less: Purchase returns and allowances........	7,000
	53,000
Less: Net purchases...................................	48,000
Purchase discounts.......................................	$ 5,000

6. (c)   The cost of goods sold is computed as follows:

Beginning inventory......................................	$ 19,000
Cost of goods purchased	184,500
Cost of goods available for sale	203,500
Ending inventory...	25,000
Cost of goods sold..	$178,500

7. (b)   Beginning inventory is determined as follows:

Cost of goods sold..	$ 82,000
Add: Ending inventory	34,000
Cost of good available for sale	116,000
Less: Cost of goods purchased......................	76,000
Beginning inventory......................................	$ 40,000

8. (b)   Under the FIFO method, the costs of the most recent purchases are assigned to the goods on hand as follows:

Date	Units		Unit Cost		Total Cost
Nov. 8	6,000	X	$7.00	=	$42,000
June 18	2,000	X	8.00	=	16,000
	8,000				$58,000

9. (c)   Under the LIFO method, the costs of the earliest units purchased remain in inventory as follows:

Date	Units		Unit Cost		Total Cost
Jan. 1	300	X	$32.00	=	$ 9,600
Jan. 15	150	X	33.00	=	4,950
	450				$14,550

10. (d) Under the FIFO method, the costs of the most recent purchases are assigned to the goods on hand as follows:

Date	Units		Unit Cost		Total Cost
Jan. 25	100	X	$22.00	=	$2,200
Jan. 17	50	X	20.00	=	1,000
	150				$3,200

11. (b) Under the LIFO method, the cost of the earliest units purchased remains in inventory as follows:

Date	Units		Unit Cost		Total Cost
Jan. 1	150	X	$18.00	=	$2,700

12. (c) Average cost must be computed at the end of the accounting period based on the weighted average unit cost of goods available for sale during the period. The computation is as follows:

Date	Units		Unit Cost		Total Cost
Jan. 1	400	X	$1.00	=	$ 400
Jan. 8	600	X	1.10	=	660
	1,000				$1,060

$1,060 ÷ 1,000 = $1.06

13. (b) In a period of rising prices, FIFO will have a lower cost of goods sold than LIFO. This is because under FIFO, the earliest costs are assigned to cost of goods sold whereas under LIFO, the latest costs are assigned to cost of goods sold. Net purchases will be the same under either method.

14. (b) The use of LIFO method will result in a better matching of costs and revenues. The use of FIFO method will result in a more realistic inventory value (a). The use of the LIFO method will result in lower income taxes and lower net income not higher as answer (c) and (d) indicate.

15. (b) The ending inventory on December 31, 2002, is the beginning inventory on January 1, 2003. When beginning inventory is overstated, then cost of goods sold will be overstated and net income will be understated. The Sales account will not be affected.

16. (c) By counting an inventory item twice, the ending inventory will be overstated. When ending inventory is overstated, net income is overstated and, therefore, owner's equity is overstated. The overstatement will have no effect on liabilities.

*17. (a) The estimated cost of ending inventory at March 31 under the gross profit method is as follows:

Net sales	$300,000
Less: Estimated gross profit ($30% X $300,000).......	90,000
Estimated cost of goods sold	$210,000
Beginning inventory..	$ 59,000
Cost of goods purchased	155,000
Cost of goods available for sale	214,000
Less: Estimated cost of goods sold.........................	210,000
Estimated cost of ending inventory	$ 4,000

*18. (a) The estimated cost of ending inventory at December 31 under the gross profit method is as follows:

Net sales	$3,000,000
Less: Estimated gross profit (30% X $3,000,000)......	900,000
Estimated cost of goods sold	$2,100,000
Beginning inventory..	$ 550,000
Cost of goods purchased	2,250,000
Cost of goods available for sale	2,800,000
Less: Estimated cost of goods sold.........................	2,100,000
Estimated cost of ending inventory	$ 700,000

Therefore the estimated cost of missing inventory is $100,000 ($700,000 - $600,000).

*19. (c) The cost to retail ratio is based on the cost of goods available for sale. The ratio is 75% ($97,500 ÷ $130,000).

*20. (c) The cost to retail ratio (75%) times the ending inventory at retail ($58,000) equals the ending inventory at cost ($43,500).

*21. (c) The cost of the 25 units sold on May 15: (20 X $20) + (5 X $22) = $510. The cost of the 10 units sold on May 24 is 10 X $22 = $220.

*22. (a) The cost of the 25 units sold on May 15: (20 X $22) + (5 X $20) = $540. The cost of the 10 units sold on May 24 is 10 X $25 = $250.

*23. (b) A moving average cost is computed after each purchase. The average unit cost is $21 after the May 14 purchase [($400 + $440) ÷ 40]. Thus, the cost of the May 15 sale is 25 X $21 = $525. After the May 21 purchase, average cost is $22.60 [($315 + $250) ÷ 25]. Thus, the cost of the May 24 sale is 10 X $22.60 = $226.

MATCHING

1.	g	5.	c	9.	j
2.	a	6.	e	10.	h
3.	b	7.	i		
4.	d	8.	f		

EXERCISES

EX. 6-1

MAILER COMPANY
Income Statement
For the Year Ended December 31, 2002

Sales revenues			
Sales			$505,000
Less: Sales returns and allowances		$ 13,850	
Sales discounts		7,750	21,600
Net sales			483,400
Cost of goods sold			
Inventory, January 1		42,000	
Purchases	$300,000		
Less: Purchase returns			
and allowances	$14,350		
Purchase discounts	22,000	36,350	
Net purchases		263,650	
Add: Freight-in		12,700	
Cost of goods purchased		276,350	
Cost of goods available for sale		318,350	
Inventory, December 31		40,500	
Cost of goods sold			277,850
Gross profit			205,550
Operating expenses			
Selling expenses			
Sales commissions expense	35,000		
Advertising expense	9,500		
Utilities expense ($23,000 X 40%)	9,200		
Freight-out	6,000		
Depreciation expense ($4,000 X 40%)	1,600		
Total selling expenses		61,300	
Administrative expenses			
Office salaries	83,000		
Utilities expense ($23,000 X 60%)	13,800		
Depreciation (4,000 X 60%)	2,400		
Total administrative expenses		99,200	
Total operating expenses			160,500
Income from operations			45,050
Other revenues and gains			
Interest revenue		10,900	
Other expenses and losses			
Interest expense		8,700	2,200
Net income			$ 47,250

EX. 6-2

For each of the inventory methods, the number of units available for sale and cost of goods available for sale should be computed as follows:

Pool of Costs
Cost of Goods Available for Sale

Date	Units		Unit Cost		Total Cost
1/1	200	X	$30	=	$ 6,000
5/5	240	X	28	=	6,720
8/8	350	X	31	=	10,850
11/29	300	X	33	=	9,900
	1,090				$33,470

Since 500 units are in ending inventory, 590 (1,090 - 500) units were sold.

FIFO Method

Ending inventory:

Date	Units		Unit Cost		Total Cost
11/29	300	X	$33	=	$ 9,900
8/8	200	X	31	=	6,200
	500				$16,100

Cost of goods sold: $33,470 - $16,100 = $17,370.

LIFO Method

Ending inventory:

Date	Units		Unit Cost		Total Cost
1/1	200	X	$30	=	$ 6,000
5/5	240	X	28	=	6,720
8/8	60	X	31	=	1,860
	500				$14,580

Cost of goods sold: $33,470 - $14,580 = $18,890.

Average Cost Method

Weighted average cost: = $33,470 ÷ 1,090 = $30.71 (rounded).

Ending inventory: = 500 X $30.71 = $15,355.

Cost of goods sold: = $33,470 - $15,355 = $18,115 or 590 units sold X $30.71 = $18,115 (rounded).

*EX. 6-3

(a)

	Cost	Retail
Beginning inventory	$122,500	$175,000
Goods purchased	149,600	220,000
Goods available for sale	$272,100	395,000
Net sales		230,000
(1) Ending inventory at retail		$165,000

(2) Cost to retail ratio = ($272,100 ÷ $395,000) = 68.89%.

(3) Ending inventory at cost = ($165,000 X 68.89%) = $113,688.50.

(b)

Net sales	$230,000
Less: Estimated gross profit (30% X $230,000)	69,000
Estimated cost of goods sold	$161,000
Beginning inventory	$122,500
Cost of goods purchased	149,600
Cost of goods available for sale	272,100
Less: Estimated cost of goods sold	161,000
Estimated cost of ending inventory	$111,100

1											1
2											2
3											3
4											4
5											5
6											6
7											7
8											8
9											9
10											10
11											11
12											12
13											13
14											14
15											15
16											16
17											17
18											18
19											19
20											20
21											21
22											22
23											23
24											24
25											25
26											26
27											27
28											28
29											29
30											30
31											31
32											32
33											33
34											34
35											35
36											36
37											37
38											38
39											39
40											40

1												1
2												2
3												3
4												4
5												5
6												6
7												7
8												8
9												9
10												10
11												11
12												12
13												13
14												14
15												15
16												16
17												17
18												18
19												19
20												20
21												21
22												22
23												23
24												24
25												25
26												26
27												27
28												28
29												29
30												30
31												31
32												32
33												33
34												34
35												35
36												36
37												37
38												38
39												39
40												40

1																		1
2																		2
3																		3
4																		4
5																		5
6																		6
7																		7
8																		8
9																		9
10																		10
11																		11
12																		12
13																		13
14																		14
15																		15
16																		16
17																		17
18																		18
19																		19
20																		20
21																		21
22																		22
23																		23
24																		24
25																		25
26																		26
27																		27
28																		28
29																		29
30																		30
31																		31
32																		32
33																		33
34																		34
35																		35
36																		36
37																		37
38																		38
39																		39
40																		40

Chapter 7

ACCOUNTING INFORMATION SYSTEMS

The Navigator	✓
■ Scan Study Objectives	☐
■ Read Preview	☐
■ Read Chapter Review	☐
■ Work Demonstration Problem	☐
■ Answer True-False Statements	☐
■ Answer Multiple-Choice Questions	☐
■ Match Terms and Definitions	☐
■ Solve Exercises	☐

CHAPTER STUDY OBJECTIVES

After studying this chapter, you should be able to:
1. Identify the basic principles of accounting information systems.
2. Explain the major phases in the development of an accounting system.
3. Describe the nature and purpose of a subsidiary ledger.
4. Explain how special journals are used in journalizing.
5. Indicate how a multi-column journal is posted.

PREVIEW OF CHAPTER 7

Whether you use pen, pencil, or computers in maintaining accounting records, certain principles and procedures apply. The purpose of this chapter is to explain and illustrate these features. The content and organization of this chapter are as follows:

CHAPTER REVIEW

Accounting Information Systems

1. (S.O. 1) An **accounting information system** involves collecting and processing data and disseminating financial information to interested users. It includes each step of the accounting cycle.

2. The **basic principles** of an accounting information system are:
    a. **Cost effectiveness**. The system must be cost effective: the benefits of the information disseminated must outweigh the cost of providing it.
    b. **Usefulness.** To be useful the information must be understandable, relevant, reliable, timely, and accurate.
    c. **Flexibility.** The system should be able to accommodate a variety of users and changing information needs.

Developing an Accounting System

3. (S.O. 2) There are four phases in the development of an accounting system.
    a. **Analysis**—involves determining internal and external information needs, identifying sources of information and the records and procedures for collecting and reporting the data.
    b. **Design**—includes both the development of a new system and the redesigning of an existing system.
    c. **Implementation**—relates to making the new or revised system operational.
    d. **Follow-up**—involves the monitoring of the new or revised system for weaknesses or breakdowns.

Manual vs. Computerized Systems

4. In a **manual accounting system,** each of the steps in the accounting cycle is performed by hand.

Subsidiary Ledgers

5. (S.O. 3) A **subsidiary ledger** is a group of accounts with a common characteristic, assembled together to facilitate the recording process by freeing the general ledger from details concerning individual balances.

6. Two common subsidiary ledgers are:
    a. The accounts receivable (or customers') ledger which collects transaction data with individual customers.
    b. The accounts payable (or creditors') ledger which collects transaction data with individual creditors.

7. The summary account in the general ledger is called a **control account** and the balance in the control account must equal the composite balance of the individual accounts in the subsidiary ledger at the end of the period.

8. The advantages of using subsidiary ledgers are that they:
    a. Show transactions affecting one customer or one creditor in a single account, thus providing up-to-date information on specific account balances.
    b. Free the general ledger of excessive details. As a result, a trial balance of the general ledger does not contain vast numbers of individual account balances.
    c. Help locate errors in individual accounts by reducing the number of accounts in one ledger and by using control accounts.
    d. Make possible a division of labor in posting by having one employee post to the general ledger while a different employee(s) post to the subsidiary ledgers.

Special Journals

9. (S.O. 4) To expedite journalizing and posting transactions, most companies use **special journals** in addition to the general journal. A special journal is used to group similar types of transactions, such as all sales of merchandise on account or all cash receipts.

10. The following are types of special journals:
    a. Sales journal—all sales of merchandise on account.
    b. Cash receipts journal—all cash received (including cash sales).
    c. Purchases journal—all purchases of merchandise on account.
    d. Cash payments journal—all cash paid (including cash purchases).

11. If a transaction cannot be recorded in a special journal, it is recorded in the general journal. Special journals permit greater division of labor and reduce the time necessary to complete the posting process.

Sales Journal

12. For the **sales journal,**
    a. Each entry results in a debit to Accounts Receivable and a credit to Sales at selling price; and a debit to Cost of Goods Sold and a credit to Merchandise Inventory at cost.
    b. Only one line is needed to record each transaction.
    c. All entries are made from sales invoices.
    d. Postings are made daily to the individual accounts receivable in the subsidiary ledger and monthly, in total, to Accounts Receivable, Sales, Cost of Goods Sold and Merchandise Inventory in the general ledger.

Cash Receipts Journal

13. The **cash receipts journal** is a columnar journal with debit columns for cash and sales discounts, and credit columns for accounts receivable, sales, and "other" accounts. In addition there is a separate column for a debit to Cost of Goods Sold and a credit to Merchandise Inventory. In journalizing cash receipts transactions:
    a. Only one line is needed for each entry.
    b. Each sale entry is accompanied by another entry that debits Cost of Goods Sold and credits Merchandise Inventory for cost.

14. (S.O. 5) The **posting of a columnar journal** such as the cash receipts journal involves the following procedures:
    a. All column totals except the total for the Other Accounts column are posted once at the end of the month to the account title or titles specified in the column heading.

b.   The total of the Other Accounts column is not posted. Instead, the individual amounts comprising the total are posted separately to the general ledger accounts specified in the Accounts Credited column.

c.   The individual amounts in a column, posted in total to a control account, are posted daily to the subsidiary ledger account specified in the Accounts Credited column.

Purchases Journal

15.   For the **purchases journal,**
a.   Each entry results in a debit to Merchandise Inventory and a credit to Accounts Payable.
b.   Only one line is needed to record each transaction.
c.   All entries are made from purchase invoices.
d.   Postings are made daily to the individual creditor accounts in the accounts payable subsidiary ledger and monthly, in total, to Merchandise Inventory and Accounts Payable in the general ledger.

16.   The purchases journal can be expanded into a columnar journal by adding columns for office supplies, store supplies, and other accounts.

Cash Payments Journal

17.   The **cash payments journal** has multiple columns because cash payments may be made for a variety of purposes.
a.   The journalizing procedures are similar to those described earlier for the cash receipts journal.
b.   All entries are made from prenumbered checks.
c.   The posting procedures are similar to those described earlier for the cash receipts journal.

Effects of Special Journals on General Journal

18.   Only transactions that cannot be entered in a special journal are recorded in the **general journal.**   When the entry involves both control and subsidiary accounts the following modifications are required:
a.   In journalizing, both the control and subsidiary accounts must be identified.
b.   In posting, there must be a dual posting: once to the control account and once to the subsidiary account.

The Navigator

DEMONSTRATION PROBLEM (S.O. 4 and 5)

The Gauguin Company uses a five column cash payments journal with columns for Cash (Cr.), Merchandise Inventory (Cr.), Store Supplies (Dr.), Accounts Payable (Dr.), and Other Accounts (Dr.). Cash payments for the month of October are as follows:

October	2	Check No. 101 for $1,100 is issued to Toulouse-Lautrec Realty for October rent.
	5	Check No. 102 for $600 is issued for the purchase of merchandise.
	9	Check No. 103 for $8,820 is sent to Cassatt Inc. in payment of October 4 invoice for $9,000 less a 2% discount.
	13	Check No. 104 for $550 is issued for store supplies.
	17	Check No. 105 for $8,000 is sent to Picasso Company in payment of October 3 invoice for $8,000.
	21	Check No. 106 for $400 is issued to Paul Gauguin as a cash withdrawal for personal use.
	28	Check No. 107 for $300 is issued for store supplies.

Instructions
Journalize the transactions in the cash payments journal.

The
Navigator

SOLUTION TO DEMONSTRATION PROBLEM

Cash Payments Journal

Date	Ck. No.	Accounts Debited	Explanation	Ref.	Other Accounts Dr.	Accounts Payable Dr.	Store Supplies Dr.	Merchandise Inventory Cr.	Cash Cr.
Oct. 2	101	Rent Expense	Toulouse-Lautrec, Realty		1,100				1,100
5	102	Merchandise Inventory	Buy merchandise.		600				600
9	103	Cassatt, Inc.	Pay in full.			9,000		180	8,820
13	104		Purchase supplies.				550		550
17	105	Picasso Company	Pay in full.			8,000			8,000
21	106	Paul Gauguin, Drawing	Withdraw cash.		400				400
28	107		Purchase supplies.				300		300
					2,100	17,000	850	180	19,770

REVIEW QUESTIONS AND EXERCISES

TRUE—FALSE

Indicate whether each of the following is true (T) or false (F) in the space provided.

_____ 1. (S.O. 1) An accounting information system involves data collection, data processing, and information dissemination.

_____ 2. (S.O. 1) The basic principles of an accounting information system are cost aware-ness, usefulness, and fixed structure.

_____ 3. (S.O. 2) The final phase in the development of an accounting system is implement-ation.

_____ 4. (S.O. 3) A subsidiary ledger is a group of accounts with a common characteristic.

_____ 5. (S.O. 3) The summary account in the general ledger that controls the subsidiary ledger is called a special account.

_____ 6. (S.O. 3) Each general ledger control account balance must equal the composite balance of the individual accounts in the related subsidiary ledger at the end of an accounting period.

_____ 7. (S.O. 3) An advantage of using a subsidiary ledger control account is that it assists in locating errors in individual accounts by reducing the number of accounts combined in one ledger.

_____ 8. (S.O. 4) A special journal is used to group unusual types of transactions.

_____ 9. (S.O. 4) If a transaction cannot be recorded in a special journal, it should not be recorded.

_____ 10. (S.O. 4) When special journals are employed, all postings must be monthly or daily but cannot be both.

_____ 11. (S.O. 4) A disadvantage of the sales journal is that recording transactions takes longer.

_____ 12. (S.O. 4) At the end of the month, the column totals in the sales journal need only to be posted to the Sales account.

_____ 13. (S.O. 4) A cash sale of merchandise will result in the use of one line in the cash receipts journal.

_____ 14. (S.O. 4) Totaling the columns of a journal and proving the equality of the totals is called footing and cross-footing a journal.

_____ 15. (S.O. 4) The cash receipts journal will usually include a Sales Discounts column.

_____ 16. (S.O. 5) All purchases of merchandise on account are recorded in the purchases journal.

_____ 17. (S.O. 5) Entries in the purchases journal are made from sales invoices.

_____ 18. (S.O. 5) Postings from the one-column purchases journal are made daily to the accounts payable subsidiary ledger and monthly to the general ledger.

_____ 19. (S.O. 5) The total of the Other Accounts column of the cash payments journal is posted to the general ledger at the end of the month.

_____ 20. (S.O. 5) Only transactions that cannot be entered in a special journal are recorded in the general journal.

The
Navigator

MULTIPLE CHOICE

Circle the letter that best answers each of the following statements.

1. (S.O. 1) Which of the following statements is **incorrect?**
    a. A major consideration in developing an accounting system is cost awareness.
    b. When an accounting system is designed, no consideration needs to be given to the needs and knowledge of the various users.
    c. The accounting system should be able to accommodate a variety of users and changing information needs.
    d. To be useful, information must be understandable, relevant, reliable, timely, and accurate.

2. (S.O. 2) The development of an accounting system does not involve:
    a. analysis and design.
    b. analysis and implementation.
    c. implementation and follow up.
    d. all of the above are involved in the development of an accounting system.

3. (S.O. 2) The four phases of developing an accounting system are:
    a. analysis, design, implementation and follow-up.
    b. analysis, recording, measurement and implementation.
    c. design, recording, measurement and follow-up.
    d. analysis, design, revision and measurement.

4. (S.O. 3) Which of the following accounts may a business not use as a controlling account and subsidiary ledger?
    a. Inventory.
    b. Accounts Payable.
    c. Selling and Administrative Expenses.
    d. A business may use all of the above as controlling accounts and subsidiary ledgers.

5. (S.O. 3) Which of the following is **not** an advantage of a subsidiary ledger?
    a. Shows transactions affecting one customer or one creditor in a single account.
    b. Help locate errors in individual accounts.
    c. Puts greater detail in the general ledger.
    d. Makes possible a division of labor.

6. (S.O. 4) Which of the following is a journal that most merchandising enterprises will not use?
    a. Cash payments journal.
    b. Purchases journal.
    c. Sales journal.
    d. Equipment journal.

7. (S.O. 4) When the totals of the sales journal are posted at the end of the month there will be credits to:
    a. Sales and Merchandise Inventory and debits to Accounts Receivable and Cost of Goods Sold.
    b. Accounts Receivable and Cost of Goods Sold and debits to Sales and Merchandise Inventory.
    c. Sales and debits to each individual customer account.
    d. the Sales account only, and no debits.

8. (S.O. 4) The entries in the sales journal must be posted daily to the:
    a. Sales Account.
    b. Accounts Receivable subsidiary ledger.
    c. the Accounts Payable subsidiary ledger.
    d. none of the above.

9. (S.O. 4) A cash receipts journal will be used for:

	Cash sales	Sales discounts	Cost of Goods Sold
a.	yes	yes	yes
b.	yes	no	yes
c.	no	yes	yes
d.	yes	yes	no

10. (S.O. 4) Which of the following transactions will not involve the cash receipts journal?
    a. Cash sales of merchandise totaling $2,000.
    b. Cash is received by signing a note for $3,000.
    c. The owner makes a cash investment in the business.
    d. A company gives a purchase refund to a purchaser following a cash purchase.

11. (S.O. 4) The Other Accounts column of a columnar journal is often referred to as the:
    a. Sundry Accounts column.
    b. Controlling Account column.
    c. Credit Account column.
    d. Debit Account column.

12.   (S.O. 4) In the cash receipts journal, debits are made in which columns?
   a.   Cash, Sales Discounts, and Cost of Goods Sold.
   b.   Accounts Receivable, Cash, and Cost of Goods Sold.
   c.   Sales Discounts, Sales, and Merchandise Inventory.
   d.   Accounts Receivable, Sales, and Merchandise Inventory.

13.   (S.O. 5) The purchases journal will include:

	Cash purchases	Credit purchases	Merchandise Inventory ·
a.	yes	yes	yes
b.	yes	no	yes
c.	no	yes	no
d.	no	yes	yes

14.   (S.O. 5) In the expanded purchases journal, debits are made in which columns?
   a.   Accounts Payable, Merchandise Inventory, and Office Supplies.
   b.   Merchandise Inventory, Office Supplies, and Store Supplies.
   c.   Cash, Office Supplies, and Store Supplies.
   d.   Accounts Payable, Cash, and Merchandise Inventory.

15.   (S.O. 5) The cash payments journal may include a column for:
   a.   store supplies.
   b.   accounts receivable.
   c.   sales.
   d.   sales discounts.

16.   (S.O. 5) If a customer returns goods for credit, an entry is normally made in the:
   a.   cash receipts journal.
   b.   sales journal.
   c.   cash payments journal.
   d.   general journal.

17.   (S.O. 5) If a customer takes a sales discount, an entry is made in the:
   a.   cash receipts journal.
   b.   sales journal.
   c.   cash payments journal.
   d.   general journal.

18.   (S.O. 5) Totaling the columns of a multi-column journal and proving the equality of the totals is called:
   a.   totaling and balancing.
   b.   footing and cross-footing.
   c.   totaling and cross-footing.
   d.   footing and balancing.

The Navigator

MATCHING

Match each term with its definition by writing the appropriate letter in the space provided.

Terms

_____ 1. Subsidiary ledger.

_____ 2. Control account.

_____ 3. Special journal.

_____ 4. Sales journal.

_____ 5. Cash receipts journal.

_____ 6. Purchases journal.

_____ 7. Cash payments journal.

_____ 8. Accounting information system.

_____ 9. Multi-column journal.

Definitions

a. An account in the general ledger that controls a subsidiary ledger.

b. A special journal used to record all sales of merchandise on account.

c. A group of accounts with a common characteristic that is controlled by an account in the general ledger.

d. A special journal used to record all cash paid.

e. A journal that is used to group similar types of transactions such as all credit sales or all cash receipts.

f. A special journal used to record all purchases of merchandise on account.

g. A special journal used to record all cash received.

h. A system that involves data collection, data processing, and information dissemination.

i. A special journal with more than one column.

The Navigator

EXERCISES

EX. 7-1   (S.O. 4 and 5) Cartoonist Inc., had the following transactions during the month.
1.   Merchandise is sold on credit to Gary Trudeau for $2,500.
2.   Merchandise is sold to Charles Schulz for $1,000 cash.
3.   Merchandise purchased by Charlie Brown on account is returned for credit.
4.   A check for $2,940 is received from Al Capp in payment of invoice no. 101 for $3,000 less 2% discount.
5.   Merchandise is purchased on credit from Disney Company for $2,000, terms 1/20, n/30.
6.   Check no. 101 for $3,100 is issued for store supplies bought from Jim Davis.
7.   Check no. 102 for $1,980, $2,000 less the 1% discount is mailed to Disney Company to pay for merchandise purchased on credit.
8.   Merchandise is purchased for $1,000 (check no. 103) cash from Mary Worth.
9.   Equipment is purchased from Mort Walker for $4,000 on credit.
10.   Cash is received from R. Dagwood in payment of a $5,000 note receivable, plus $75 of accrued interest.

Instructions
(a)   Indicate the journal in which each transaction should be entered using the following letters:

G =   General journal
S =   Sales journal
P =   Purchases journal (one-column)

CR =   Cash receipts journal
CP =   Cash payments journal

(b)   For each journal selected in (a) above, indicate by inserting a check mark in the appropriate column whether the journalized data should be posted (1) only at the end of the month, (2) daily and at the end of the month, or (3) only daily. (Note: Assume that the columnar journals have the same columns as those in the chapter and subsidiary and control accounts are used.)

	(a)	(b) Posting		
		Monthly Only	Daily and Monthly	Daily Only
Transaction	**Journal**			
1.				
2.				
3.				
4.				
5.				
6.				
7.				
8.				
9.				
10.				

EX. 7-2   (S.O. 5) The following transactions were made by George Baker Company during the month of October 2002.

Oct. 3 Received a $3,000 payment from Chic Young in full for invoice no. 101 when terms were n/30.

6 Bought store supplies from Chester Gould Co. for $500—used check no. 101.

9 Purchased merchandise from Harold Gray Company for $3,500—used check no. 102.

13 Received $2,000 cash from Harold Gray Company as an allowance for defective goods purchased on Oct. 9.

16 Purchased merchandise from Hank Ketcham Company for $1,500 on credit.

20 Sold merchandise to Jack Kirby for $2,250 on credit—used sales invoice no. 10. The cost of goods sold was $1,600.

23 Purchased merchandise from Bob Montana, Inc. for $6,000 on credit.

25 Received $2,205 from Jack Kirby for the sale made on Oct. 20 less a 2% discount.

27 Paid Hank Ketcham Company $1,485 cash for the purchase on Oct. 16 less a 1% discount--used check no. 103.

Instructions
In the journals provided, enter the transactions for the George Baker Company for the month ended October 31, 2002.

Sales Journal

S1

Date	Account Debited	Invoice No.	Ref.	Accts. Receivable Dr. Sales Cr.	Cost of Goods Sold Dr. Merchandise Inventory Cr.
2002					

Purchases Journal

P1

Date	Account Credited	Terms	Ref.	Merchandise Inventory Dr. Accounts Payable Cr.
2002				

Cash Receipts Journal

CR1

Date	Account Credited	Ref.	Cash Dr.	Sales Discounts Dr.	Accounts Receivable Cr.	Sales Cr.	Other Accounts Cr.	Cost of Goods Sold Dr. Merchandise Inventory Cr.
2002								

Cash Payments Journal

CP1

Date	Ck No.	Accounts Debited	Ref.	Other Accounts Dr.	Accounts Payable Dr.	Store Supplies Dr.	Merchandise Inventory Cr.	Cash Cr.
2002								

The Navigator

SOLUTIONS TO REVIEW QUESTIONS AND EXERCISES

TRUE-FALSE

1.   (T)
2.   (F)   The last principle is flexibility, not fixed structure.
3.   (F)   The final phase is follow-up.
4.   (T)
5.   (F)   The summary account in the general ledger is called a control account.
6.   (T)
7.   (T)
8.   (F)   A special journal is used to group similar types of transactions.
9.   (F)   If a transaction cannot be recorded in a special journal, it is recorded in the general journal.
10. (F)   When special journals are employed, daily postings are usually made to the subsidiary ledgers and monthly postings to the general ledger.
11. (F)   An advantage of the sales journal is that one-line entry for each sales transaction saves time.
12. (F)   The column totals of the Sales journal are posted to the Sales account and the Accounts Receivable account, and the Cost of Goods Sold account and the Merchandise Inventory account.
13. (T)
14. (T)
15. (T)
16. (T)
17. (F)   Entries in the purchases journal are made from purchase invoices. Sales invoices are used to make entries in the sales journal.
18. (T)
19. (F)   The total of the Other Accounts column is not posted because each individual transaction is posted to the appropriate account affected.
20. (T)

MULTIPLE CHOICE

1.   (b)   When an accounting system is designed, consideration must be given to the needs and knowledge of the various users so that the system's output will be useful. Answers (a), (c), and (d), are all correct statements.

2.   (d)   The development of an accounting system involves analysis, design, implementation and follow-up.

3.   (a)   The four phases of developing an accounting system are analysis, design, implementation and follow-up.

4. (d)   Two common subsidiary ledgers are the accounts receivable ledger and the accounts payable ledger. Businesses may also use controlling accounts and subsidiary ledgers for other accounts such as inventory, equipment, and selling and administrative expenses.

5. (c)   Advantages of the subsidiary ledger are: (a) shows transactions affecting one customer or one creditor in a single account, (b) helps locate errors in individual accounts, and (d) makes possible a division of labor. Another advantage is that subsidiary ledgers free the general ledger of excessive details.

6. (d)   Most merchandising enterprises use a (c) sales journal, (b) purchases journal, and (a) cash payments journal as well as a cash receipts journal. An equipment journal is generally not used as a special journal because there are not that many equipment purchases during an accounting period.

7. (a)   At the end of the month, the totals are posted to the general ledger as debits to Accounts Receivable and Cost of Goods Sold, and as credits to Sales and Merchandise Inventory.

8. (b)   Postings from the sales journal are made daily to the individual accounts receivable in the subsidiary ledger and monthly to the general ledger.

9. (a)   The cash receipts journal will be used for cash sales, collections of accounts, and other receipts of cash. Since the sales discount is not determined until the receipt of cash, it also is recorded in the cash receipts journal. Cost of Goods Sold is also debited when goods are sold.

10. (d)   The cash receipts journal is used for all receipts of cash. When a refund is given on a cash purchase, cash is paid. Thus, the entry should be made in the cash payments journal.

11. (a)   The Other Accounts column is often referred to as the sundry accounts column because a variety of general ledger account titles may be used. The other choices are not used referring to a miscellaneous accounts column.

12. (a)   In the cash receipts journal, debits are made in the cash and sales discounts columns. In the same journal, credits are made in the accounts receivable, sales, and other accounts columns. In addition debits and credits are made in the Cost of Goods Sold and Merchandise Inventory column.

13. (d)   The purchases journal is a special journal that is used to record all purchases of merchandise on account. Cash purchases are recorded in the cash payments journal.

14. (b)   In the Purchases Journal, credits are made to the Accounts Payable column and debits to the Merchandise Inventory, Office Supplies, Store Supplies and Other Accounts columns.

15. (a)   The cash payments journal may have a column for Store Supplies because supplies may be purchased for cash. It would not have columns for the other choices because they pertain to sales and cash receipts.

16. (d) The return of goods for credit cannot be made in any of the special journals. Therefore, the entry must be made in the general journal.

17. (a) The sales discount is not taken until the cash is received. Therefore, the entry is made in the cash receipts journal.

18. (b) The correct terminology is footing and cross-footing.

MATCHING

1.	c	4.	b	7.	d
2.	a	5.	g	8.	h
3.	e	6.	f	9.	i

EXERCISES

EX. 7-1

		(b) Posting		
Transaction	(a) Journal	Monthly Only	Daily and Monthly	Daily Only
1.	S		✓	
2.	CR	✓		
3.	G			✓
4.	CR		✓	
5.	P		✓	
6.	CP	✓		
7.	CP		✓	
8.	CP	✓		
9.	G			✓
10.	CR		✓	

EX. 7-2

Sales Journal

S1

Date	Account Debited	Invoice No.	Ref.	Accts. Receivable Dr. Sales Cr.	Cost of Goods Sold Dr. Merchandise Inventory Cr.
2002					
Oct. 20	Jack Kirby	10		2,250	1,600

Purchases Journal

P1

Date	Account Credited	Terms	Ref.	Merchandise Inventory Dr. Accounts Payable Cr.
2002 Oct. 16	Hank Ketcham Company			1,500
23	Bob Montana, Inc.			6,000

Cash Receipts Journal

CR1

Date	Account Credited	Ref.	Cash Dr.	Sales Discounts Dr.	Accounts Receivable Cr.	Sales Cr.	Other Accounts Cr.	Cost of Goods Sold Dr. Merchandise Inventory Cr.
2002 Oct. 3	Chic Young		3,000		3,000			
13	Merchandise Inventory		2,000				2,000	
25	Jack Kirby		2,205	45	2,250			

Cash Payments Journal

CP1

Date	Ck No.	Accounts Debited	Ref.	Other Accounts Dr.	Accounts Payable Dr.	Store Supplies Dr.	Merchandise Inventory Cr.	Cash Cr.
2002 Oct. 6	101					500		500
9	102	Merchandise Inventory		3,500				3,500
27	103	Hank Ketcham Company			1,500		15	1,485

1													1
2													2
3													3
4													4
5													5
6													6
7													7
8													8
9													9
10													10
11													11
12													12
13													13
14													14
15													15
16													16
17													17
18													18
19													19
20													20
21													21
22													22
23													23
24													24
25													25
26													26
27													27
28													28
29													29
30													30
31													31
32													32
33													33
34													34
35													35
36													36
37													37
38													38
39													39
40													40

	1																					1
	2																					2
	3																					3
	4																					4
	5																					5
	6																					6
	7																					7
	8																					8
	9																					9
	10																					10
	11																					11
	12																					12
	13																					13
	14																					14
	15																					15
	16																					16
	17																					17
	18																					18
	19																					19
	20																					20
	21																					21
	22																					22
	23																					23
	24																					24
	25																					25
	26																					26
	27																					27
	28																					28
	29																					29
	30																					30
	31																					31
	32																					32
	33																					33
	34																					34
	35																					35
	36																					36
	37																					37
	38																					38
	39																					39
	40																					40

Chapter 8

The Navigator ✓
- ■ Scan Study Objectives ☐
- ■ Read Preview ☐
- ■ Read Chapter Review ☐
- ■ Work Demonstration Problem ☐
- ■ Answer True-False Statements ☐
- ■ Answer Multiple-Choice Questions ☐
- ■ Match Terms and Definitions ☐
- ■ Solve Exercises ☐

INTERNAL CONTROL AND CASH

CHAPTER STUDY OBJECTIVES

After studying this chapter, you should be able to:
1. Define internal control.
2. Identify the principles of internal control.
3. Explain the applications of internal control principles to cash receipts.
4. Explain the applications of internal control principles to cash disbursements.
5. Describe the operation of a petty cash fund.
6. Indicate the control features of a bank account.
7. Prepare a bank reconciliation.
8. Explain the reporting of cash.

PREVIEW OF CHAPTER 8

The organization and content of Chapter 8 are as follows:

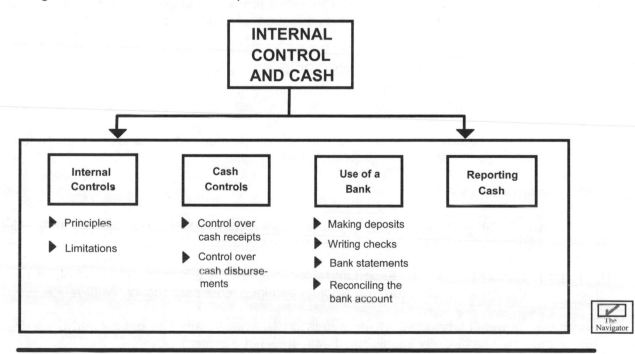

CHAPTER REVIEW

Internal Control

1. (S.O. 1) **Internal control** consists of the plan of organization and all the related methods and measures adopted within a business to (a) safeguard its assets and (b) enhance the accuracy and reliability of its accounting records.

2. (S.O. 2) An essential characteristic of internal control is the **establishment of responsibility** to specific employees. Control is most effective when only one person is responsible for a given task.

3. The rationale for segregation of duties is this: The work of one employee should, without a duplication of effort, provide a reliable basis for evaluating the work of another employee.

4. The responsibility for related transactions should be assigned to different individuals, and the responsibility for establishing the **accountability for an asset** should be separate from the physical custody of that asset.

5. **Documentation procedures** provide evidence that transactions and events have occurred.

6. **Physical, mechanical, and electronic controls** relate primarily to the safeguarding of assets and include such measures as safes for the storage of cash prior to deposit, bank vaults for the deposit of cash, safety deposit boxes for the storage of important business papers, fences around storage areas, and locked warehouses for inventories.

7. Mechanical and electronic controls include electronic burglar alarms, television monitors, sensors on garments, cash registers, time clocks and built-in hardware controls.

8. Most systems of internal control provide for **independent internal verification.** This principle involves the review, comparison, and reconciliation of data prepared by one or several employees.

9. In large companies, independent internal verification is often assigned to internal auditors. **Internal auditors** are employees of the company who evaluate the effectiveness of the company's system of internal control on a continuous basis.

10. **Other control measures** include bonding of employees who handle cash, rotating employees' duties, and requiring employees to take vacations.

Limitations of Internal Control

11. The concept of **reasonable assurance** rests on the premise that the costs of establishing control procedures should not exceed their expected benefits.

12. The **human element** is also an important factor in every system of internal control. A good system can become ineffective through employee fatigue, carelessness, or indifference.

13. **Collusion** may result when two or more individuals work together to get around prescribed controls and may significantly impair the effectiveness of a system.

Cash

14. Cash consists of coins, currency (paper money), checks, money orders, and money on hand or on deposit in a bank or similar depository. To safeguard cash and to assure the accuracy of the accounting records for cash, effective internal control over cash is imperative.

Internal Control Over Cash Receipts

15. (S.O. 3) The application of internal control principles to **cash receipts transactions** includes: (1) only designated personnel should be authorized to handle or have access to cash receipts; (2) different individuals should be assigned the duties of receiving cash, recording cash receipt transactions, and having custody of cash; (3) documents should include remittance advices, cash register tapes, and deposit slips; (4) cash should be stored in company safes and bank vaults, access to storage areas should be limited to authorized personnel, and cash registers should be used in executing over-the-counter receipts; (5) daily cash counts and daily comparisons of total receipts should be made; and (6) all personnel who handle cash receipts should be bonded and required to take vacations.

16. Control of over-the-counter receipts is centered on cash registers that are visible to customers.

Internal Control Over Cash Disbursements

17. (S.O. 4) Generally, internal control over cash disbursements is more effective when payments are made by check rather than by cash, except for incidental amounts that are paid out of petty cash.

18. The application of internal control principles to **cash disbursements transactions** includes: (1) only specified individuals should be authorized to sign checks; (2) different departments or individuals should be assigned the duties of approving an item for payment and paying it; (3) prenumbered checks should be used and each check should be supported by an approved invoice or other document; (4) blank checks should be stored in a safe and access should be restricted to authorized personnel, and a check writer machine should be used to imprint the amount on the check in indelible ink; (5) each check should be compared with the approved invoice before it is issued; and (6) following payment, the approved invoice (or form) should be stamped PAID.

Voucher System

19. A **voucher system** is often used to enhance the internal control over cash disbursements. A voucher system is an extensive network of approvals by authorized individuals acting independently to ensure that all disbursements by check are proper. A voucher system includes the use of authorization forms called **vouchers** which are recorded by the accounting department in the voucher register.

Electronic Funds Transfer

20. **Electronic Funds Transfer (EFT)** is a disbursement system that uses wire, telephone, telegraph or computer to send cash from one location to another.

Petty Cash Fund

21. (S.O. 5) A petty cash fund is a cash fund used to pay relatively small amounts.
    a. The operation of the fund, often called an imprest system, involves (1) establishing the fund, (2) making payments from the fund, and (3) replenishing the fund.
    b. Accounting entries are required when (1) the fund is established, (2) the fund is replenished, and (3) the amount of the fund is changed.

Use of a Bank

22. (S.O. 6) The use of a bank minimizes the amount of currency that must be kept on hand and therefore contributes significantly to good internal control over cash.

23. A check is a written order signed by the depositor directing the bank to pay a specified sum of money to a designated recipient. The three parties to a check are as follows:
    a. The maker (or drawer) who issues the check.
    b. The bank (or payer) on which the check is drawn.
    c. The payee to whom the check is payable.

24. A bank statement shows (a) checks paid and other debits charged against the account, (b) deposits and other credits made to the account, and (c) the account balance after each day's transactions.

25. A bank debit memoranda is usually included with the bank statement to indicate charges against the depositor's account such as a bank service charge, cost of printing checks, issuing traveler's checks, and when a previously deposited customer's check "bounces" because of insufficient funds (NSF check).

26. A bank credit memoranda shows such items as the collection of a note receivable for the depositor by the bank.

Reconciling the Bank Account

27. (S.O. 7) A **reconciliation** of a bank account is necessary because the balance per bank and balance per books are seldom in agreement. The lack of agreement may be the result of **time lags** and **errors.**

28. To obtain maximum benefit from a **bank reconciliation,** the reconciliation should be prepared by an employee who has no other responsibilities pertaining to cash.

29. In reconciling the bank statement, it is customary to reconcile the balance per books and balance per bank to their adjusted cash balances. The reconciliation schedule consists of two sections. The steps in preparing a bank reconciliation are:

a. Determine deposits in transit.
b. Determine outstanding checks.
c. Note any errors discovered.
d. Trace bank memoranda to the records.

30. Each reconciling item used in determining the adjusted cash balance per books should be recorded by the depositor.

Reporting Cash

31. (S.O. 8) Cash on hand, cash in banks, and petty cash are often combined and reported simply as **Cash.** Because it is the most liquid asset, cash is listed first in the current asset section of the balance sheet under the title "cash and cash equivalents." **Cash equivalents** are highly liquid investments, with maturities of 3 months or less when purchased, that can be converted into a specific amount of cash. They include money market funds, money market savings certificates, bank certificates of deposit, and U.S. Treasury bills and notes.

DEMONSTRATION PROBLEM (S.O. 7)

The information below relates to the Cash in Bank account in the ledger of Mozart Corporation for November, 2002:

Balance November 1—$27,100.	Cash deposited—$94,500.
Balance November 30—$28,200.	Checks written—$93,400.

The November bank statement shows:

Balance, November 30	$26,950
Credit memorandum:	
Collection of note by bank including $27 of interest	1,000
Debit memorandum:	
NSF check: G.F. Handel	425
Bank service charge	25

At November 30, deposits in transit amounted to $7,200 and outstanding checks totaled $5,400.

Instructions
Prepare the bank reconciliation at November 30, 2002.

SOLUTION TO DEMONSTRATION PROBLEM

MOZART CORPORATION
Bank Reconciliation
November 30, 2002

Cash balance per bank statement		$26,950
Add: Deposits in transit...		7,200
		34,150
Less: Outstanding checks...		5,400
Adjusted cash balance per bank...		$28,750
Cash balance per books		$28,200
Add: Collection of note receivable		1,000
		29,200
Less: NSF check...	$425	
Bank service charge...	25	450
Adjusted cash balance per books...		$28,750

REVIEW QUESTIONS AND EXERCISES

TRUE—FALSE

Indicate whether each of the following is true (T) or false (F) in the space provided.

_____ 1. (S.O. 1) Internal control consists of the plan of organization and all of the related methods and measures adopted within a business to (a) safeguard its assets, and (b) enhance the accuracy and reliability of its accounting records.

_____ 2. (S.O. 2) Internal control is most effective when only one person is responsible for a given task.

_____ 3. (S.O. 2) The responsibility for related transactions should be assigned to one person.

_____ 4. (S.O. 2) The responsibility for establishing the accountability for an asset should be separate from the physical custody of that asset.

_____ 5. (S.O. 2) In general, documents should be prenumbered and all documents should be accounted for.

_____ 6. (S.O. 2) Internal auditors are specialists hired from other companies to evaluate the effectiveness of the company's system of internal control.

_____ 7. (S.O. 2) The concept of reasonable assurance rests on the premise that the costs of establishing control procedures should not exceed their expected benefits.

_____ 8. (S.O. 2) The human element is an important factor in every system of internal control.

_____ 9. (S.O. 2) Collusion may result when one individual circumvents prescribed controls and may significantly impair the effectiveness of a system.

_____ 10. (S.O. 3) Only designated personnel should be authorized to handle or have access to cash receipts.

_____ 11. (S.O. 3) Personnel who handle cash receipts should have the option of taking a vacation or not.

_____ 12. (S.O. 3) Control of over-the-counter receipts is centered on cash registers that are visible to customers.

_____ 13. (S.O. 4) The duties of approving an item for payment and paying the item should be done by different departments or individuals.

_____ 14. (S.O. 4) Electronic Funds Transfer is a system that uses computers to send cash from one location to another.

_____ 15. (S.O. 5) The custodian of the petty cash fund has the responsibility of recording a journal entry every time cash is used from the fund.

_____ 16. (S.O. 6) The three parties to a check are the maker, the drawer, and the bank.

_____ 17. (S.O. 6) A debit memoranda could show the collection of a note receivable by the bank.

_____ 18. (S.O. 7) The lack of agreement between the balance of the bank and the balance of the books may be the result of time lags and errors.

_____ 19. (S.O. 7) To obtain maximum benefit from a bank reconciliation, the reconciliation should be prepared by an employee who has no other responsibilities pertaining to cash.

_____ 20. (S.O. 7) In a bank reconciliation, outstanding checks are added to the balance per books to obtain the adjusted balance per books.

MULTIPLE CHOICE

Circle the letter that best answers each of the following statements.

1. (S.O. 1) Which of the following is **not** considered a part of the definition of internal control?
   a. Safeguard its assets.
   b. Enhance the accuracy and reliability of its accounting records.
   c. Assignment of responsibility to specific individuals.
   d. The plan of organization.

2. (S.O. 2) An example of poor internal control is:
   a. The accountant should not have physical custody of the asset nor access to it.
   b. The custodian of an asset should not maintain or have access to the accounting records.
   c. One person should be responsible for handling related transactions.
   d. A salesperson should make the sale, and a different person ships the goods.

3. (S.O. 2) Independent internal verification is not involved when an independent person:
   a. reconciles the cash balance per books with the cash balance per the bank.
   b. reviews the accounts receivable subsidiary ledger.
   c. makes a surprise count of the petty cash fund.
   d. is responsible for making sales and recording the entries in the books.

4. (S.O. 2) Internal auditors

	are employees of the company	review activities of departments for compliance with prescribed internal controls
a.	yes	yes
b.	yes	no
c.	no	yes
d.	no	no

5. (S.O. 2) Which of the following is **not** a physical, mechanical, or electronic control?
    a. Bonding employees who handle cash.
    b. Employee identification badges.
    c. Safety deposit boxes.
    d. Fences around storage areas.

6. (S.O. 2) Which of the following is **not** an example of an effective internal control measure?
    a. Requiring employees to take vacations.
    b. Prenumbering sales invoices.
    c. Bonding employees who handle cash.
    d. Permitting collusion among employees.

7. (S.O. 2) Which of the following statements concerning the limitations of internal control is **correct?**
    a. The human factor is unimportant.
    b. The costs of establishing control procedures should not exceed their expected benefit.
    c. Collusion among employees may result in more effective control.
    d. A system of internal control should be infallible.

8. (S.O. 3) Which of the following is **not** cash?
    a. Money orders.
    b. Postdated checks.
    c. Bank deposits.
    d. Currency.

9. (S.O. 3) Effective control over cash receipts transactions does **not** result when:
    a. cash registers are used in executing cash receipts transactions.
    b. personnel who handle cash receipts are bonded.
    c. company safes and vaults are used for the storage of cash prior to deposit.
    d. one individual is responsible for the receiving, recording, and custody of cash receipts.

10. (S.O. 3) Independent internal verification over cash receipts transactions does **not** occur when:
    a. cashiers make daily cash counts of cash register totals.
    b. the treasurer's office makes daily comparisons of total receipts and receipts deposited in the bank.
    c. an internal auditor reconciles bank and book balances monthly.
    d. none of the above.

11. (S.O. 3) Storing cash in a company safe is an application of which internal control principle?
    a. Segregation of duties.
    b. Documentation procedures.
    c. Physical controls.
    d. Establishment of responsibility.

12. (S.O. 4) All but one of the following statements about internal control over cash disbursements are correct. The **incorrect** statement is:
    a. More effective internal control results when payments are made by check rather than in cash.
    b. The bank reconciliation should be prepared by the employee who writes the checks.
    c. The use of a bank contributes significantly to good internal control over cash disbursements.
    d. Prenumbered checks should be used and all checks in a series should be accounted for.

13. (S.O. 4) An application of good internal control over cash disbursements is:
    a. Following payment, the approved invoice should be stamped PAID.
    b. Blank checks should be stored in the treasurer's desk.
    c. Each check should be compared with the approved invoice after the check is issued.
    d. Check signers should record the cash disbursements.

14. (S.O. 5) When making a payment from the petty cash fund for postage stamps, the following journal entry is made.
    a. Office Supplies......................... XXXX
          Petty Cash XXXX
    b. Postage Expense.................... XXXX
          Petty Cash XXXX
    c. Miscellaneous Expense XXXX
          Petty Cash XXXX
    d. No entry is made.

15. (S.O. 5) A $100 petty cash fund contains $92 in receipts and $7 in cash. The entry to record replenishments of the fund will include a debit to:
    a. Petty Cash for $100.
    b. Cash Over and Short for $1.
    c. Expenses for $93.
    d. Petty Cash for $8.

16. (S.O. 6) Which of the following statements is **false?**
    a. The use of a bank contributes significantly to good internal control over cash.
    b. Many companies have only one bank account.
    c. Use of a bank minimizes the amount of currency that must be kept on hand.
    d. A company can safeguard its cash by using a bank as a depository and clearing house for checks received and checks written.

17. (S.O. 6) The person who issues the check is known as the:
    a. maker.
    b. payer.
    c. payee.
    d. drawee.

18.   (S.O. 6) A bank may issue a credit memoranda for:
   a.   a bank service charge.
   b.   an NSF (not sufficient funds) check from a customer.
   c.   the collection of a note receivable for the depositor by the bank.
   d.   the cost of printing checks.

19.   (S.O. 7) Which of the following reconciling items would be added to the balance per bank statement to determine the adjusted balance per bank?

	Deposits in transit	Outstanding checks	NSF checks
a.	yes	yes	yes
b.	no	yes	no
c.	yes	no	no
d.	yes	yes	no

20.   (S.O. 8) Cash equivalents are highly liquid investments that can be converted into a specific amount of cash with maturities of:
   a.   1 month or less when purchased.
   b.   3 months or less when purchased.
   c.   6 months or less when purchased.
   d.   1 year or less when purchased.

The
Navigator

MATCHING

Match each term with its definition by writing the appropriate letter in the space provided.

Terms

_____ 1. Internal control.

_____ 2. Cash.

_____ 3. NSF check.

_____ 4. Internal auditors.

_____ 5. Outstanding checks.

_____ 6. Deposits in transit.

_____ 7. Bank statement.

_____ 8. Petty cash fund.

_____ 9. Electronic funds transfer.

Definitions

a. Resources that consist of coins, currency, checks, money orders, and money on hand or on deposit in a bank.

b. Company employees who evaluate the effectiveness of the company's system of internal control on a continuous basis.

c. A cash fund used to pay small amounts.

d. A check that is not paid by a bank because of insufficient funds in a customer's bank account.

e. The plan of organization and all of the related methods and measures adopted within a business to safeguard its assets and enhance the accuracy and reliability of its accounting records.

f. A statement received monthly from the bank that shows the depositor's bank transactions and balances.

g. A disbursement system that uses wire, telephone, telegraph or computer to transfer cash from one location to another.

h. Deposits recorded by the depositor that have not been recorded by the bank.

i. Checks issued and recorded by the company that have not been paid by the bank.

The Navigator

EXERCISES

EX. 8-1   Avison Company uses a petty cash fund for small cash disbursements. The following transactions occurred during July.

July   1   Established a petty cash fund of $200.

4   Paid freight costs on goods purchased $52. Issued receipt ticket No. 1.

8   Paid $37 postage expense. Issued receipt ticket No. 2.

15   Paid miscellaneous expenses $29. Issued receipt tickets Nos. 3 and 4.

20   Paid delivery costs on goods sold $44. Issued receipt ticket No. 5.

24   Paid $35 for office supplies expense. Issued receipt ticket No. 6.

25   Replenished petty cash fund by issuing a check for $197.

31   Increased petty cash fund to $300.

Instructions
Journalize the entries that affect the Petty Cash account by using the general journal on the next page.

	General Journal		J1
Date	**Account Title**	**Debit**	**Credit**

EX. 8-2 (S.O. 6) As of January 31, 2002, the Beethoven Company had the following facts concerning cash in bank.
1. Balance per bank, $55,000.
2. Balance per books, $53,965.
3. Deposits in transit, $4,000.
4. Outstanding checks: No. 305, $1,000; No. 308, $2,500; and No. 310, $3,000.
5. Error: Check No. 301 for $3,416 was correctly paid by the bank but was recorded by the company for $3,461. This check was a payment on account to a creditor.
6. Two bank debit memoranda are unrecorded.
   a. NSF check from Franz Schubert for $3,000 on account.
   b. A bank service charge of $10.
7. One bank credit memorandum is unrecorded. A note receivable for $1,450 plus interest of $75 was collected by the bank. The bank charged $25 for this service. The interest has been accrued by Beethoven Company.

Instructions
(a) Prepare a bank reconciliation for the Beethoven Company for the month ended January 31, 2002.
(b) Journalize the adjusting entries for Beethoven Company on January 31, 2002.

(a)   **BEETHOVEN COMPANY**
                                   Bank Reconciliation
                                   January 31, 2002

(b)

General Journal			J1
Date	**Account Title**	**Debit**	**Credit**

SOLUTIONS TO REVIEW QUESTIONS AND EXERCISES

TRUE-FALSE

1.   (T)
2.   (T)
3.   (F)   The responsibility for related transactions should be assigned to different individuals.
4.   (T)
5.   (T)
6.   (F)   Internal auditors are employees of the company.
7.   (T)
8.   (T)
9.   (F)   Collusion results when two or more individuals circumvent prescribed controls and may significantly impair the effectiveness of the system.
10. (T)
11. (F)   For good internal control, all persons who handle cash should be required to take vacations.
12. (T)
13. (T)
14. (T)
15. (F)   An entry is not made every time petty cash is used.
16. (F)   The maker and drawer are one and the same. The three parties to a check are the maker (or drawer), the bank (or payer), and the payee.
17. (F)   A debit memoranda shows charges to the account such as a bank service charge, and the cost of printing checks. A credit memoranda will show the collection of a note receivable.
18. (T)
19. (T)
20. (F)   Outstanding checks are subtracted from the balance per bank to obtain the adjusted balance per bank.

MULTIPLE CHOICE

1.   (c)   Internal control consists of the plan of organization and all of the related methods and measures adopted within a business to safeguard its assets and enhance the accuracy and reliability of its accounting data.

2.   (c)   Answers (a), (b), and (d) are all considered a part of good internal control. The responsibility for related transactions should be assigned to different individuals.

3.   (d)   Independent internal verification involves the review, comparison, and reconciliation of information from two different sources. Answers (a), (b), and (c) are all considered to be independent internal verification. Answer (d) has nothing to do with internal verification and actually is considered poor internal control.

4.   (a)   Internal auditors are employees of the company who evaluate the effectiveness of the company's system of internal control on a year-round basis. In addition, they review the activities of departments for compliance with prescribed internal controls.

5. (a) Physical, mechanical, and electronic controls relate primarily to the safeguarding of assets and include the measures identified in (b), (c), and (d). Another control measure, but not a physical control, is the bonding of employees who handle cash.

6. (d) Answers (a), (b), and (c) are effective internal control measures. Permitting collusion among employees is bad internal control, because collusion between two or more individuals to circumvent prescribed controls may significantly impair the effectiveness of a system.

7. (b) The human factor (a) is important because internal control may become ineffective through employee fatigue and indifference. Answer (c) may significantly impair the system of internal control because collusion circumvents prescribed controls. No internal control system is infallible.

8. (b) Cash consists of coins, currency (paper money), checks, money orders, and money on deposit in a bank or similar depository. Postdated checks are classified as accounts receivable.

9. (d) Answers (a), (b), and (c) are valid statements. Answer (d) is a violation of the principle of segregation of duties.

10. (a) A cashier department supervisor should make the daily cash count, not the cashiers, because the cashiers would be checking their own work. Answers (b) and (c) are applications of independent internal verification.

11. (c) Storing cash in a company safe is an application of physical controls.

12. (b) This answer choice is a violation of the principle of independent internal verification. An independent individual should prepare the bank reconciliation.

13. (a) Following payment, the approved invoice (or form) should be stamped PAID to prevent it from being resubmitted for payment at a later date. Answer (b) is incorrect because blank checks should be stored in a safe. Answer (c) is incorrect because the comparison should be made before the check is issued. Answer (d) is a violation of segregation of duties; check signers should not record the checks.

14. (d) No entry is made when a petty cash payment occurs. Each payment, though, must be documented on a prenumbered petty cash receipt.

15. (b) The entry is:

Expenses..	92.00	
Cash Over and Short...	1.00	
Cash		93.00

16. (b) Many companies have more than one bank account. They use regional bank accounts, payroll bank accounts and other accounts to obtain short-term loans.

17. (a) The three parties to a check are (1) the maker (or drawer) who issues the check, (2) the bank (or payer) on which the check is drawn, and (3) the payee to whom the check is payable.

18. (c) The collection of a note receivable results in a credit memoranda. The bank service charge (a), NSF checks (b), and the cost of printing checks (d) all result in debit memoranda.

19. (c) Deposits in transit are added to the balance per bank statement, outstanding checks are deducted from the balance per bank, and NSF checks are deducted from the balance per books.

20. (b) A cash equivalent is defined as a highly liquid investment with a maturity of 3 months or less when purchased, that can be converted into a specific amount of cash.

MATCHING

1.	e.	4.	b.	7.	f.
2.	a.	5.	i.	8.	c.
3.	d.	6.	h.	9.	g.

EXERCISES

EX. 8-1

General Journal			J1
Date	**Account Title**	**Debit**	**Credit**
July 1	Petty Cash	200	
	Cash in Bank		200
	(To establish petty cash fund)		
25	Freight-in	52	
	Postage Expense	37	
	Miscellaneous Expense	29	
	Delivery Expense	44	
	Office Supplies Expense	35	
	Cash in Bank		197
	(To replenish petty cash fund)		
31	Petty Cash	100	
	Cash in Bank		100
	(To increase petty cash fund)		

EX. 8-2

(a)

BEETHOVEN COMPANY
Bank Reconciliation
January 31, 2002

Cash balance per bank statement			$55,000
Add:	Deposits in transit		4,000
			59,000
Less:	Outstanding checks		
	No. 305	$1,000	
	No. 308	2,500	
	No. 310	3,000	6,500
Adjusted cash balance per bank			$52,500
Cash balance per books			$53,965
Add:	Collection of note receivable	$1,500	
	Error in recording check No. 301	45	1,545
			55,510
Less:	NSF check	3,000	
	Bank service charge	10	3,010
Adjusted cash balance per books			$52,500

(b)

	General Journal		J1
Date	**Account Title**	**Debit**	**Credit**
2002 Jan. 31	Cash in Bank	1,500	
	Miscellaneous Expense	25	
	Notes Receivable		1,450
	Interest Receivable		75
	(To record collection of note		
	receivable by bank)		
31	Cash in Bank	45	
	Accounts Payable		45
	(To correct error in recording		
	check No. 301)		
31	Accounts Receivable — Franz Schubert	3,000	
	Cash in Bank		3,000
	(To record NSF check)		
31	Miscellaneous Expense	10	
	Cash in Bank		10
	(To record January bank service		
	charge)		

1															1
2															2
3															3
4															4
5															5
6															6
7															7
8															8
9															9
10															10
11															11
12															12
13															13
14															14
15															15
16															16
17															17
18															18
19															19
20															20
21															21
22															22
23															23
24															24
25															25
26															26
27															27
28															28
29															29
30															30
31															31
32															32
33															33
34															34
35															35
36															36
37															37
38															38
39															39
40															40

1											1
2											2
3											3
4											4
5											5
6											6
7											7
8											8
9											9
10											10
11											11
12											12
13											13
14											14
15											15
16											16
17											17
18											18
19											19
20											20
21											21
22											22
23											23
24											24
25											25
26											26
27											27
28											28
29											29
30											30
31											31
32											32
33											33
34											34
35											35
36											36
37											37
00											38
39											39
40											40

	1 2 3 4 5 6 7 8 9 10 11 12 13 14 15 16 17 18 19 20 21 22 23 24 25 26 27 28 29 30 31 32 33 34 35 36 37 38 39 40

Chapter 9

ACCOUNTING FOR RECEIVABLES

The Navigator ✓
- ■ Scan Study Objectives ☐
- ■ Read Preview ☐
- ■ Read Chapter Review ☐
- ■ Work Demonstration Problem ☐
- ■ Answer True-False Statements ☐
- ■ Answer Multiple-Choice Questions ☐
- ■ Match Terms and Definitions ☐
- ■ Solve Exercises ☐

CHAPTER STUDY OBJECTIVES

After studying this chapter, you should be able to:
1. Identify the different types of receivables.
2. Explain how accounts receivable are recognized in the accounts.
3. Distinguish between the methods and bases used to value accounts receivable.
4. Describe the entries to record the disposition of accounts receivable.
5. Compute the maturity date of and interest on notes receivable.
6. Explain how notes receivable are recognized in the accounts.
7. Describe how notes receivable are valued.
8. Describe the entries to record the disposition of notes receivable.
9. Explain the statement presentation and analysis of receivables.

PREVIEW OF CHAPTER 9

The content and organization of this chapter is as follows:

CHAPTER REVIEW

Types of Receivables

1. (S.O. 1) **Receivables** are claims that are expected to be collected in cash. The three major classes of receivables are usually classified as: (a) accounts, (b) notes, and (c) other.

2. **Accounts receivable** are amounts owed by customers on account. **Notes receivable** represent claims for which formal instruments of credit are issued as evidence of debt. And **other receivables** include nontrade receivables such as interest receivable, loans to company officers, advances to employees, and income taxes refundable.

Recognizing Accounts Receivable

3. (S.O. 2) When a business sells merchandise to a customer on credit, Accounts Receivable is debited and Sales is credited.

4. If a payment is received by a customer within the discount period, the following entry is made:

Cash...	XXX	
Sales Discounts	XXX	
Accounts Receivable..		XXX

Valuing Accounts Receivable

5. (S.O. 3) To ensure that receivables are not overstated on the balance sheet, they are stated at their cash (net) realizable value. Cash (net) realizable value is the net amount expected to be received in cash.

6. In accounting, credit losses are debited to Bad Debts Expense or Uncollectible Accounts Expense. Such losses are considered to be a normal and necessary risk of doing business. Two methods are used in accounting for uncollectible accounts: (a) the allowance method and (b) the direct write-off method.

7. The **allowance method** is required when bad debts are material in amount. Its essential features are:
   a. Uncollectible accounts are estimated and the expense for the uncollectible accounts is matched against sales in the same accounting period in which the sales occurred.
   b. **Estimated uncollectibles** are debited to Bad Debts Expense and credited to Allowance for Doubtful Accounts through an adjusting entry at the end of each period.
   c. **Actual uncollectibles** are debited to Allowance for Doubtful Accounts and credited to Accounts Receivable at the time a specific account is written off.

8. When there is a recovery of an account that has been written off as uncollectible, it is necessary to:
   a. reverse the entry made when the account was written off, and
   b. record the collection in the usual manner.

9. There are two bases that are used to determine the amount of expected uncollectibles. One is the percentage of sales basis, and the other is the percentage of receivables basis.

Percentage of Sales Basis

10. Under the **percentage of sales basis,**
    a. Management establishes a percentage relationship between the amount of credit sales and expected losses from uncollectible accounts.
    b. The expected bad debt losses are determined by applying the percentage to the sales base of the current period.
    c. This basis better matches expenses with revenues.

Percentage of Receivables Basis

11. Under the **percentage of receivables basis,**
    a. The balance in the allowance account is derived from an analysis of individual customer accounts. The analysis is often called **aging the accounts receivable.**
    b. The amount of the adjusting entry is the difference between the required balance and the existing balance in the allowance account.
    c. This basis produces the better estimate of **cash realizable value** of the accounts receivable.

Direct Write-off Method

12. Under the direct write-off method, bad debt losses are not anticipated and no allowance account is used.
    a. No entries are made for bad debts until an account is determined to be uncollectible at which time the loss is charged to Bad Debts Expense.
    b. This method makes no attempt to match bad debts expense to sales revenue in the income statement or to show the cash realizable value of the accounts receivable in the balance sheet.
    c. This method is not acceptable for financial reporting purposes, unless bad debt losses are insignificant.

Disposing Accounts Receivable

13. (S.O. 4) In order to accelerate the receipt of cash from receivables, owners frequently (1) sell to a factor such as finance company or bank, or (2) make credit card sales.

14. A factor buys receivables from businesses for a fee and then collects the payments directly from the customers. The entry for a sale to a factor is:

Cash..	XXX	
Service Charge Expense	XXX	
Accounts Receivable..		XXX

15. Credit cards are frequently used by retailers because the retailer does not have to be concerned with the customer's credit history and the retailer can receive cash more quickly from the credit card issuer. However, the credit card issuer usually receives a fee of from 2-6% of the invoice price from the retailer.

Notes Receivable

16. (S.O. 5) A **promissory note** is a written promise to pay a specified amount of money on demand or at a definite time. The party making the promise is called the maker; the party to whom payment is made is called the payee.

17. When the life of a note is expressed in terms of months, the due date is found by counting the months from the date of issue. When the due date is stated in terms of days, it is necessary to count the days. In counting days, the date of issue is omitted but the due date is included.

18. The basic formula for computing interest on an interest bearing note is:

$$\begin{array}{ccccc} & \text{Annual} & & \text{Time} & \\ \text{Face Value} & \text{X} \ \text{Interest} & \text{X} & \text{in Terms} & = \ \text{Interest} \\ \text{of Note} & \text{Rate} & & \text{of One} & \\ & & & \text{Year} & \end{array}$$

Recognizing Notes Receivable

19. (S.O. 6) Entries for notes receivable are required when the note is received and at maturity. To illustrate, assume that on June 1, 2002, Raider Company receives a $2,000, 3-month, 12% note receivable from Paul Revere in settlement of an open account. The entry is:

June 1 Notes Receivable	2,000	
Accounts Receivable		2,000

Valuing Notes Receivable

20. (S.O. 7) Like accounts receivable, short-term notes receivable are reported at their cash (net) realizable value and an Allowance for Doubtful Accounts is used.

Disposing Notes Receivable

21. (S.O. 8) On September 1, the maturity date, Paul Revere honors the note by paying the face amount, $2,000 plus interest of $60 ($2,000 X 12% X 3/12). Assuming that interest has not been accrued, the entry is:

Sept. 1 Cash...	2,060	
Notes Receivable...		2,000
Interest Revenue...		60

22. (S.O. 9) In the balance sheet, short-term receivables are reported within the current assets section below temporary investments. Both the gross amount of receivables and the allowance for doubtful accounts should be reported. In a multiple-step income statement, Bad Debts Expense and Service Charge Expense are reported as selling expenses in the operating expenses section.

DEMONSTRATION PROBLEM (S.O. 3, 4, 5, 6, 7, and 8)

The December 31, 2002 balance sheet of Zunich Company reported the following amounts:

Accounts Receivable...	$190,000
Allowance for Doubtful Accounts (credit balance)....................	4,200

During 2003, Zunich had the following transactions:

February   5   Wrote off as uncollectible an account receivable from Stoldt Co. for $750 and an account receivable from Scanlon for $1,200.

March   31   Credit sales for the first quarter were $125,000. Zunich records its bad debts expense at the end of each quarter based on 2% of credit sales.

May   25   Received $1,200 from Scanlon for the account receivable written off on February 5th.

June   30   Credit sales for the second quarter were $130,000.

July   17   Received a two-month, 11% note from Hammond to replace her account receivable balance of $5,000.

September 17   Hammond dishonored her note. It is expected that Hammond will still pay in the future.

September 30   Credit sales for the third quarter were $90,000.

December   15   Hammond declared bankruptcy. Her account is written off as uncollectible.

December   31   Credit sales for the fourth quarter were $120,000.

Instructions
Prepare the journal entries for Zunich's transactions.

SOLUTION TO DEMONSTRATION PROBLEM

February	5	Allowance for Doubtful Accounts	750	
		Accounts Receivable		750
		(Write-off account of Stoldt)		
		Allowance for Doubtful Accounts	1,200	
		Accounts Receivable		1,200
		(Write-off account of Scanlon)		
March	31	Bad Debts Expense ($125,000 X 2%)	2,500	
		Allowance for Doubtful Accounts		2,500
		(To record estimated bad debts)		
May	25	Accounts Receivable	1,200	
		Allowance for Doubtful Accounts		1,200
		(Reverse the write-off entry)		
		Cash..	1,200	
		Accounts Receivable		1,200
		(Record collection from Scanlon)		
June	30	Bad Debts Expense ($130,000 X 2%)	2,600	
		Allowance for Doubtful Accounts		2,600
		(To record estimated bad debts)		
July	17	Notes Receivable...	5,000	
		Accounts Receivable		5,000
September	17	Accounts Receivable	5,092	
		Interest Revenue ($5,000 X 11% X 2/12)		92
		Notes Receivable...		5,000
		(Hammond dishonored note)		
September	30	Bad Debts Expense ($90,000 X 2%)	1,800	
		Allowance for Doubtful Accounts		1,800
		(To record estimated bad debts)		
December	15	Allowance for Doubtful Accounts	5,092	
		Accounts Receivable		5,092
		(Hammond account write-off)		
December	31	Bad Debts Expense ($120,000 X 2%)	2,400	
		Allowance for Doubtful Accounts		2,400
		(To record estimated bad debts)		

REVIEW QUESTIONS AND EXERCISES

TRUE—FALSE

Indicate whether each of the following is true (T) or false (F) in the space provided.

_____ 1. (S.O. 1) Accounts receivable generally are expected to be collected within 90-120 days.

_____ 2. (S.O. 1) Notes receivable represent claims for which formal instruments of credit are issued as evidence of debt.

_____ 3. (S.O. 3) The two methods of accounting for uncollectible accounts are (a) percentage of sales and (b) percentage of receivables.

_____ 4. (S.O. 3) Under the allowance method, estimated uncollectibles are debited to Bad Debts Expense and credited to Allowance for Doubtful Accounts through an adjusting entry at the end of each period.

_____ 5. (S.O. 3) Actual uncollectibles are debited to Accounts Receivable and credited to Allowance for Doubtful Accounts at the time the specific account is written off.

_____ 6. (S.O. 3) Allowance for Doubtful Accounts is a contra asset account that shows the portion of gross claims on customers that is expected to become uncollectible in the future.

_____ 7. (S.O. 3) The account Allowance for Doubtful Accounts is closed out at the end of the year.

_____ 8. (S.O. 3) To record the recovery of a bad debt, the only entry needed is the entry that reverses the customer's account.

_____ 9. (S.O. 3) Under both the percentage of sales basis and the percentage of receivables basis, it is necessary to determine the company's past experience with bad debt losses.

_____ 10. (S.O. 3) The percentage of sales basis for estimating uncollectibles emphasizes income statement relationships.

_____ 11. (S.O. 3) Under the percentage of receivables basis for estimating uncollectibles, the balance in the allowance account is derived from an analysis of individual customer accounts.

_____ 12. (S.O. 3) Under the direct write-off method, bad debt losses are not anticipated and an allowance account is not used.

_____ 13. (S.O. 3) The direct write-off method is not acceptable in accounting unless bad debt losses are insignificant.

_____ 14. (S.O. 4) In order to accelerate the receipt of cash from receivables, owners may sell the receivables to another company for cash.

_____ 15. (S.O. 4) National credit cards involve three parties: (a) the credit card issuer, (b) the customer, and (c) a bank.

_____ 16. (S.O. 5) A promissory note is a written promise to pay a specified amount of money at some unknown time in the future.

_____ 17. (S.O. 5) When counting the exact number of days to determine the maturity date of a note, the date of issue is included but the due date is omitted.

_____ 18. (S.O. 8) A note is dishonored when it is not fully paid at maturity.

_____ 19. (S.O. 9) Short-term receivables are reported in the current asset section before temporary investments.

_____ 20. (S.O. 9) Bad Debts Expense is reported in the income statement as a selling expense in the operating expenses section.

MULTIPLE CHOICE

Circle the letter that best answers each of the following statements.

1.   (S.O. 1) Which of the following are also called trade receivables?
a.   Accounts receivable.
b.   Other receivables.
c.   Advances to employees.
d.   Income taxes refundable.

2.   (S.O. 2) On February 1, 2002, Chudzick Company sells merchandise on account to Livingston Company for $5,000. The entry to record this transaction by Chudzick Company is:

a.	Sales..	5,000	
	Accounts Payable..		5,000
b.	Cash	5,000	
	Sales..		5,000
c.	Accounts Receivable	5,000	
	Sales..		5,000
d.	Notes Receivable..	5,000	
	Accounts Receivable		5,000

Questions 3 and 4 are based on the following information: On March 1, 2002, Etheredge, Inc. sells merchandise on account to Brooks Company for $7,000 terms 2/10, n/30. On March 3, Brooks returns $500 of the merchandise to Etheredge. On March 9, payment is received from Brooks for the balance due.

3. (S.O. 2) The entry on March 3 by Etheredge is:

   a. Sales...   500
         Cash...   500
   b. Sales...   500
         Accounts Receivable   500
   c. Sales Discount...   500
         Cash...   500
   d. Sales Returns and Allowances   500
         Accounts Receivable   500

4. (S.O. 2) The entry on March 9 by Etheredge is:

   a. Cash   7,000
         Accounts Receivable   7,000
   b. Cash   6,500
         Accounts Receivable   6,500
   c. Cash   6,360
         Sales Discount..   140
         Accounts Receivable   6,500
   d. Cash   6,370
         Sales Discount..   130
         Accounts Receivable   6,500

5. (S.O. 3) When the allowance method of recognizing bad debts expense is used, the entry to recognize that expense:
   a. increases net income.
   b. decreases current assets.
   c. has no effect on current assets.
   d. has no effect on net income.

6. (S.O. 3) A basis of estimating uncollectible accounts that focuses on the income statement rather than the balance sheet is the:
   a. direct write-off of receivables.
   b. aging of the accounts receivable.
   c. percentage of sales.
   d. percentage of receivables.

7.   (S.O. 3) White Company provides for bad debts expense at the rate of 2% of credit sales. The following data are available for 2002:

Allowance for doubtful accounts, 1/1/02 (Cr.) .... $ 21,000
Accounts written off as uncollectible during 2002 13,000
Credit sales in 2002 3,000,000

The Allowance for Doubtful Accounts balance at December 31, 2002, should be:
a. $68,000.
b. $60,000.
c. $50,000.
d. $13,000.

8.   (S. O. 3) In 2002, the Slowe Company had credit sales of $600,000 and granted sales discounts of $12,000. On January 1, 2002, Allowance for Doubtful Accounts had a credit balance of $15,000. During 2002, $25,000 of uncollectible accounts receivable were written off. Past experience indicates that 3% of net credit sales become uncollectible. What should be the adjusted balance of Allowance for Doubtful Accounts at December 31, 2002?
a. $7,640.
b. $8,000.
c. $17,640.
d. $33,000.

9.   (S.O. 3) An analysis and aging of the accounts receivable of Green Company at December 31 revealed the following data:

Accounts Receivable... $600,000
Allowance for Doubtful Accounts per books
   before adjustment (Cr.) 75,000
Amounts expected to become uncollectible........................... 82,000

The cash realizable value of the accounts receivable at December 31, after adjustment, is:
a. $593,000.
b. $525,000.
c. $518,000.
d. $443,000.

10.   (S.O. 3) Voight Company's account balances at December 31 for Accounts Receivable and Allowance for Doubtful Accounts were $1,400,000 and $70,000 (Cr.), respectively. An aging of accounts receivable indicated that $108,000 are expected to become uncollectible. The amount of the adjusting entry for bad debts at December 31 is:
a. $108,000.
b. $38,000.
c. $178,000.
d. $70,000.

11. (S.O. 3) Bonnie Company decides that the past-due account of Sheldon Stahl is uncollectible. Under the allowance method, the $865 balance owed by Sheldon Stahl is written off as follows:

    a. Bad Debts Expense 865
            Accounts Receivable—S. Stahl   865
    b. Allowance for Doubtful Accounts 865
            Accounts Receivable—S. Stahl   865
    c. Accounts Receivable—S. Stahl 865
            Allowance for Doubtful Accounts   865
    d. Allowance for Doubtful Accounts 865
            Bad Debt Expense   865

12. (S.O. 3) Aurora Company has insignificant bad debt losses and therefore uses the direct write-off method. On October 19, the $300 balance of Mary Vonesh becomes uncollectible. The entry to record the write-off is:

    a. Allowance for Doubtful Accounts 300
            Accounts Receivable—Mary Vonesh.........................   300
    b. Bad Debts Expense 300
            Allowance for Doubtful Accounts   300
    c. Accounts Receivable—Mary Vonesh.............................. 300
            Bad Debts Expense   300
    d. Bad Debts Expense 300
            Accounts Receivable—Mary Vonesh.........................   300

13. On March 1, 2002, Tom Zarle purchased a suit at Madden's Fine Apparel Store. The suit cost $350 and Tom used his Madden credit card. Madden charges 2% per month interest if payment on credit charges are not made within 30 days. On April 30, 2002, Tom had not yet made his payment. What entry should Madden make on April 30th?

    a. Uncollectible Account 350
            Accounts Receivable   350
    b. Bad Debts Expense 343
            Interest Expense.. 7
            Accounts Receivable   350
    c. Accounts Receivable 357
            Interest Revenue...   7
            Sales   350
    d. Accounts Receivable 7
            Interest Revenue...   7

14. (S.O. 4) Gudenas Co., makes a credit card sale to a customer for $250. The credit card sale has a grace period of 30 days and then an interest charge of 18% per year or 1.5% per month is added to the balance. If the unpaid balance on the above sale is $150 at the end of the grace period, the interest charge is:

    a. $3.75.
    b. $3.00.
    c. $1.50.
    d. $2.25.

15. (S.O. 4) On October 1, 2002, Arteberry Company sells (factors) $300,000 of receivables to Church Factors, Inc. Church assesses a service charge of 3% of the amount of receivables sold. The journal entry to record the sale by Arteberry will include:
     a. a debit of $300,000 to Accounts Receivable.
     b. a credit of $309,000 to Cash.
     c. a debit of $309,000 to Cash.
     d. a debit of $9,000 to Service Charge Expense.

16. (S.O. 5) On April 3, 2002, Sublette, Inc. issued a promissory note to Biterman Company that was to mature in 90 days. The maturity date of the 90-day note is:
     a. July 1, 1999.
     b. July 2, 1999.
     c. July 3, 1999.
     d. July 4, 1999.

17. (S.O. 5) On February 1, Lowery Company received a $5,000, 10%, four-month note receivable. The cash to be received by Lowery Company when the note becomes due is:
     a. $167.
     b. $5,000.
     c. $5,167.
     d. $5,500.

Questions 18 and 19 are based on the following information: On February 15, 2002, Gilbert Company received a two-month, 10%, $2,000 note from Vincent Nathan for the settlement of his open account.

18. (S.O. 6) The entry by Gilbert Company on February 15, 2002 is:
     a. Notes Receivable... 2,000
             Accounts Receivable—V. Nathan.............................   2,000
     b. Accounts Receivable—V. Nathan.................................. 2,000
             Notes Receivable..   2,000
     c. Cash 2,000
             Notes Receivable..   2,000
     d. Cash 2,000
             Accounts Receivable—V. Nathan.............................   2,000

19. (S.O. 8) The entry by Gilbert Company on April 15, 2002 if Nathan dishonors the note and collection is expected is:
     a. Accounts Receivable—V. Nathan.................................. 2,000
             Notes Receivable..   2,000
     b. Accounts Receivable—V. Nathan.................................. 2,033
             Notes Receivable..   2,000
             Interest Revenue   33
     c. Accounts Receivable—V. Nathan.................................. 1,067
         Interest Lost..   33
             Notes Receivable..   2,000
     d. Bad Debts Expense 2,033
             Notes Receivable..   2,033

20. (S.O. 9) Which of the following statements concerning receivables is **incorrect?**
    a. Notes receivable are often listed last under receivables.
    b. The contingent liability from selling notes receivable should be disclosed.
    c. Both the gross amount of receivables and the allowance for doubtful accounts should be reported.
    d. Interest revenue and gain on sale of notes receivable are shown under other revenues and gains.

MATCHING

Match each term with its definition by writing the appropriate letter in the space provided.

Terms	Definitions
_____ 1. Promissory note.	a. Management establishes a percentage relationship between the amount of credit sales and expected losses from uncollectible accounts.
_____ 2. Aging of accounts receivable.	
_____ 3. Percentage of sales basis.	b. The net amount expected to be received in cash.
_____ 4. Allowance method.	c. A method of accounting for bad debts that is required when bad debts are material.
_____ 5. Percentage of receivables basis.	d. The party who promises to pay a promissory note.
_____ 6. Cash net realizable value.	e. A note that is not paid in full at maturity.
_____ 7. Dishonored note.	f. A written promise to pay a specified amount of money on demand or at a definite time.
_____ 8. Honored note.	g. Management establishes a percentage relationship between the amount of receivables and the expected losses from uncollectible accounts.
_____ 9. Maker.	h. An analysis of individual customer accounts by the length of time they have been unpaid.
_____ 10. Payee.	i. The party to whom a promissory note is to be paid.
_____ 11. Direct write-off method.	j. A note that is paid in full at maturity.
	k. A method of accounting for bad debts that is only acceptable when bad debts are insignificant.

EXERCISES

EX. 9-1   (S.O. 3) The N. Hawthorne Co. had a credit balance in Allowance for Doubtful Accounts of $10,000 at January 1, 2002. During 2002 credit sales totaled $300,000. A summary of the aging of accounts receivable at December 31, 2002 is as follows:

Classification by Month of Sale	Balance in Each Category	Estimated % Uncollectible
Nov.—Dec., 2002	$ 60,000	2%
Jul.—Oct., 2002	30,000	10
Jan.—June, 2002	10,000	25
Prior to 1/1/02	5,000	75
	$105,000	

On April 2, 2002, $750 was received from Hermann Hesse; his account for $750 had been written off as uncollectible in 2001. During 2002, accounts receivable totaling $8,400 were written off as uncollectible.

Instructions
(a)   Prepare the journal entries on April 2 for the collection of the account previously written off and a summary entry on December 31 for the accounts written off in 2002.
(b)   Assuming N. Hawthorne Co. estimates uncollectibles as 2% of credit sales, prepare the adjusting entry at December 31, 2002.
(c)   Assuming the N. Hawthorne Co. estimates uncollectibles by using the percentage of accounts receivables, prepare the adjusting entry at December 31, 2002 (use an aging schedule).

	General Journal		J1
Date	**Account Title**	**Debit**	**Credit**
2002 (a)			

	General Journal		J
Date	**Account Title**	**Debit**	**Credit**
(b)			
(c)			

EX. 9-2 (S.O. 5, 6, 7, and 8) Hemingway Company had the following transactions for the year ended December 31, 2002.

July   1   Received a $2,000, three-month 10% promissory note from Damon Runyon in settlement of an open account.

Aug.   1   Received a $1,000, three-month 12% note receivable from Carl Sandburg for cash borrowed by Sandburg.

Oct.   1   Received notice that the Damon Runyon note had been dishonored. It is expected that Runyon will eventually pay the amount owed.

Nov.   1   Sandburg honored the note receivable in full. (Assume that interest has not been accrued.)

Instructions
Prepare the entries for the transactions above.

	General Journal		J1
Date	Account Title	Debit	Credit

The
Navigator

SOLUTIONS TO REVIEW QUESTIONS AND EXERCISES

TRUE-FALSE

1. (F) Accounts receivable generally are expected to be collected within 30 to 60 days.
2. (T)
3. (F) The two methods are (a) the allowance method and (b) the direct write-off method.
4. (T)
5. (F) Actual uncollectibles are debited to Allowance for Doubtful Accounts and credited to Accounts Receivable at the time the specific account is written off.
6. (T)
7. (F) The account Allowance for Doubtful Accounts is a contra asset account on the balance sheet and is therefore a permanent account that is not closed out.
8. (F) Two entries are required to record the recovery of a bad debt: (1) the entry made in writing off the account is reversed to reinstate the customer's account, and (2) the collection is journalized in the usual manner.
9. (T)
10. (T)
11. (T)
12. (T)
13. (T)
14. (T)
15. (F) The three parties are (a) the credit card issuer, (b) the retailer, and (c) the customer.
16. (F) A promissory note is a written promise to pay a specified amount of money on demand or at a definite time.
17. (F) When counting the exact number of days to determine the maturity date, the date of issue is omitted but the due date is included.
18. (T)
19. (F) Short-term receivables are reported in the current asset section immediately after temporary investments.
20. (T)

MULTIPLE CHOICE

1. (a) Accounts receivables, also called trade receivables, are amounts owed by customers on account. Answer (b), other receivables, include non-trade receivables. Advances to employees (c) and income taxes refundable (d) are included under the category of other receivables.

2. (c) When a business sells merchandise on credit they must recognize an asset by debiting Accounts Receivable and revenue earned by crediting Sales.

3. (d) When merchandise is returned, the seller must recognize the return by debiting Sales Returns and Allowance, which is a contra account to Sales. A decrease in assets must be recognized by crediting Accounts Receivable.

4.   (d)   The sales discount is $130 ($6,500 X 2%). The correct entry is Cash (Dr.) $6,370, Sales Discounts (Dr.) $130, and Accounts Receivable (Cr.) $6,500.

5.   (b)   Estimated uncollectibles are debited to Bad Debts Expense and credited to Allowance for Doubtful Accounts through an adjusting entry at the end of each period. Bad Debts Expense, being an expense decreases net income. The Allowance for Doubtful Accounts is a contra asset account to accounts receivable, thus decreasing current assets.

6.   (c)   The allowance method using the percentage of sales basis focuses on the income statement. The direct write-off of receivables (a) is not an allowance method. The aging of the accounts receivable (b) and a percentage of the accounts receivable (d) are the same; they focus on the balance sheet.

7.   (a)   The balance in the Allowance for Doubtful Accounts prior to adjustment is a credit of $8,000 ($21,000 - $13,000). The adjusting entry under the percentage of sales method is $60,000 ($3,000,000 X 2%). Thus, the adjusted balance is $68,000 ($8,000 + $60,000).

8.   (a)   The balance in Allowance for Doubtful Accounts prior to adjustment is a debit of $10,000 ($25,000 - $15,000). The adjusting entry is $17,640 [$600,000 - $12,000) X .03]. Thus the ending balance is $7,640 ($17,640 - $10,000).

9.   (c)   The cash realizable value of the accounts receivable at December 31 should be accounts receivable ($600,000) less the amounts deemed uncollectible ($82,000) or $518,000.

10.   (b)   Under the percentage of receivables basis, the allowance account is adjusted to the estimated uncollectibles. In this case, the required balance is $108,000 and the amount of the adjusting entry is $38,000 ($108,000 - $70,000).

11.   (b)   Under the allowance method, every bad debt write-off is made against the allowance account and not to Bad Debts Expense. A debit to Bad Debts Expense would be incorrect because the expense is recognized when the adjusting entry is made for estimated bad debts. The write-off of the account reduces both Accounts Receivable and the Allowance for Doubtful Accounts.

12.   (d)   Under the direct write-off method, bad debt loses are not anticipated and an allowance account is not used. No entries are made for bad debts until an account is determined to be uncollectible, at which time the loss is charged to Bad Debts Expense and credited to Accounts Receivable.

13.   (d)   Madden should recognize revenue earned of $7 ($350 X 2%). The amount is simply added to the accounts receivable balance.

14.   (d)   The interest charge is $150 X 1.5% or $2.25.

15. (d) The entry to record the sale (factor) of receivables by Arteberry is as follows:

Cash	291,000	
Service Charge Expense	9,000	
Accounts Receivable		300,000

16. (b) In calculating the maturity date, the date the note is issued is omitted but the due date is included.

Term on the note		90
April (30 - 3)	27	
May	31	
June	30	88
Maturity date, July		2

17. (c) The cash to be received by Lowery Company will be the face value, $5,000, plus the interest earned, $167 ($5,000 X 10% X 4/12).

18. (a) A transfer from one asset account, Accounts Receivable, to another asset account, Notes Receivable, is made by debiting Notes Receivable and crediting Accounts Receivable.

19. (b) By dishonoring the note, the Notes Receivable is reverted back to Accounts Receivable. The amount of interest that has been earned $33 - ($2,000 X .10 X 2/12) is recognized by crediting interest revenue and by increasing Accounts Receivable.

20. (a) Notes receivable are often listed first under receivables because they can be quickly realized in cash through sale. Answers (b), (c), and (d) are all correct statements.

MATCHING

1.	f	5.	g	9.	d		
2.	h	6.	b	10.	i		
3.	a	7.	e	11.	k		
4.	c	8.	j				

EXERCISES

EX. 9-1

	General Journal		J1
Date	**Account Title**	**Debit**	**Credit**
2002 (a)			
Apr. 2	Accounts Receivable — H. Hesse	750	
	Allowance for Doubtful Accounts		750
	(To reverse write-off of H. Hesse		
	account)		
2	Cash	750	
	Accounts Receivable — H. Hesse		750
	(To record collection from H. Hesse)		
Dec. 31	Allowance for Doubtful Accounts	8,400	
	Accounts Receivable		8,400
	(Write-off of 1999 uncollectibles)		
(b)			
Dec. 31	Bad Debts Expense ($300,000 X 2%)	6,000	
	Allowance for Doubtful Accounts		6,000
	(To record estimated bad debts		
	for year)		
(c)			
Dec. 31	Bad Debts Expense	8,100	
	Allowance for Doubtful Accounts		8,100
	(To adjust allowance account to total		
	estimated uncollectibles)		

Aging Schedule

Classification by Month of Sale	Balance in Each Category	Estimated % Uncollectible	Estimated Bad Debts
Nov.—Dec. 2002	$ 60,000	2%	$ 1,200
July—Oct. 2002	30,000	10	3,000
Jan.—June 2002	10,000	25	2,500
Prior to 1/1/02	5,000	75	3,750
	$105,000		$10,450

The balance in Allowance for Doubtful Accounts prior to adjustment is $2,350 (Cr.) ($10,000 + $750 - $8,400). Therefore, the adjusting entry is $8,100 ($10,450 - $2,350).

EX. 9-2

	General Journal		J1
Date	**Account Title**	**Debit**	**Credit**
2002			
July 1	Notes Receivable	2,000	
	Accounts Receivable—D. Runyon		2,000
	(To record acceptance of D. Runyon note)		
Aug. 1	Notes Receivable	1,000	
	Cash		1,000
	(To record acceptance of C. Sandburg note)		
Oct. 1	Accounts Receivable	2,050	
	Notes Receivable		2,000
	Interest Revenue ($2,000 X 10% X 3/12)		50
	(To record collection of D. Runyon note)		
Nov. 1	Cash	1,030	
	Notes Receivable		1,000
	Interest Revenue ($1,000 X 12% X 3/12)		30
	(To record honoring of C. Sandburg note)		

1																				1
2																				2
3																				3
4																				4
5																				5
6																				6
7																				7
8																				8
9																				9
10																				10
11																				11
12																				12
13																				13
14																				14
15																				15
16																				16
17																				17
18																				18
19																				19
20																				20
21																				21
22																				22
23																				23
24																				24
25																				25
26																				26
27																				27
28																				28
29																				29
30																				30
31																				31
32																				32
33																				33
34																				34
35																				35
36																				36
37																				37
38																				38
39																				39
40																				40

	1	2	3	4	5	6	7	8	9	10
1										
2										
3										
4										
5										
6										
7										
8										
9										
10										
11										
12										
13										
14										
15										
16										
17										
18										
19										
20										
21										
22										
23										
24										
25										
26										
27										
28										
29										
30										
31										
32										
33										
34										
35										
36										
37										
38										
39										
40										

1																		1
2																		2
3																		3
4																		4
5																		5
6																		6
7																		7
8																		8
9																		9
10																		10
11																		11
12																		12
13																		13
14																		14
15																		15
16																		16
17																		17
18																		18
19																		19
20																		20
21																		21
22																		22
23																		23
24																		24
25																		25
26																		26
27																		27
28																		28
29																		29
30																		30
31																		31
32																		32
33																		33
34																		34
35																		35
36																		36
37																		37
38																		38
39																		39
40																		40

Chapter 10

*P*LANT ASSETS, NATURAL RESOURCES AND INTANGIBLE ASSETS

The Navigator ✓
- ■ Scan Study Objectives ☐
- ■ Read Preview ☐
- ■ Read Chapter Review ☐
- ■ Work Demonstration Problem ☐
- ■ Answer True-False Statements ☐
- ■ Answer Multiple-Choice Questions ☐
- ■ Match Terms and Definitions ☐
- ■ Solve Exercises ☐

CHAPTER STUDY OBJECTIVES

After studying this chapter, you should be able to:
1. Describe the application of the cost principle to plant assets.
2. Explain the concept of depreciation.
3. Compute periodic depreciation using different methods.
4. Describe the procedure for revising periodic depreciation.
5. Distinguish between revenue and capital expenditures, and prepare the entries for these expenditures.
6. Explain how to account for the disposal of a plant asset through retirement, sale, or exchange.
7. Compute periodic depletion of natural resources.
8. Contrast the accounting for intangible assets with the accounting for plant assets.
9. Indicate how plant assets, natural resources, and intangible assets are reported and analyzed.

The Navigator

PREVIEW OF CHAPTER 10

In this chapter, we explain the application of the cost principle of accounting to natural resources and intangible assets. We also describe the methods that may be used to allocate an asset's cost over its useful life. In addition, the accounting for expenditures incurred during the useful life of assets is discussed. The organization and content of this chapter are as follows:

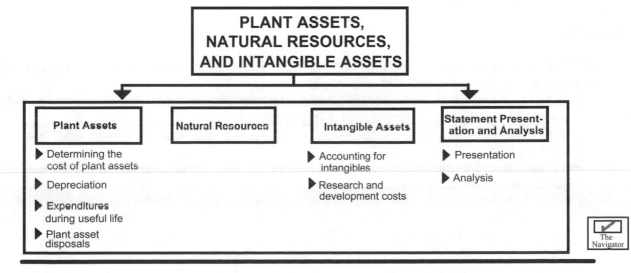

CHAPTER REVIEW

Plant Assets

1. (S.O. 1) **Plant assets** are tangible resources that are used in the operations of a business and are not intended for sale to customers. Plant assets are subdivided into four classes: (a) land, (b) land improvements, (c) buildings, and (d) equipment.

Cost of Plant Assets

2. Plant assets are recorded at cost in accordance with the **cost principle** of accounting. Cost consists of all expenditures necessary to (1) acquire the asset and (2) make it ready for its intended use.

3. The cost of **land** includes the cash purchase price plus other related costs. The cost might include closing costs such as title and attorney's fees, real estate brokers' commissions, and accrued property taxes and other liens on the land assumed by the purchaser. All necessary costs incurred in making land ready for its intended use are debited to the Land Account.

4. The cost of **land improvements** includes all expenditures needed to make the improvements ready for their intended use such as the cost of a new parking lot, fencing, and lighting.

5. The cost of **buildings** includes **all** necessary costs related to the purchase or construction of a building:
   a. When a building is purchased, such costs include the purchase price, closing costs, and real estate broker's commission.
   b. Costs to make the building ready for its intended use include expenditures for remodeling and replacing or repairing the roof, floors, wiring, and plumbing.
   c. When a new building is constructed, cost consists of the contract price plus payments for architects' fees, building permits, interest payments during construction, and excavation costs.

6. The cost of **equipment** consists of the cash purchase price, sales taxes, freight charges, and insurance paid by the purchaser during transit. Cost includes all expenditures required in assembling, installing, and testing the unit. Recurring costs such as licenses and insurance are expensed as incurred.

Depreciation

7. (S.O. 2) **Depreciation** is the process of allocating to expense the cost of a plant asset over its useful (service) life in a rational and systematic manner.
   a. The cost allocation is designed to provide for the proper matching of expenses with revenues in accordance with the **matching principle.**
   b. During an asset's life, its usefulness may decline because of wear and tear or obsolescence.
   c. Recognition of depreciation does not result in the accumulation of cash for the replacement of the asset.

8.   Three factors that affect the computation of depreciation are (1) cost, (2) useful life, and (3) salvage value.

9.   Three methods of recognizing depreciation are (a) straight-line, (b) units of activity, and (c) declining-balance.
a.   Each method is acceptable under generally accepted accounting principles.
b.   Management selects the method that is appropriate in the circumstances.
c.   Once a method is chosen, it should be applied consistently.

Straight-Line Method

10.   Under the **straight-line method** depreciation is the same for each year of the asset's useful life.
a.   The formula for computing annual depreciation expense is:

Depreciable Cost ÷ Useful Life (in years) = Depreciation Expense

b.   To illustrate the computation, assume that the Benson Company purchased a delivery truck for $11,000 on January 1 with an estimated salvage value of $1,000 at the end of its four-year service life. Annual depreciation is $2,500 [($11,000 - $1,000 ÷ 4)].
c.   The straight-line method predominates in practice.
d.   This method is simple to apply and it matches expenses and revenues appropriately when the use of the asset is reasonably uniform throughout the service life.

Units-of-Activity Method

11.   Under the **units-of-activity method,** service life is expressed in terms of the total units of production or expected use from the asset, rather than time.
a.   The formulas for computing depreciation expense are:

(1)   Depreciable Cost ÷ Total Units of Activity = Depreciation Cost per Unit

(2)   Depreciation Cost per Unit X Units of Activity During the Year = Depreciation
Expense

b.   To illustrate the computation, assume that Benson Company expects to drive the truck purchased in (10b) above for 100,000 miles and that 30,000 miles are driven in the first year. Depreciation for the first year is $3,000.

(1) $10,000 ÷ 100,000 = $.10 per mile.

(2) $.10 X 30,000 = $3,000.

c.   In using this method, it is often difficult to make a reasonable estimate of total activity.
d.   When the productivity of an asset varies significantly from one period to another, this method results in the best matching of expenses with revenues.

Declining-Balance Method

12.   The **declining-balance method** produces a decreasing annual depreciation expense over the useful life of the asset.
a.   The formula for computing depreciation expense is:

Book Value at Beginning of Year X Declining Balance Rate = Depreciation Expense

    b. To illustrate the computation, assume that Benson Company uses a declining-balance rate that is double the straight-line rate of 25%. Depreciation in the first year is $5,500 ($11,000 X 50%).

    c. Under this method, the depreciation rate remains constant from year to year, but the book value to which the rate is applied declines each year.

    d. This method is compatible with the matching principle because the higher depreciation in early years is matched with the higher benefits received in these years.

13. Taxpayers must use on their tax returns either the straight-line method or a special accelerated depreciation method called the Modified Accelerated Cost Recovery System (MACRS).

Revising Periodic Depreciation

14. (S.O. 4) If wear and tear or obsolescence indicate that annual depreciation is inadequate or excessive, a change in the periodic amount should be made.

    a. When a change is made, (1) there is no correction of previously recorded depreciation expense, and (2) depreciation expense for current and future years is revised.

    b. To determine the new annual depreciation expense, the depreciable cost at the time of the revision is divided by the remaining useful life.

Expenditures During Useful Life

15. (S.O. 5) **Ordinary repairs** are expenditures to maintain the operating efficiency and expected productive life of the plant asset. They are debited to Repairs Expense as incurred and are often referred to as **revenue expenditures.**

16. **Additions and improvements** are costs incurred to increase the operating efficiency, productive capacity, or expected useful life of the plant asset. These expenditures are usually material in amount and occur infrequently during the period of ownership.

17. **Capital expenditures** increase the company's investment in productive facilities. These expenditures include additions and improvements.

Plant Asset Disposals

18. (S.O. 6) Plant assets may be disposed of by (a) retirement, (b) sale, or (c) exchange.

19. At the time of disposal, it is necessary to determine the **book value** of the plant asset.

    a. If the disposal occurs during the year, depreciation for the fraction of the year to the date of disposal must be recorded.

    b. The book value is then eliminated by debiting the Accumulated Depreciation account for the total depreciation to the date of disposal and crediting the asset account for the cost of the asset.

Retirement of Plant Assets

20. In accounting for a disposal by **retirement,**
    a. if the asset is fully depreciated, the entry is a debit to Accumulated Depreciation and a credit to the plant asset account.
    b. if the asset is retired before it is fully depreciated and no scrap or salvage value is received, a loss on disposal occurs.
    c. the loss on disposal is reported in the Other Expenses and Losses section of the income statement.

Sale of Plant Assets

21. In a disposal by **sale,** the book value of the asset is compared with the **proceeds** received from the sale.
    a. If the proceeds of the sale exceed the book value, a **gain on disposal** occurs which is reported in the Other Revenues and Gains section of the income statement.
    b. If the proceeds of the sale are less than the book value of the asset, a **loss on disposal** occurs which is reported in the Other Expenses and Losses section of the income statement.

Exchanges of Plant Assets

22. An **exchange of similar assets** involves assets of the same type. In this type of exchange, the new asset performs the same function as the old asset. The accounting depends on whether there is a gain or loss on the old asset.
    a. When a gain occurs in the exchange of similar assets:
       (1) The acquisition cost of the new asset is equal to the fair market value of the old asset exchanged plus any cash or other consideration given up.
       (2) The gain or loss is the difference between the fair market value and the book value of the asset given up.
       (3) The gain is then offset against the cost of the new asset (instead of being credited to Gain on Disposal).
    b. When a loss occurs in the exchange of similar assets, the loss is recognized immediately—it is not deferred.

Natural Resources

23. (S.O. 7) **Natural resources** consist of standing timber and underground deposits of oil, gas, and minerals. These assets are frequently called wasting assets.

Acquisition Cost

24. The acquisition cost of a natural resource is the price needed to acquire the resource and prepare it for its intended use.

Depletion

25. **Depletion** is the systematic write-off of the cost of natural resources. The **units of activity method** is generally used to compute depletion because periodic depletion is generally a function of the units extracted during the year. The formulas for computing depletion expense are:
    a. Total Cost minus Salvage Value ÷ Total Estimated Units = Depletion Cost per Unit.
    b. Depletion Cost per Unit X Number of Units Extracted and Sold = Depletion Expense.

26. To record depletion expense, Depletion Expense is debited and a contra asset account, Accumulated Depletion, is credited.
    a. Depletion expense is reported as a cost of producing the product.
    b. Accumulated Depletion is deducted from the cost of the natural resource in the balance sheet.

Intangible Assets

27. (S.O. 8) **Intangible assets** are rights, privileges, and competitive advantages that result from the ownership of long lived assets that do not possess physical substance. Intangibles may arise from government grants, acquisition of another business, and private monopolistic arrangements.

28. In general, **accounting for intangible assets** parallels the accounting for plant assets. Intangible assets are (a) recorded at cost, (b) cost is written off over useful life in a rational and systematic manner, and (c) at disposal, book value is eliminated and gain or loss, if any, is recorded.

29. Differences between the accounting for intangible assets and the accounting for plant assets include:
    a. The systematic write-off of an intangible asset is referred to as **amortization.**
    b. To record amortization, Amortization Expense is debited and the specific intangible asset is credited.
    c. The amortization period cannot be longer than 40 years.
    d. Amortization is typically computed on a straight-line basis.

Patents

30. A **patent** is an exclusive right issued by the U.S. Patent Office that enables the recipient to manufacture, sell, or otherwise control his or her invention for a period of seventeen years from the date of grant.
    a. The initial cost of a patent is the cash or cash equivalent price paid when the patent is acquired.
    b. When legal costs are incurred in successfully defending the patent, they are added to the Patent account and amortized over the remaining useful life of the patent.
    c. The cost of the patent should be amortized over its legal life (20 years) or useful life, whichever is shorter.

Copyrights

31. Copyrights are granted by the federal government, giving the owner the exclusive right to reproduce and sell an artistic or published work.

Trademark or Trade name

32. A **trademark** or **trade name** is a word, phrase, jingle, or symbol that distinguishes or identifies a particular enterprise or product.

Franchise

33. A **franchise** is a contractual arrangement under which the franchisor grants the franchisee the right to sell certain products, to render specific services, or to use certain trademarks or trade names, usually within a designated geographical area. Another type of franchise, commonly referred to as a **license** or **permit,** is entered into between a governmental body and a business enterprise and permits the enterprise to use public property in performing its services.

Goodwill

34. **Goodwill** is the value of all favorable attributes that relate to a business enterprise such as exceptional management, desirable location, good customer relations, high-quality products, fair pricing policies, and harmonious relations with labor unions.
     a. Goodwill can be identified only with the business as a whole.
     b. Goodwill is recorded only when there is an exchange transaction that involves the purchase of an entire business.
     c. When an entire business is purchased, goodwill is the excess of cost over the fair market value of the net assets (assets less liabilities) acquired.

35. Goodwill is written off over its useful life, not to exceed 40 years. The amortization entry generally results in a debit to Goodwill Expense and a credit to Goodwill.

Research and Development

36. **Research and development** costs are costs that are spent on developing new products and processes. Such costs are usually recorded as an expense when incurred.

Financial Statement Presentation

37. (S.O. 9) In the balance sheet, plant assets and natural resources are usually combined under Property, Plant, and Equipment and intangibles are shown separately under Intangible Assets.
     a. There should be disclosure of the balances in the major classes of assets and accumulated depreciation of major classes of assets or in total.
     b. Depreciation and amortization methods used should be described and the amount of depreciation and amortization expense for the period disclosed.

The Navigator

DEMONSTRATION PROBLEM (S.O. 2 and 3)

On January 1, 2001, Hume Company purchases a machine that includes a cash price of $7,000, freight charges of $250, insurance during transit of $50, assembly costs of $150, and a license of $35 per year. Hume depreciates the machine using the straight-line method based on a five-year useful life with an estimated salvage value of $700.

Instructions
(a)   Make the entry for the purchase on January 1, 2001.
(b)   Make the depreciation expense entries for December 31, 2001, 2002, and 2003.

SOLUTION TO DEMONSTRATION PROBLEM

(a)   2001
Jan.   1   Equipment   7,450
           License Expense   35
               Cash...   7,485
               ($7,000 + $250 + $50 + $150)

(b)   2001, 2002, and 2003
Dec. 31   Depreciation Expense   1,350
               Accumulated Depreciation—Equipment   1,350
               [($7,450 - $700) ÷ 5]

REVIEW QUESTIONS AND EXERCISES

TRUE—FALSE

Indicate whether each of the following is true (T) or false (F) in the space provided.

_____   1.   (S.O. 1) To be classified as a plant asset, an asset must possess physical substance.

_____   2.   (S.O. 1) All plant assets should be depreciated over their useful life.

_____   3.   (S.O. 1) The cost of tearing down an old building on a newly purchased lot to make the site suitable for a new building should be debited to Buildings.

_____   4.   (S.O. 1) The cost of driveways and parking lots is debited to Land.

_____   5.   (S.O. 1) When constructing a building, a company is permitted to include the acquisition cost and certain interest costs incurred in financing the project.

_____ 6. (S.O. 1) The cost of equipment includes the cash price, freight charges, expenditures required in the assembling, motor vehicle licenses, and accident insurance.

_____ 7. (S.O. 2) Recognition of depreciation permits the accumulation of cash for the replacement of the asset.

_____ 8. (S.O. 3) Under the straight-line method, depreciation decreases for each year of service life of the asset.

_____ 9. (S.O. 3) Under the units of activity method, the decline in service potential is attributed to time rather than activity.

_____ 10. (S.O. 3) The declining-balance method is often called an accelerated depreciation method.

_____ 11. (S.O. 3) The declining-balance method is compatible with the matching principle.

_____ 12. (S.O. 3) When an asset is purchased during the year, it is not necessary to record depreciation expense in the first year under the declining-balance depreciation method.

_____ 13. (S.O. 3) Taxpayers must use either the straight-line method or a special accelerated depreciation method called Modified Accelerated Cost Recovery System on their tax returns.

_____ 14. (S.O. 3) The book value of a plant asset is the difference between the asset's fair market value and accumulated depreciation.

_____ 15. (S.O. 6) The retirement of a fully depreciated plant asset will usually result in a loss.

_____ 16. (S.O. 6) If the proceeds from the sale of a plant asset exceed the asset's book value, a gain should be recognized.

_____ 17. (S.O. 6) A gain can be recognized on the exchange of similar assets.

_____ 18. (S.O. 6) A loss on the exchange of plant assets occurs when the fair market value of the old asset is less than its book value.

_____ 19. (S.O. 6) Gains resulting from the exchange of similar assets are deferred and reduce the cost basis of the new asset acquired.

_____ 20. (S.O. 7) Wasting assets are natural resources which no longer have any value.

_____ 21. (S.O. 7) The acquisition cost of a natural resource is the cash or cash equivalent price necessary to acquire the resource and prepare it for its intended use.

_____ 22. (S.O. 7) The units of activity method is generally used to compute depletion.

_____ 23. (S.O. 7) Depletion expense is reported in the income statement as an operating expense.

_____ 24. (S.O. 8) In general, the accounting for intangible assets parallels the accounting for plant assets.

_____ 25. (S.O. 8) The straight-line method is generally used to compute amortization expense on intangible assets.

_____ 26. (S.O. 8) The cost of successfully defending a patent in an infringement suit should be expensed when incurred.

_____ 27. (S.O. 8) Goodwill is not recognized in accounting unless it is acquired from another business enterprise.

_____ 28. (S.O. 8) Research and development costs should be charged to expense when incurred.

MULTIPLE CHOICE

Circle the letter that best answers each of the following statements.

1. (S.O. 1) A term which is not synonymous with property, plant, and equipment is:
    a.   plant assets.
    b.   fixed assets.
    c.   intangible assets.
    d.   long-lived tangible assets.

2. (S.O. 1) Plant assets are often subdivided into four groups. Which of the following would not be classified as a plant asset?
    a.   Land.
    b.   Land improvements.
    c.   Supplies.
    d.   Buildings.

3. (S.O. 1) Plato Company acquired land with a purchase price of $150,000 plus attorney's fee $6,000, demolition and removal costs of an old building $4,000, and grading and filling the land $3,000. The land should be recorded at:
    a. $137,000.
    b. $150,000.
    c. $157,000.
    d. $163,000.

4. (S.O. 1) Land improvements do **not** include:
   a. building sites.
   b. driveways.
   c. parking lots.
   d. fencing.

5. (S.O. 1) Schopenhauer Company purchased a delivery truck and incurred the following costs:

Cash price..	$15,000
Sales tax	750
Painting...	600
Motor vehicle license	75
2-year accident insurance policy	700
Total costs	$17,125

   What amount should be recorded as the cost of the delivery truck?
   a. $15,750.
   b. $16,350.
   c. $16,425.
   d. $17,125.

6. (S.O. 2) The factor that is not relevant in computing depreciation is:
   a. Replacement value.
   b. Cost.
   c. Salvage value.
   d. Useful life.

7. (S.O. 3) Using the straight-line method, depreciation expense is calculated with the formula:
   a. (Cost ÷ Useful life) - Salvage value.
   b. (Cost + Salvage value) ÷ Useful life.
   c. (Cost - Salvage value) ÷ Useful life.
   d. (Cost ÷ Useful life) + Salvage value.

8. (S.O. 3) Bruno Company purchased equipment on January 1, 2002 at a total invoice cost of $280,000; additional costs of $5,000 for freight and $25,000 for installation were incurred. The equipment has an estimated salvage value of $10,000 and an estimated useful life of five years. The amount of accumulated depreciation at December 31, 2003 if the straight-line method of depreciation is used is:
   a. $108,000.
   b. $110,000.
   c. $120,000.
   d. $124,000.

9.   (S.O. 3) Spinoza Enterprises purchased a truck for $27,000 on January 1, 2002. The truck will have an estimated salvage value of $2,000 at the end of five years. Using the units of activity method, the accumulated depreciation at December 31, 2003 can be computed by the following formula:
   a.   ($27,000 ÷ Total estimated activity) X Units of activity for 2003.
   b.   ($25,000 ÷ Total estimated activity) X Units of activity for 2003.
   c.   ($27,000 ÷ Total estimated activity) X Units of activity for 2002 and 2003.
   d.   ($25,000 ÷ Total estimated activity) X Units of activity for 2002 and 2003.

10.   (S.O. 3) Nietzsche Company purchased a machine on January 1, 2002, for $350,000. The machine has an estimated useful life of five years and a salvage value of $50,000. The machine is being depreciated using the double-declining balance method. The book value at December 31, 2003 is:
   a. $126,000.
   b. $158,000.
   c. $170,000.
   d. $224,000.

11.   (S.O. 4) Santayana Company purchased a machine on January 1, 2000, for $8,000 with an estimated salvage value of $2,000 and an estimated useful life of 8 years. On January 1, 2002, Santayana decides the machine will last 12 years from the date of purchase. The salvage value is still estimated at $2,000. Using the straight-line method the new annual depreciation will be:
   a. $450.
   b. $500.
   c. $600.
   d. $667.

12.   (S.O. 5) Which of the following would be considered an ordinary repair?
   a.   Constructing a new wing on a building.
   b.   A major motor overhaul of a new truck.
   c.   Painting of buildings.
   d.   Replacing a stairway with an escalator.

13.   (S.O. 5) Improvements are:
   a.   revenue expenditures.
   b.   debited to an appropriate asset account when they increase useful life.
   c.   debited to accumulated depreciation when they do not increase useful life.
   d.   debited to an appropriate asset account when they do not increase useful life.

14.   (S.O. 6) Which of the following is an example of a plant asset disposal?
   a.   Retirement.
   b.   Sale.
   c.   Exchange.
   d.   All of the above are examples.

15.   (S.O. 6) A plant asset cost $27,000 when it was purchased on January 1, 1995. It was depreciated by the straight-line method based on a 9-year life with no salvage value. On June 30, 2002, the asset was discarded with no cash proceeds. What gain or loss should be recognized on the retirement?
   a.   No gain or loss.
   b. $6,000 loss.
   c. $4,500 loss.
   d. $3,000 gain.

Use the following information for questions 16 and 17:

On May 1, 2002, Bentham Company sells office furniture for $60,000 cash. The office furniture originally cost $150,000 when purchased on January 1, 1995. Depreciation is recorded by the straight-line method over 10 years with a salvage value of $15,000.

16. (S.O. 3) What depreciation expense should be recorded on this asset in 2002?
    a. $4,500.
    b. $5,000.
    c. $6,750.
    d. $13,500.

17. (S.O. 6) What gain should be recognized on the sale?
    a. $4,500.
    b. $9,000.
    c. $9,500.
    d. $18,000.

18. (S.O. 6) On January 1, Averroes Company sold a machine that had a book value of $7,500 for $8,000 cash. The entry by Averroes Company on January 1, will include a:
    a. debit to Loss on Disposal.
    b. credit to Loss on Disposal.
    c. debit to Gain on Disposal.
    d. debit to Cash.

19. (S.O. 6) In exchanges of similar assets:
    a. neither gains nor losses are recognized immediately.
    b. gains, but not losses, are recognized immediately.
    c. losses, but not gains, are recognized immediately.
    d. both gains and losses are recognized immediately.

20. (S.O. 6) Hobbes Company exchanges a used truck (original cost, $41,000) plus $20,000 cash for a new truck costing $45,000. At the time of exchange, accumulated depreciation on the used truck is $23,000. What gain or loss should Hobbs recognize on the exchange?
    a. $16,000 loss.
    b. $7,000 loss.
    c. $0 gain or loss.
    d. $7,000 gain.

21. (S.O. 6) Voltaire Company exchanged an old machine, with a book value of $53,000 and a fair market value of $49,000, and paid $7,000 cash for a similar used machine. At what amount should the machine acquired in the exchange be recorded on the books of Voltaire?
    a. $49,000.
    b. $53,000.
    c. $56,000.
    d. $60,000.

22. (S.O. 7) Natural resources include all of the following except:
    a. standing timber.
    b. land improvements.
    c. oil deposits.
    d. mineral deposits.

23. (S.O. 7) The entry to record depletion expense:
    a. decreases owner's equity and assets.
    b. decreases net income and increases liabilities.
    c. decreases assets and liabilities.
    d. decreases assets and increases liabilities.

24. (S.O. 7) Abelard Company expects to extract 15 million tons of coal from a mine that cost $25 million. If no salvage value is expected, and 3,000,000 tons are mined in the first year, the entry to record depletion in the first year will include a:
    a. debit to Accumulated Depletion of $3,000,000.
    b. credit to Depletion Expense of $5,000,000.
    c. debit to Depletion Expense of $5,000,000.
    d. credit to Accumulated Depletion of $1,800,000.

25. (S.O. 8) All of the following are intangible assets except:
    a. franchises.
    b. copyrights.
    c. accounts receivable.
    d. goodwill.

26. (S.O. 8) A purchased patent has a legal life of 15 years. It should be:
    a. expensed in the year of acquisition.
    b. amortized over 15 years regardless of its useful life.
    c. amortized over its useful life if less than 15 years.
    d. amortized over 40 years.

27. (S.O. 8) Eloise Company incurred $350,000 of research and development costs in its laboratory to develop a patent granted on January 1, 2002. On July 31, 2002, Eloise paid $52,000 for legal fees in a successful defense of the patent. The total amount debited to Patents through July 31, 2002, should be:
    a. $350,000.
    b. $52,000.
    c. $402,000.
    d. $298,000.

28. (S.O. 8) Goodwill from the acquisition of a business enterprise:
    a. should be expensed in the year of acquisition.
    b. is an asset that is not subject to amortization.
    c. is an intangible asset.
    d. is granted by the federal government.

MATCHING

Match each term with its definition by writing the appropriate letter in the space provided.

Terms

_____ 1. Revenue expenditures.

_____ 2. Declining-balance method.

_____ 3. Natural resources.

_____ 4. Cash equivalent price.

_____ 5. Additions and improvements.

_____ 6. Ordinary repairs.

_____ 7. Units of activity method.

_____ 8. Straight-line method.

_____ 9. Patent.

_____ 10. Intangible assets.

_____ 11. Copyright.

_____ 12. Full cost approach.

_____ 13. Successful efforts approach.

_____ 14. Depletion.

_____ 15. Amortization

_____ 16. Franchise.

_____ 17. Goodwill.

_____ 18. Trademark.

_____ 19. Research and development costs.

Definitions

a. A depreciation method where the computation of periodic depreciation is based on the book value of the asset which declines each year.

b. Expenditures that are immediately charged against revenues as an expense.

c. An exclusive right that enables the recipient to manufacture, sell, or otherwise control his or her invention for a period of seventeen years from the date of grant.

d. A depreciation method in which the decline in service potential is attributable to activity rather than time.

e. The fair market value of the asset given up or the fair market value of the asset received, whichever is more clearly determinable.

f. Costs incurred to increase the operating efficiency, productive capacity, or expected productive life of the unit.

g. Expenditures to maintain the operating efficiency and expected productive life of the unit.

h. The value of all favorable attributes that relate to a business enterprise.

i. A depreciation method where periodic depreciation is the same throughout the service life of the asset.

j. Rights, privileges, and competitive advantages that result from the ownership of long-lived assets that do not possess physical substance.

k. Costs relating to the development of new products and processes that are usually recorded as expense when incurred.

l. The costs of both successful and unsuccessful explorations are capitalized.

m. Assets that consist of standing timber and underground deposits of oil, gas, and minerals.

n. Only the costs of successful explorations are capitalized.

o. A word, phrase, or symbol that distinguishes or identifies a particular enterprise or product.

Definitions (continued)

p. A right granted by the federal government giving the owner the exclusive right to reproduce and sell an artistic or published work.

q. A contractual agreement granting rights to sell certain products, or render specific services, or to use certain trademarks.

r. The systematic write-off of the cost of natural resources.

s. The rational and systematic write-off of the cost of an intangible asset.

EXERCISES

EX. 10-1 (S.O. 1 and 5)   During 2002, Bergson Company had the following plant asset transactions.

Jan.   1   Purchased a bus for company tours. The bus had a purchase price of $23,000 plus costs of $500 for delivery charges, $250 for insurance during transit to the company, $700 for painting and lettering, $300 for sales tax, $30 for motor vehicle license, and $800 for accident insurance for two years.

July   1   Purchased a factory machine by making a $500 down payment and signing a $2,500 1-year, 10% note.

Instructions
Journalize the transactions. (Omit explanations.)

	General Journal		J1
Date	Account Title	Debit	Credit

EX. 10-2 (S.O. 3) On January 1, 2002, Dewey Company purchased a mainframe computer for $150,000. The computer is estimated to have a $30,000 salvage value after its four-year useful life.

Instructions
(a) Fill in the appropriate amounts concerning the depreciation on the computer for the depreciation methods identified below.
(b) Show the depreciation schedules for each method for the years 2002 and 2003.

	Straight-Line Method	Declining Balance Method
Depreciation Expense: 2002	$_____	$_____
Book Value: 12/31/02	$_____	$_____
Depreciation Expense: 2003	$_____	$_____
Book Value: 12/31/03	$_____	$_____

Schedules

Straight-Line Method

Year	Computation Depreciable Cost	X	Depreciation Rate	=	Depreciation Expense	End of Year Accumulated Depreciation	Book Value

Declining-Balance Method

Year	Computation Book Value Beginning of Year	X	Depreciation Rate	=	Depreciation Expense	End of Year Accumulated Depreciation	Book Value

EX. 10-3 (S.O. 6) During 2003, the Leibniz Company had the following plant asset transactions.

Jan. 1 Exchange a delivery truck and $3,000 of cash for another delivery truck from Goethe Company. The Leibniz truck had a book value of $5,000 (accumulated depreciation of $2,500) and a fair market value of $7,000. The Goethe truck had a book value of $4,000 (accumulated depreciation of $9,500).

July 1 Sold machinery costing $17,000 for $2,200 cash. The machinery had accumulated depreciation of $12,000 at December 31, 2002, based on annual depreciation of $2,000 per year.

Instructions
(a) Journalize the plant asset transactions.
(b) Assume the same facts in the January 1 exchange except that the fair market value of the Leibniz truck was $3,500. Journalize this exchange transaction.

	General Journal		J1
Date 2002 (a)	Account Title	Debit	Credit
(b)			

EX. 10-4 (S.O. 8) On December 31, 2001, the intangible asset section of Mill Company's balance sheet was:

Patents (net of $9,000 accumulated amortization)	$109,000
Trademarks (net of $10,000 accumulated amortization)	90,000
Copyrights (net of $48,000 accumulated amortization)	12,000
Total intangibles	$211,000

Mill owns two patents, one purchased for $50,000 on 1/1/01 with a total useful life of 10 years , and the other purchased for $68,000 on 1/1/01 with a total useful life of 17 years. The trademark was obtained on 1/1/98 for $100,000 and is being amortized over 40 years. The copyrights were also capitalized on 1/1/98 at a cost of $60,000, and are being amortized over 5 years. During 2002, Mill purchased a patent on July 1 at a cost of $72,000. This patent has a total useful life of 12 years from 7/1/02.

Instructions
Prepare the December 31, 2002 intangible asset section of Mill Company's balance sheet.

MILL COMPANY
Partial Balance Sheet
December 31, 2002

The
Navigator

SOLUTIONS TO REVIEW QUESTIONS AND EXERCISES

TRUE-FALSE

1. (T)
2. (F) Land is a plant asset that is not depreciated over its useful life.
3. (F) The cost of tearing down the old building should be debited to Land.
4. (F) The cost of driveways and parking lots is debited to Land Improvements.
5. (T)
6. (F) The cost of equipment includes the cash price, freight charges, expenditures required in assembling, etc. Motor vehicle licenses and accident insurance are expensed as incurred because they represent annual recording expenditures.
7. (F) Recognition of depreciation permits a matching of expenses and revenues, but does not result in the accumulation of cash for the replacement of the asset.
8. (F) Under the straight-line method, depreciation is the same for each year of service life of the asset.
9. (F) Under the units of activity method the decline in service potential is attributed to activity rather than time.
10. (T)
11. (T)
12. (F) When an asset is purchased during the year, it is necessary to prorate the declining balance depreciation in the first year on a time basis.
13. (T)
14. (F) Book value is cost less accumulated depreciation.
15. (F) A fully depreciated plant asset has no book value, so a retirement at a loss is impossible. Generally, the entry would consist of a debit to accumulated depreciation and an equal credit to the asset account.
16. (T)
17. (F) A gain cannot be recognized on the exchange of similar assets.
18. (T)
19. (T)
20. (F) Wasting assets have value but they are not replaceable.
21. (T)
22. (T)
23. (F) Depletion expense is reported as part of the cost of producing the product.
24. (T)
25. (T)
26. (F) The cost of defending the patent should be added to the Patent account and amortized over the remaining life of the patent.
27. (T)
28. (T)

MULTIPLE CHOICE

1. (c) Property, plant and equipment, plant assets (a), fixed assets (b), and long-lived tangible assets (d) are all terms which mean tangible long-lived resources that are used in the operations of the business and are not intended for sale to customers. Intangible assets are not considered to be plant assets.

2. (c) Plant assets are subdivided into the four classes of (a) Land, (b) Land improvements, (c) Buildings, and (d) Equipment. Supplies is classified as a current asset.

3. (d) The acquisition of land will consist of the purchase price ($150,000), attorney's fee ($6,000), demolition and removal costs of an old building ($4,000), and grading and filling ($3,000) for a total of $163,000.

4. (a) Land improvements include driveways (b), parking lots (c), fencing (d), underground sprinkler systems, and similar assets. Building sites (a) are recorded in the Land account.

5. (b) The cost of a plant asset consists of all expenditures necessary to acquire the asset and make it ready for its intended use ($15,000 + $750 + $600 = $16,350). The payment for the license is expensed as incurred because it is an annual recurring expenditure. The insurance premium is recorded as prepaid insurance and expensed over its two-year life.

6. (a) Replacement value is not relevant in computing depreciation.

7. (c) The formula for calculating depreciation expense under the straight-line method is (Cost - Salvage value) ÷ Useful life.

8. (c) The cost of the equipment includes the invoice cost of $280,000, freight costs of $5,000 and installation costs of $25,000. The annual depreciation is then calculated as follows:

   ($310,000 - $10,000) ÷ 5 = $60,000 X 2 = $120,000

9. (d) The salvage value is subtracted from the cost to compute the depreciable cost. The depreciable cost is divided by the total estimated activity (e.g., miles) to compute the depreciable cost per unit. Since the accumulated depreciation for the years 2002 and 2003 is needed, the depreciable cost per unit should be multiplied by the units of activity for both 2002 and 2003.

10. (a) Annual depreciation expense is computed by multiplying the book value at the beginning of the year times the declining balance rate. Salvage value is ignored. The depreciation rate is double the straight-line rate: 1/5 or 20% X 2 = 2/5 or 40%.

	Book Value at Beginning of Year		**Depreciation Rate**	**Annual Depreciation**	**Book Value**
2002	$350,000	X	40%	$140,000	$210,000
2003	210,000	X	40%	84,000	126,000

11. (a) To determine the new annual depreciation expense, the depreciable cost is divided by the revised remaining useful life as follows:

Book value, 1/1/02 ($8,000 - $1,500)	$6,500
Less: Salvage value	2,000
Depreciable cost	$4,500
Remaining useful life (12-2)	10 years
Revised annual depreciation ($4,500 ÷ 10)	$450

12. (c) Ordinary repairs include such expenses as motor tune-ups on delivery trucks, the painting of buildings and the replacing of worn-out tires on delivery trucks. Additions and improvements include costs for (a) constructing a new wing on a building, (b) a major motor overhaul of a new truck, and (d) replacing a stairway with an escalator.

13. (d) Improvements are capital expenditures, not revenue expenditures (a). When the expenditure does not increase useful life, it should be debited to an appropriate asset account.

14. (d) Plant assets may be disposed of by retirement, sale, or exchange.

15. (c) On June 30, 2002, the plant asset would have a book value of $4,500:

Cost	$27,000
Depreciation, 1995-01 (7 X $3,000)	(21,000)
Depreciation, 1/1/99-6/30/99 (6/12 X $3,000)	(1,500)
Book value, 6/30/01	$ 4,500

Since the asset was discarded with no cash proceeds, a loss of $4,500 should be recognized.

16. (a) In 2002, depreciation expense should be recorded for four months (1/1/02 to 5/1/02). This amount is computed below:

$$\text{Annual depreciation} = \frac{\$150,000 - \$15,000}{10} = \underline{\$13,500}.$$

Four months' depreciation = $13,500 X 4/12 = $4,500.

17. (b) On May 1, 2002, the office furniture would have a book value of $51,000, as computed below:

Cost	$150,000
Depreciation, 1995-01 (7 X $13,500)	(94,500)
Depreciation, 1/1/02-5/1/02 (4/12 X $13,500)	(4,500)
Book value, 5/1/02	$ 51,000

The gain recognized is the excess of the proceeds ($60,000) over the book value ($51,000) or $9,000.

18. (d) The $8,000 cash is recorded with a debit to Cash and since the amount of cash received is more than the book value of the asset, a gain would be recorded with a credit to Gain on Disposal. Therefore, answers (a), (b), and (c) are all incorrect.

19. (c) In exchanges of similar assets, any loss on the old asset is recognized immediately.

20. (c) The book value of the used truck is $18,000 ($41,000 - $23,000), while its fair market value is $25,000 ($45,000 value of land obtained less $20,000 in cash paid). In an exchange of **similar** assets, any gain ($7,000 in this case) is deferred. Thus, zero gain or loss is recognized.

21. (c) Because a loss occurs in this exchange, the acquisition cost is equal to the fair market value of the asset given up ($49,000) plus any cash paid by the purchaser ($7,000) or a total of $56,000. The entry is as follows:

Machine..	56,000	
Loss on Disposal...	4,000	
Machine		53,000
Cash..		7,000

22. (b) Natural resources consist of standing timber and underground deposits of oil, gas, and minerals. Land improvements are reported as plant assets.

23. (a) The entry to record depletion expense results in a debit to Depletion Expense and a credit to Accumulated Depletion. The debit to Depletion Expense decreases net income and owner's equity.

24. (c) The computations for depletion are:

$$\frac{\$25,000,000}{15,000,000} = \$1.67 \text{ and } \$1.67 \times 3,000,000 = \$5,000,000.$$

The entry is as follows:

Depletion Expense	5,000,000	
Accumulated Depletion		5,000,000

25. (c) Intangible assets are rights, privileges and competitive advantages that result from the ownership of long-lived assets that do not possess physical substance. They include patents, copyrights, trademarks, trade names, franchises, licenses, and goodwill. Accounts receivable are included in current assets.

26. (c) The cost of a patent should be amortized over its legal life or useful life, whichever is shorter; therefore, if its useful life is less than 15 years, then it should be amortized over its useful life.

27. (b) The research and development costs of $350,000 should be expensed when incurred. The legal fees in a successful defense of the patent of $52,000 are debited to the Patent account.

28. (c) Goodwill is an intangible asset that is not recognized in accounting unless it is acquired from another business enterprise. Goodwill is amortized over its useful life, but not in excess of 40 years.

MATCHING

1.	b	6.	g	11.	p	16.	q
2.	a	7.	d	12.	l	17.	h
3.	m	8.	i	13.	n	18.	o
4.	e	9.	c	14.	r	19.	k
5.	f	10.	j	15.	s		

EXERCISES

EX. 10-1

General Journal			J1
Date	**Account Title**	**Debit**	**Credit**
2002			
Jan. 1	Bus	24,750	
	License Expense	30	
	Prepaid Insurance	800	
	Cash		25,580
July 1	Factory Machinery	3,000	
	Cash		500
	Notes Payable		2,500

EX. 10-2

	Straight-Line Method	Declining Balance Method
Depreciation Expense: 2002	$ 30,000	$ 75,000
Book Value: 12/31/02	$120,000	$ 75,000
Depreciation Expense: 2003	$ 30,000	$ 37,500
Book Value: 12/31/03	$ 90,000	$ 37,500

Schedules

Straight-Line Method

	Computation			End of Year	
Year	Depreciable Cost	X Depreciation Rate	= Depreciation Expense	Accumulated Depreciation	Book Value
2002	$120,000	25%	$30,000	$30,000	$120,000
2003	120,000	25%	30,000	60,000	90,000

Declining-Balance Method

	Computation			End of Year	
Year	Book Value Beginning of Year	X Depreciation Rate	= Depreciation Expense	Accumulated Depreciation	Book Value
2002	$150,000	50%	$75,000	$ 75,000	$75,000
2003	75,000	50%	37,500	112,500	37,500

EX. 10-3

	General Journal		J1
Date 2003	**Account Title**	**Debit**	**Credit**
(a) Jan. 1	Delivery Equipment	8,000	
	Accumulated Depreciation — Delivery Equipment	2,500	
	Delivery Equipment		7,500
	Cash		3,000
	(To record exchange of similar assets		
	The $2,000 gain reduces the cost of the		
	new truck from $10,000 to $8,000.)		
July 1	Depreciation Expense	1,000	
	Accumulated Depreciation — Machinery		1,000
	(To record six-months' depreciation:		
	$2,000 ÷ 2)		
1	Cash	2,200	
	Accumulated Deprectiaion — Machinery		
	($12,000 + $1,000)	13,000	
	Loss on Disposal ($4,000 - $2,200)	1,800	
	Machinery		17,000
	(To record sale of machinery)		
2003 (b) Jan. 1	Delivery Equipment ($3,000 + $3,500)	6,500	
	Accumulated Depreciation — Delivery Equipment	2,500	
	Loss on Disposal ($5,000 - $3,500)	1,500	
	Delivery Equipment		7,500
	Cash		3,000
	(To record exchange of assets and		
	loss on disposal)		

EX. 10-4

MILL COMPANY
Partial Balance Sheet
December 31, 2002

Intangible assets:

Patents: (net of $21,000 accumulated amortization)	$169,000
Trademarks: (net of $12,500 accumulated amortization)	87,500
Total intangibles	$256,500

Computations:

Patents: $50,000 + $68,000 + $72,000 =..	$190,000
Accumulated amortization: $9,000 + $5,000 + $4,000 + $3,000 = ...	(21,000)
Patents, net	$169,000
Trademarks:...	$100,000
Accumulated amortization: $10,000 + $2,500 = ...	(12,500)
Trademarks, net..	$ 87,500
Copyrights:..	$ 60,000
Accumulated amortization: $48,000 + $12,000 = ...	(60,000)
Organization costs, net	$ -0-

	1	2	3	4	5	6	7	8	9	10
1										
2										
3										
4										
5										
6										
7										
8										
9										
10										
11										
12										
13										
14										
15										
16										
17										
18										
19										
20										
21										
22										
23										
24										
25										
26										
27										
28										
29										
30										
31										
32										
33										
34										
35										
36										
37										
38										
39										
40										

	1	2	3	4	5	6	7	8	9	10	11	12
1												
2												
3												
4												
5												
6												
7												
8												
9												
10												
11												
12												
13												
14												
15												
16												
17												
18												
19												
20												
21												
22												
23												
24												
25												
26												
27												
28												
29												
30												
31												
32												
33												
34												
35												
36												
37												
38												
39												
40												

Chapter 11

CURRENT LIABILITIES AND PAYROLL ACCOUNTING

The Navigator	✓
■ *Scan Study Objectives*	☐
■ *Read Preview*	☐
■ *Read Chapter Review*	☐
■ *Work Demonstration Problem*	☐
■ *Answer True-False Statements*	☐
■ *Answer Multiple-Choice Questions*	☐
■ *Match Terms and Definitions*	☐
■ *Solve Exercises*	☐

CHAPTER STUDY OBJECTIVES

After studying this chapter, you should be able to:
1. Explain a current liability, and identify the major types of current liabilities.
2. Describe the accounting for notes payable.
3. Explain the accounting for other current liabilities.
4. Explain the financial statement presentation and analysis of current liabilities.
5. Describe the accounting and disclosure requirements for contingent liabilities.
6. Discuss the objectives of internal control for payroll.
7. Compute and record the payroll for a pay period.
8. Describe and record employer payroll taxes.
9. Identify additional fringe benefits associated with employee compensation.

PREVIEW OF CHAPTER 11

All enterprises have liabilities for payroll. In addition, they also have many other types of liabilities. Examples are the purchase of supplies on account, the borrowing of money on a bank loan, and the obligation to pay interest. Liabilities are classified as current or long-term on the balance sheet. We will explain current liabilities in this chapter and long-term liabilities in Chapter 16. The content and organization of this chapter are as follows:

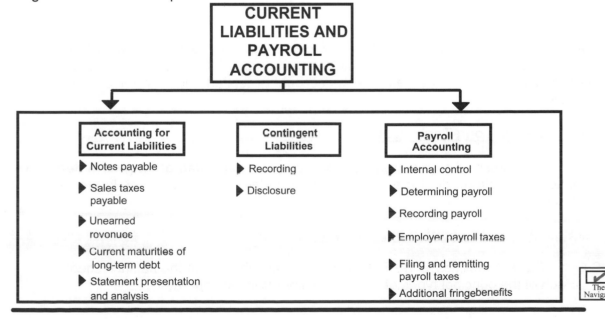

CHAPTER REVIEW

Current Liabilities

1.   (S.O. 1) A **current liability** is a debt that can reasonably be expected to be paid (1) from existing current assets or in the creation of other current liabilities, and (2) within one year or the operating cycle whichever is longer. Current liabilities include notes payable, accounts payable, unearned revenues, and accrued liabilities.

Notes Payable

2.   (S.O. 2) **Notes payable** are obligations in the form of written promissory notes that usually require the borrower to pay interest. Notes due for payment within one year of the balance sheet date are usually classified as current liabilities.

3.   When an **interest-bearing note** is issued, the assets received generally equal the face value of the note.
     a.   During the term of the note, it is necessary to accrue interest expense.
     b.   At maturity, Notes Payable is debited for the face value of the note and Interest Payable is debited for accrued interest.

Sales Taxes Payable

4.   (S.O. 3) A **sales tax** is expressed as a stated percentage of the sales price on goods sold to customers by a retailer. The entry by the retailer to record sales taxes is as follows:

Cash..	XXXX	
Sales...		XXXX
Sales Taxes Payable...		XXXX

     When sales taxes are not rung up separately on the cash register, total receipts are divided by 100% plus the sales tax percentage to determine the sales.

Unearned Revenues

5.   **Unearned Revenues** (advances from customers) are recorded by a debit to Cash and a credit to a current liability account identifying the source of the unearned revenue. When the revenue is earned, the unearned revenue account is debited and an earned revenue account is credited.

Current Maturities of Long-Term Debt

6.   Another item classified as a current liability is **current maturities of long-term debt.** Current maturities of long-term debt are often identified on the balance sheet as long-term debt due within one year.

Financial Statement Presentation and Analysis

7.   (S.O. 4) Current liabilities is the first category under liabilities on the balance sheet.
     a.   Each of the principal types of current liabilities is listed separately.

b.   Current liabilities are usually in order of magnitude with the largest obligations being listed first. However, many companies, as a matter of custom, show notes payable and accounts payable first regardless of amount.

8.   The excess of current assets over current liabilities is **working capital.** The **current ratio** is current assets divided by current liabilities.

Contingent Liabilities

9.   (S.O. 5) A **contingent liability** is a potential liability that may become an actual liability in the future. The accounting guidelines require that:
    a.   If the contingency is probable and the amount can be reasonably estimated, the liability should be recorded in the accounts.
    b.   If the contingency is only reasonably possible, then it need be disclosed only in the notes accompanying the financial statements.
    c.   If the contingency is remote, it need not be recorded or disclosed.

10.   Product warranties are a good example of a contingent liability. They are recorded by estimating the cost of honoring product warranty contracts and expensing the amount in the period in which the sale occurs. Warranty expense is reported under selling expenses in the income statement, and estimated warranty liability is classified as a current liability on the balance sheet.

Payroll Accounting

11.   The term **payroll** pertains to all salaries and wages paid to employees. Payments made to professional individuals who are independent contractors are called fees.   Government regulations relating to the payment and reporting of payroll taxes apply only to employees.

Internal Controls for Payroll

12.   (S.O. 6)   The objectives of **internal accounting control** concerning payroll are (a) to safeguard company assets from unauthorized payments of payrolls, and (b) to ensure the accuracy and reliability of the accounting records pertaining to payrolls.

13.   The payroll activities consist of four functions (a) hiring employees, (b) timekeeping, (c) preparing the payroll, and (d) paying the payroll. These four functions should be assigned to different departments or individuals.

14.   The **personnel department** is responsible for the posting of job openings, the screening and interviewing of applicants, and the hiring of employees. The personnel department is also responsible for authorizing changes in pay rates during employment and terminations of employment.

15.   In **timekeeping,** employees usually are required to record time worked on a time card by punching a time clock. A supervisor often monitors the time clock procedures.

16.   The **payroll department** prepares the payroll based on (a) personnel department authorizations and (b) approved time cards. The payroll department is also responsible for preparing payroll checks, maintaining payroll records, and preparing payroll tax returns.

17. The **treasurer's department** is responsible for the payment of the payroll.
   a. Payment by check minimizes the risk of loss from theft, and the endorsed check provides proof of payment.
   b. All checks must be signed by the treasurer and their distribution should be controlled by the treasurer's department.

Gross Earnings

18. (S.O. 7) **Gross earnings** is the total compensation earned by an employee. It consists of: wages or salaries, plus any bonuses and commissions.
   a. Total wages are determined by applying the hourly rate of pay to the hours worked.
   b. Most companies are required to pay a minimum of one and one-half times the regular hourly rate for overtime work.

Payroll Deductions

19. Mandatory payroll deductions consist of FICA taxes and income taxes.
   a. These deductions do not result in payroll tax expense to the employer.
   b. **FICA taxes** are designed to provide workers with supplemental retirement, employment disability, and medical benefits.
   c. FICA taxes are also known as social security taxes.

20. **Income taxes** are required to be withheld from employees each pay period and the amount is determined by three variables: (a) the employees' gross earnings; (b) the number of allowances claimed by the employee; and (c) the length of the pay period.

21. **Voluntary deductions** pertain to withholdings for charitable, retirement, and other purposes. All voluntary deductions from gross earnings should be authorized in writing by the employee.

22. **Net pay** is determined by subtracting payroll deductions from gross earnings.

Recording the Payroll

23. The **employee earnings record** provides a cumulative record of each employee's gross earnings, deductions, and net pay during the year. This record is used by the employer in:
   a. Determining when an employee has earned the maximum earnings subject to FICA taxes.
   b. Filing state and federal payroll tax returns.
   c. Providing each employee with a statement of gross earnings and tax withholdings for the year.

24. Many companies use a **payroll register** to accumulate the gross earnings, deductions, and net pay by employee for each period. In some cases, this record is a journal or book of original entry.

25. The typical journal entry to record a payroll is as follows:

Office Salaries Expense..	XXX	
Wages Expense	XXX	
FICA Taxes Payable..		XXX
Federal Income Taxes Payable		XXX
State Income Taxes Payable..		XXX
United Fund Payable		XXX
Union Dues Payable		XXX
Salaries and Wages Payable..		XXX

26. When the payroll is paid, Salaries and Wages Payable is debited and Cash is credited. Each payroll check is usually accompanied by a detachable **statement of earnings** document that shows the employee's gross earnings, payroll deductions, and net pay.

Employer Payroll Taxes

27. (S.O. 8) There are three taxes imposed on employers by government agencies that result in payroll tax expense.
    a. **FICA Taxes.** The employer must match each employee's FICA contribution.
    b. **Federal Unemployment Taxes.** The employer is required to pay a tax on the first $7,000 of gross wages paid to each employee during a calendar year.
    c. **State Unemployment Taxes.** All states have unemployment compensation programs that require the employer to pay a tax on the first $7,000 of gross wages paid to each employee during a calendar year.

28. The typical entry for recording payroll tax expense is as follows:

Payroll Tax Expense	XXXX	
FICA Taxes Payable..		XXXX
Federal Unemployment Taxes Payable.............................		XXXX
State Unemployment Taxes Payable.................................		XXXX

29. Preparation of payroll tax returns is the responsibility of the payroll department; payment of the taxes is made by the treasurer's department.

30. The employer is required to provide each employee with a **Wage and Tax Statement (Form W-2)** by January 31 following the end of a calendar year. This statement shows gross earnings, FICA taxes withheld, and income taxes withheld for the year.

Additional Fringe Benefits

31. (S.O. 9) When the compensation for **paid absences** (paid vacations, sick pay benefits, and paid holidays) is probable and the amount can be reasonably estimated, a liability should be accrued. When the amount cannot be reasonably estimated, the potential liability should be disclosed.

Postretirement Benefits

32. **Postretirement benefits** consist of payments by employers to retired employees for (1) health care and life insurance and (2) pensions. Both types of postretirement benefits are accounted for on the accrual basis.

33. A **pension plan** is an agreement whereby an employer provides benefits to employees after they retire. Three parties are generally involved in a pension plan:
    a. The employer sponsors the plan.
    b. The plan administrator receives the contributions, invests the pension assets, and makes the benefit payments.
    c. The retired employees receive the pension payments.

DEMONSTRATION PROBLEM (S.O. 1, 2, and 3)

On January 1, 2002, the ledger of Reichenbacher Company contains the following liability accounts:

Note Payable	$52,000
Accounts Payable	61,500
Interest Payable	520
Sales Taxes Payable	7,700
Advances from Customers	4,000

The note payable was issued on November 30, 2001. It bears 12% interest and matures on May 31, 2002. During 2002, the following selected transactions occurred:

Feb.	5	Sold merchandise for cash totaling $13,650 which includes 5% sales tax.
Mar.	13	Provided services for customers who had made advance payments of $2,000.
Apr.	22	Paid $32,000 of accounts payable.
May	31	Accrued interest on note payable for five months.
May	31	Paid the note due.
June	15	Borrowed $22,000 in cash from Sandwich Bank on a 10% interest-bearing, three-month note having a face value of $22,000.
Aug.	7	Sold merchandise on credit totaling $28,350 which includes 5% sales tax.
Sept.	15	Recognized interest expense on Sandwich Bank note.
Sept.	15	Paid the note due.
Nov.	30	Borrowed $30,000 in cash from Somonauk Bank on a six-month, 12%, $30,000 note.

Instructions
(a) Journalize the 2002 transactions.
(b) Journalize the adjusting entry at December 31, 2002 for the outstanding notes payable.

			SOLUTION TO DEMONSTRATION PROBLEM		

Feb. 5   Cash   13,650
           Sales ($13,650 ÷ 105%)   13,000
           Sales Taxes Payable   650
         (To record sales and sales taxes)

Mar. 13   Advances From Customers   2,000
           Sales   2,000
         (To record services performed)

Apr. 22   Accounts Payable   32,000
           Cash   32,000
         (To record payment of Accounts Payable)

May 31   Interest Expense   2,600
           Interest Payable   2,600
         (To record accrued interest: $52,000 X 12% X
         5/12)

May 31   Notes Payable   52,000
      Interest Payable ($520 + $2,600)   3,120
           Cash   55,120
         (To record payment of interest-bearing note)

June 15   Cash   22,000
           Notes Payable   22,000
         (To record receipt of cash and issuance of 3-
         month, 10% interest-bearing note)

Aug. 7   Accounts Receivable   28,350
           Sales   27,000
           Sales Taxes Payable   1,350
         (To record sales and sales taxes)

Sept. 15   Interest Expense   550
           Interest Payable   550
         (To recognize interest expense for 3 months)

Sept. 15   Notes Payable   22,000
      Interest Payable   550
           Cash   22,550
         (To recognize payment of 10% interest-bearing
         note)

Nov. 30   Cash   30,000
           Notes Payable   30,000
         (To record receipt of cash and issuance of
         12%, 6-month note)

(b)
Dec. 31   Interest Expense ($30,000 X 12% X 1/12)   300
                Interest Payable   300
                (To record interest expense for one month
                on $30,000 interest-bearing note)

REVIEW QUESTIONS AND EXERCISES

TRUE—FALSE

Indicate whether each of the following is true (T) or false (F) in the space provided.

_____ 1.   (S.O. 1)   A debt that is expected to be paid within one year through the creation of long-term debt is a current liability.

_____ 2.   (S.O. 2)   Obligations in the form of written promissory notes are recorded as accounts payable.

_____ 3.   (S.O. 2)   Notes payable usually are issued to meet long-term financing needs.

_____ 4.   (S.O. 3)   A company does not report sales taxes as an expense but merely forwards the amount paid by the customer to the government.

_____ 5.   (S.O. 3)   Unearned Revenues are classified as a current asset.

_____ 6.   (S.O. 3)   Current maturities of long-term debt are often identified as long-term debt due within one year on the balance sheet.

_____ 7.   (S.O. 3)   Current liabilities are usually listed in the order of maturity.

_____ 8.   (S.O. 5)   If it is possible that a contingency will happen and it is reasonably estimable, the liability should be recorded in the accounts.

_____ 9.   (S.O. 5)   In a given year, total warranty expense is the sum of actual warranty costs incurred on units sold plus the estimated cost of servicing those units in the future.

_____ 10. (S.O. 6)   Payments made for personal service to the company by professionals, such as an attorney, should be included as a part of salaries and wages.

_____ 11. (S.O. 6)   The objectives of internal accounting control for payrolls are (a) to safeguard company assets from unauthorized payments of payrolls, and (b) to assure the accuracy and reliability of the accounting records pertaining to payrolls.

_____ 12. (S.O. 6)   The posting of job openings, the screening and interviewing of applicants, and the hiring of employees is the responsibility of the payroll department.

_____   13.   (S.O. 6)   For good internal control, payroll checks should be prenumbered and signed by the treasurer.

_____   14.   (S.O. 7)   FICA taxes are a voluntary deduction from employee earnings.

_____   15.   (S.O. 7)   Income taxes to be withheld are determined by (a) the employee's gross earnings; (b) the number of allowances claimed by the employee for herself or himself, his or her spouse, and other dependents; and (c) the length of the pay period.

_____   16.   (S.O. 7)   The statement of earnings document is a cumulative record of each employee's earnings during the year and provides other essential data, such as total taxes withheld for each employee.

_____   17.   (S.O. 8)   FICA taxes are a deduction from employee earnings and are also imposed upon employers as an expense.

_____   18.   (S.O. 8)   An employer is required to provide each employee with a Wage and Tax Statement (Form W-2).

_____   19.   (S.O. 8)   When the payment of a future paid absence is probable and can be reasonably estimated, a liability should be accrued.

_____   20.   (S.O. 9)   Pension expense is reported as an administrative expense in the income statement.

The
Navigator

MULTIPLE CHOICE

Circle the letter that best answers each of the following statements.

1.   (S.O. 1)   Which of the following statements concerning current liabilities is **incorrect?**
   a.   Current liabilities include unearned revenues.
   b.   A company that has more current liabilities than current assets is usually the subject of some concern.
   c.   Current liabilities include prepaid expenses.
   d.   A current liability is a debt that can reasonably be expected to be paid out of existing current assets or result in the creation of other current liabilities.

Items 2 and 3 pertain to the following information:

On October 1, 2002, Frederick Douglass Company issued a $28,000, 10%, nine-month interest-bearing note.

2.   (S.O. 2)   If the Frederick Douglass Company is preparing financial statements at December 31, 2002, the adjusting entry for accrued interest will include:
   a.   credit to Notes Payable of $700.
   b.   debit to Interest Expense of $700.
   c.   credit to Interest Payable of $1,400.
   d.   debit to Interest Expense of $1,050.

3. (S.O. 2) Assuming interest was accrued on June 30, 2003, the entry to record the payment of the note on July 1, 2003, will include a:
   a. debit to Interest Expense of $700.
   b. credit to Cash of $28,000.
   c. debit to Interest Payable of $2,100.
   d. debit to Notes Payable of $30,100.

4. (S.O. 2 and 3)   On August 1, 2002, a company borrowed cash and signed a one-year interest-bearing note on which both the face value and interest are payable on August 1, 2003. How will the note payable and the related interest be classified in the December 31, 2002, balance sheet?

	Note Payable	Interest Payable
a.	Current liability	Noncurrent liability
b.	Noncurrent liability	Current liability
c.	Current liability	Current liability
d.	Noncurrent liability	Not shown

5. (S.O. 3)   The Pam Travis Company has total proceeds (before segregation of sales taxes) from sales of $2,100. If the sales tax is 5%, the amount to be credited to the account Sales is:
   a. $2,100.
   b. $1,995.
   c. $1,900.
   d. $2,000.

6. (S.O. 5)   How should a contingency that is reasonably possible and for which the amount can be reasonably estimated be handled?

	Accrued	Disclosed
a.	Yes	No
b.	No	Yes
c.	Yes	Yes
d.	No	No

7. (S.O. 5)   A contingency need not be recorded nor disclosed when:
   a. it is probable the contingency will happen and the amount can be reasonably estimated.
   b. it is probable the contingency will happen but the amount cannot be reasonably estimated.
   c. it is reasonably possible the contingency will happen and the amount can be reasonably estimated.
   d. the possibility of the contingency happening is remote.

8. (S.O. 5)   A contingency for which the amount can be reasonably estimated should be disclosed when the outcome of the contingency is:

	Reasonably Possible	Remote
a.	Yes	No
b.	Yes	Yes
c.	No	No
d.	No	Yes

9. (S.O. 6) Which of the following is not considered a function of payroll activities?
    a. Preparing payroll tax returns.
    b. Timekeeping.
    c. Preparing the payroll.
    d. Paying independent contractors for personal service.

10. (S.O. 6) The department responsible for paying payroll is the:
    a. treasurer's department.
    b. personnel department.
    c. timekeeping department.
    d. payroll department.

11. (S.O. 6) The department responsible for authorizing the termination of employment is the:
    a. treasurer's department.
    b. personnel department.
    c. timekeeping department.
    d. payroll department.

12. (S.O. 7) Jan Turner, earns $16 per hour for a 40 hour work week and $24 per hour for overtime work. If Turner works 44 hours, her gross earnings are:
    a. $704.
    b. $736.
    c. $836.
    d. $1,056.

13. (S.O. 7) Lewis Latimer, an employee of Spottswood Company, has gross earnings for the month of October of $4,000. FICA taxes are 8% of gross earnings, federal income taxes amount to $635 for the month, state income taxes are 2% of gross earnings, and Lewis authorizes voluntary deductions of $10 per month to the United Fund. What is the net pay for Lewis Latimer?
    a. $2,961.40.
    b. $2,955.00.
    c. $2,965.00.
    d. $2,967.70.

14. (S.O. 7) The journal entry to record the payroll for Marcus Garvey Company for the week ending January 8, would probably include a:
    a. credit to Office Salaries.
    b. credit to Wages Expense.
    c. debit to Federal Income Taxes Payable.
    d. credit to FICA Taxes Payable.

15. (S.O. 7) A tax that is also known as social security taxes is:
    a. state income taxes.
    b. federal income taxes.
    c. Federal Insurance Contribution Act taxes.
    d. federal unemployment taxes.

16. (S.O. 8) The journal entry for Hansberry Corporation to record employer payroll taxes will include a:
    a. debit to Wages Expense.
    b. debit to State Unemployment Expense.
    c. debit to FICA Taxes Payable.
    d. debit to Payroll Tax Expense.

17. (S.O. 8) The record that provides a cumulative summary of each employee's gross earnings, payroll deductions, and net pay during the year and is required to be maintained to comply with state and federal law is the:
    a. payroll register.
    b. employee earnings record.
    c. statement of earnings.
    d. Wage and Tax Statement.

18. (S.O. 9) DuBois Company employees are entitled to one day's vacation for each month worked. If an employee earns an average of $150 per day in a given month, the entry to accrue vacation benefits expense for the year for one employee will be as follows:
    a. Vacation Benefits Expense.. 150
         Liability for Vacation Benefits.................................. 150
    b. Pension Expense.. 1,800
         Pension Liability... 1,800
    c. No entry.
    d. Vacation Benefits Expense.. 1,800
         Liability for Vacation Benefits.................................. 1,800

19. (S.O. 9) Postretirement benefits consist of payments by employers to retired employees for (1) health care and life insurance and (2) pensions. What basis should be used to account for both types?

	Health Care and Life Insurance	**Pensions**
a.	Cash	Cash
b.	Cash	Accrual
c.	Accrual	Cash
d.	Accrual	Accrual

20. (S.O. 9) Which of the following statements about a pension plan is **correct?**
    a. A pension plan involves two parties: the employer and the retired employees.
    b. Pension plans are usually not a concern for employers.
    c. Most pension plans are subject to the provisions of ERISA.
    d. Most pension plans are subject to the provisions of OSHA.

MATCHING

Match each term with its definition by writing the appropriate letter in the space provided.

	Terms			Definitions

Terms

_____ 1. FICA taxes.

_____ 2. Payroll register.

_____ 3. Statement of earnings.

_____ 4. Current liability.

_____ 5. Contingent liability.

_____ 6. State unemployment taxes.

_____ 7. Employee earnings record.

_____ 8. Federal unemployment taxes.

_____ 9. Wage and Tax Statement (Form W-2).

_____ 10. Employee's Withholding Allowance Certificate (Form W-4).

_____ 11. Pension plan.

_____ 12. Gross earnings.

Definitions

a. An arrangement whereby an employer provides benefits to employees after they retire.

b. A record showing the gross earnings, payroll deductions, and net pay of each employee for a pay period.

c. A document that accompanies each payroll check and indicates the employee's gross earnings, payroll deductions, and net pay.

d. A statement showing an employee's gross earnings, FICA taxes withheld, and income taxes withheld for the year.

e. A debt that can reasonably be expected to be paid from existing current assets or through the creation of other current liabilities within the next year or operating cycle, whichever is longer.

f. A cumulative record that provides information concerning each employee's gross earnings, deductions, and net pay during the year.

g. A potential liability that may become an actual liability in the future.

h. An Internal Revenue Service form showing the number of allowances claimed by an employee for the purpose of withholding income taxes from the employee's gross earnings.

i. Taxes imposed on an employer by the federal government that provide benefits to employees who lose their jobs.

j. Total compensation earned by an employee.

k. Taxes imposed on an employer by state governments that provide benefits to employees who lose their jobs.

l. Taxes designed to provide workers with supplemental retirement, employment disability, and medical benefits.

The Navigator

EXERCISES

EX. 11-1 (S.O. 2 and 3) The following transactions took place during 2002 for Revel Pots and Pans Company:

Aug. 1 Borrowed $10,000 in cash from the Third National Bank by issuing a $10,000 eight-month, 12% interest-bearing note.

Dec. 1 Borrowed $20,000 in cash from the Second Federal Savings & Loan by issuing a six-month, 10% interest-bearing note.

Dec. 24 Determined from cash register readings that sales were $24,650 and sales taxes were $1,650.

Dec. 31 Determined that it is probable and reasonably estimable that 400 units sold under warranty will be defective and that warranty repair costs will average $20 per unit. No warranty entries have been recorded during the year.

Instructions
(a) Journalize the transactions above.
(b) Prepare the adjusting entries for the two notes at December 31, 2002.
(c) Record interest expense and payment of the two notes in 2003 at their maturity dates.

	General Journal		J1
Date	**Account Title**	**Debit**	**Credit**
2002 (a)			

	General Journal		J
Date	Account Title	Debit	Credit
(a) cont.			
2003 (b)			

	General Journal		J
Date	**Account Title**	**Debit**	**Credit**
(c)			

EX. 11-2 (S.O. 7) The following information pertains to the payroll of B. T. Washington Company for the week ended January 24, 2003. All hours over 40 are paid at one and one-half times the regular hourly rate.

Employee	Total Hours Worked	Hourly Rate	Federal Income Taxes	United Fund	Union Dues
E. Bouchet	45	$13.00	$110	$10	$5
C. Cullen	44	15.00	138	12	5
M. Henson	38	10.00	64	10	5
B. Mays	48	12.00	100	14	5

Instructions
(a) Complete the schedule below. The state income tax rate is 4% of gross earnings and the FICA tax rate is 8% of gross earnings.
(b) Prepare the entry to record the payroll on January 24.
(c) Prepare the journal entry to record payment of the payroll on January 26.
(d) Record the employer's payroll taxes assuming state unemployment taxes are 5.4% and federal unemployment taxes are 0.8% (6.2% - 5.4%).

(a)

	Gross Earnings	FICA Taxes	Federal Income Taxes	State Income Taxes	United Fund	Union Dues	Net Pay
E. Bouchet							
C. Cullen							
M. Henson							
B. Mays							

	General Journal		J1
Date	**Account Title**	**Debit**	**Credit**
2003 (b)			
(c)			
(d)			

The
Navigator

SOLUTIONS TO REVIEW QUESTIONS AND EXERCISES

TRUE-FALSE

1. (F) A current liability must meet **both** of the following criteria: (1) it is expected to be paid from existing current assets or through the creation of other current liabilities, and (2) it is expected to be paid within one year or the operating cycle, whichever is longer.
2. (F) Obligations in the form of written promissory notes are recorded as notes payable.
3. (F) Notes payable usually are issued to meet short-term financing needs.
4. (T)
5. (F) Unearned Revenues are classified as a current liability.
6. (T)
7. (F) Current liabilities are seldom listed in the order of maturity because of the varying maturity dates that may exist for a specific type of obligation such as notes payable. They are usually listed in order of magnitude.
8. (F) If a contingency is probable and it is reasonably estimable, the liability should be recorded in the accounts; a contingency that is possible and reasonably estimable should only be disclosed in the notes.
9. (T)
10. (F) The term payroll does not extend to payments made for personal service to the company by professionals, such as attorneys. These and other professional individuals are independent contractors, and payments to them are called fees rather than salaries and wages.
11. (T)
12. (F) The posting of job openings, the screening and interviewing of applicants, and the hiring of employees is the responsibility of the personnel department.
13. (T)
14. (F) FICA taxes are considered a mandatory deduction from employee earnings.
15. (T)
16. (F) The statement of earnings accompanies each payroll check and indicates the employee's gross earnings, payroll deductions, and net pay. The document that shows the data given in the true-false statement is the employee earnings record which is an internal document maintained by an employer to comply with state and federal laws.
17. (T)
18. (T)
19. (T)
20. (F) Pension expense is reported as an operating expense in the income statement.

MULTIPLE CHOICE

1. (c) Prepaid expenses are current assets. Answers (a), (b), and (d) are all correct statements..

2. (b) The adjusting entry for the company is as follows:

Interest Expense	700	
Interest Payable ($28,000 X 10% X 3/12)..........		700

3. (c) The entry to record the payment of the note is as follows:

Notes Payable..	28,000	
Interest Payable	2,100	
Cash...		30,100

4. (c) Because the note and the accrued interest are payable within one year or the operating cycle whichever is longer from December 31, 2002, they both should be classified as current liabilities.

5. (d) The entry for Pam Travis Company to record sales and sales taxes is as follows:

Cash..	2,100	
Sales ($2,100 ÷ 105%)		2,000
Sales Taxes Payable ($2,000 X 5%)		100

6. (b) When a contingency is probable and reasonably estimable, the liability should be recorded in the accounts. When a contingency does not meet the two conditions for accrual described above, only disclosure of the contingency is required, unless it is remote in which case no disclosure is made.

7. (d) If the possibility of the contingency happening is remote, it need not be recorded nor disclosed.

8. (a) A contingency for which the amount of loss can be reasonably estimated should be disclosed when the outcome of the contingency is reasonably possible.

9. (d) Preparing payroll tax returns (a), timekeeping (b), and preparing the payroll (c) are all considered functions of payroll activities. Paying professionals are called fees; such payments extend beyond the term "payroll."

10. (a) The treasurer's department should be responsible for the payment of the payroll. The other departments perform other important payroll functions but not paying the payroll.

11. (b) The personnel department should be responsible for authorizing the termination of employment.

12. (b) Gross earnings are $736. (Regular 40 X $16 = $640 + overtime 4 X $24 = $96).

13. (b) The net pay is computed as follows:

Grossing earnings		$4,000.00
Payroll deductions:		
FICA taxes ($4,000 X 8%)	$320.00	
Federal income taxes	635.00	
State income taxes ($4,000 X 2%)	80.00	
United Fund	10.00	1,045.00
Net pay		$2,955.00

14. (d) An example of a typical payroll entry is as follows:

Office Salaries Expense	XXXX	
Wages Expense	XXXX	
FICA Taxes Payable		XXXX
Federal Income Taxes Payable		XXXX
State Income Taxes Payable		XXXX
United Fund Payable		XXXX
Wages Payable		XXXX

15. (c) FICA taxes are also known as social security taxes. This tax is both withheld from employees and is matched by the employer as a payroll tax expense.

16. (d) An example of a typical employer payroll taxes entry is as follows:

Payroll Tax Expense	XXXX	
FICA Taxes Payroll		XXXX
Federal Unemployment Taxes Payable		XXXX
State Unemployment Taxes Payable		XXXX

17. (b) Both the payroll register (a) and the statement of earnings (c) relate to a given pay period. The Wage and Tax Statement (d) does contain cumulative data on each employee but it does not show all payroll deductions or net pay.

18. (d) Since the employee is entitled to one day's vacation for each month worked, at the end of the year he would be entitled to 12 days. Therefore, the vacation benefits expense would amount to $1,800 and the entry in (d) would be made.

19. (d) Both (1) health care and life insurance and (2) pensions should be accounted for on the accrual basis.

20. (c) Answer (a) is incorrect because a fund administrator is also involved Answer (b) is incorrect because pension plans are usually a concern for employers to attract employees. Answer (d) is incorrect because OSHA provisions generally regulate health and safety concerns of the workplace.

MATCHING

1.	l	7.	f
2.	b	8.	i
3.	c	9.	d
4.	e	10.	h
5.	g	11.	a
6.	k	12.	j

EXERCISES

EX. 11-1

	General Journal		
			J1
Date	**Account Title**	**Debit**	**Credit**
(a) 2002			
Aug. 1	Cash	10,000	
	Notes Payable		10,000
	(To record receipt of cash and issuance		
	of $10,000, 12% eight-month note)		
Dec. 1	Cash	20,000	
	Notes Payable		20,000
	(To record receipt of cash and issuance		
	of six-month 10% interest-bearing note)		
Dec. 24	Cash	26,300	
	Sales		24,650
	Sales Taxes Payable		1,650
	(To record daily sales and sales taxes)		
Dec. 31	Warranty Expense (400 X $20)	8,000	
	Estimated Warranty Liability		8,000
	(To accrue estimated warranty costs)		

General Journal			J2
Date	**Account Title**	**Debit**	**Credit**
(b)			
Dec. 31	Interest Expense ($10,000 X 12% X 5/12)	500	
	Interest Payable		500
	(To record interest expense for five months)		
31	Interest Expense ($20,000 X 10% X 1/12)	167	
	Interest Payable		167
	(To record interest expense for one month)		
(c)			
2003			
Mar. 31	Interest Expense	300	
	Interest Payable		300
	(To record interest expense for three		
	months on 12% interest-bearing note)		
Apr. 1	Notes Payable	10,000	
	Interest Payable	800	
	Cash		10,800
	(To record payment of Third National Bank		
	note)		
May 31	Interest Expense	833	
	Interest Payable		833
	(To record interest expense for five months		
	on 10% interest-bearing note)		

	General Journal			J3
Date	Account Title		Debit	Credit
2003				
June 1	Notes Payable		20,000	
	Interest Payable		1,000	
	Cash			21,000
	(To record payment of second federal note)			

EX. 11-2

(a)

	Gross Earnings	FICA Taxes	Federal Income Taxes	State Income Taxes	United Fund	Union Dues	Net Pay
E. Bouchet	$ 617.50	$ 49.40	$110.00	$24.70	$10.00	$ 5.00	$ 418.40
C. Cullen	690.00	55.20	138.00	27.60	12.00	5.00	452.20
M. Henson	380.00	30.40	64.00	15.20	10.00	5.00	255.40
B. Mays	624.00	49.92	100.00	24.96	14.00	5.00	430.12
	$2,311.50	$184.92	$412.00	$92.46	$46.00	$20.00	$1,556.12

	General Journal		J1
Date	**Account Title**	**Debit**	**Credit**
2003 (b)			
Jan. 24	Wages Expense	2,311.50	
	FICA Taxes Payable (Employee contribs.)		184.92
	Federal Income Taxes Payable		412.00
	State Income Taxes Payable		92.46
	United Fund Payable		46.00
	Union Dues Payable		20.00
	Wages Payable		1,556.12
	(To record January 24 payroll)		
(c)			
Jan. 26	Wages Payable	1,556.12	
	Cash		1,556.12
	(To record payment of January 24 payroll)		
(d)			
Jan. 26	Payroll Tax Expense	328.23	
	FICA Taxes Payable (Employer's Contrib.)		184.92
	Federal Unemployment Taxes Payable		
	[$2,311.50 X (0.062 - 0.054)]		18.49
	State Unemployment Taxes Payable		124.82
	($2,311.50 X 0.054)		

	1		1
1			1
2			2
3			3
4			4
5			5
6			6
7			7
8			8
9			9
10			10
11			11
12			12
13			13
14			14
15			15
16			16
17			17
18			18
19			19
20			20
21			21
22			22
23			23
24			24
25			25
26			26
27			27
28			28
29			29
30			30
31			31
32			32
33			33
34			34
35			35
36			36
37			37
38			38
39			39
40			40

	1																					1
	2																					2
	3																					3
	4																					4
	5																					5
	6																					6
	7																					7
	8																					8
	9																					9
	10																					10
	11																					11
	12																					12
	13																					13
	14																					14
	15																					15
	16																					16
	17																					17
	18																					18
	19																					19
	20																					20
	21																					21
	22																					22
	23																					23
	24																					24
	25																					25
	26																					26
	27																					27
	28																					28
	29																					29
	30																					30
	31																					31
	32																					32
	33																					33
	34																					34
	35																					35
	36																					36
	37																					37
	38																					38
	39																					39
	40																					40

Chapter **12**

ACCOUNTING PRINCIPLES

The Navigator	✓
■ *Scan Study Objectives*	☐
■ *Read Preview*	☐
■ *Read Chapter Review*	☐
■ *Work Demonstration Problem*	☐
■ *Answer True-False Statements*	☐
■ *Answer Multiple-Choice Questions*	☐
■ *Match Terms and Definitions*	☐
■ *Solve Exercises*	☐

CHAPTER STUDY OBJECTIVES

After studying this chapter, you should be able to:
1. Explain the meaning of generally accepted accounting principles and identify the key items of the conceptual framework.
2. Describe the basic objectives of financial reporting.
3. Discuss the qualitative characteristics of accounting information and elements of financial statements.
4. Identify the basic assumptions used by accountants.
5. Identify the basic principles of accounting.
6. Identify the two constraints in accounting.
7. Explain the accounting principles used in international operations.

PREVIEW OF CHAPTER 12

It is important that general guidelines be available to resolve accounting issues; without these basic guidelines, each enterprise would have to develop its own set of accounting practices. If this happened, we would have to become familiar with every company's peculiar accounting and reporting rules in order to understand their financial statements. Thus, it would be difficult, if not impossible, to compare the financial statements of different companies. This chapter explores the basic accounting principles followed in developing specific accounting guidelines. The content and organization of the chapter are as follows:

CHAPTER REVIEW

GAAP

1. (S.O. 1) **Generally accepted accounting principles (GAAP)** are a set of rules and practices that are recognized as a general guide for financial reporting purposes. These principles must have "substantial authoritative support."

2. The Financial Accounting Standards Board (FASB) has developed a **conceptual framework** to serve as a basis for resolving accounting and reporting problems. This framework consists of the following:
    a. Objectives of financial reporting.
    b. Qualitative characteristics of accounting information.
    c. Elements of financial statements.
    d. Operating guidelines (assumptions, principles, and constraints).

Objectives of Financial Reporting

3. (S.O. 2) The **objectives** of financial reporting are to provide information that is useful in (a) making investment and credit decisions; (b) assessing future cash flows; and (c) identifying the economic resources (assets), the claims to those resources (liabilities), and the changes in those resources and claims.

Qualitative Characteristics

4. (S.O. 3) The accounting alternative selected or policy adopted should be one that generates the most useful financial information for decision making. To be useful, information should possess the following **qualitative characteristics:**
    a. **Relevance.** The information must be capable of making a difference in a decision. Relevant information has either predictive or feedback value; and is also timely.
    b. **Reliability.** The information should be free of error and bias and be dependable.
    c. **Comparability.** The information should be comparable with accounting information about other enterprises.
    d. **Consistency**. The same accounting principles and methods should be used from year to year within a company.

Elements of Financial Statements

5. The **elements of financial statements** are a set of definitions of the basic terms used in accounting. These elements include such terms as assets, liabilities, equity, revenues, and expenses.

6. The **operating guidelines** used by accountants to solve practical problems include assumptions, principles, and constraints.

Accounting Assumptions

7. (S.O. 4) The accounting assumptions are:
    a. **Monetary unit assumption**—states that only transaction data that can be expressed in terms of money should be included in the accounting. An important corollary is the added assumption that the unit of measure remains relatively constant over time.
    b. **Economic entity assumption**—states that the activities of the entity be kept separate and distinct from the activities of the owner and of all other economic entities.

c. **Time period assumption**—states that the economic life of a business can be divided into artificial time periods.

d. **Going concern assumption**—assumes that the enterprise will continue in operation long enough to carry out its existing objectives.

Principles

8. (S.O. 5) On the basis of these assumptions, the accounting profession has developed principles that dictate how transactions and other economic events should be recorded and reported.

9. The **revenue recognition principle** dictates that revenue should be recognized in the accounting period in which it is earned. When a sale is involved, revenue is recognized at the point of sale.

10. In long-term construction contracts, revenue and income are recognized in proportion to the contract work performed each year using the **percentage-of-completion method.**
    a. A project's progress toward completion is measured by comparing the costs incurred in a year to total estimated costs of the entire project.
    b. The formulas for this method are:
       (1) Costs Incurred During the Period ÷ Total Estimated Cost X Total Revenue = Revenues Recognized for the Period.
       (2) Revenue Recognized (Current Period) - Cost Incurred (Current Period) = Gross Profit (Current Period).

11. If collection of a sale is very uncertain, revenue and income are recorded over time in proportion to the cash collected using the **installment method.**
    a. Each cash collection is considered to be revenue and to consist of (1) partial recovery of the cost of goods sold and (2) partial gross profit from the sale.
    b. The formula to recognize gross profit is:
       Cash Collections from Customers X Gross Profit Percentage = Gross Profit Recognized (Current Period).

12. The **matching principle** requires that expenses be matched with revenues in the period in which efforts are expended to generate revenues. Expenses are not recognized when cash is paid, or the work performed; they are recognized when the labor (service) or product actually makes its contributions to revenue.
    a. Incurred costs that will only generate revenues in the current period are expensed immediately. These costs are expired costs.
    b. Incurred costs that will generate revenues in current and future periods are recognized as **assets** when incurred; these costs are unexpired costs.
    c. Unexpired costs become expenses either as cost of goods sold or operating expenses.

13. The **full disclosure principle** requires that circumstances and events that make a difference to financial statement users be disclosed. Compliance with this principle occurs through the data contained in the financial statements and the information in the notes that accompany the statements. The first note in most cases is a **summary of significant accounting policies.**

14. The most basic principle of accounting is the **cost principle.**
    a. Cost is relevant because it represents the price paid, the assets sacrificed, or the commitment made at the date of acquisition.
    b. Cost is reliable because it is objectively measurable, factual and verifiable.

Price-Level Adjusted Data

15. While admitting that some changes in prices do occur, the accounting profession believes the unit of measure (e.g., the dollar) has remained sufficiently constant over time to produce meaningful financial information. If presented, the disclosure of price-level adjusted data is in the form of supplemental information presented with financial statements.

Constraints

16. (S.O. 6) There are **two constraints** in applying the operating guidelines.
    a. **Materiality** means that an item is likely to influence the decision of a reasonably prudent investor.
    b. **Conservatism** means that when in doubt choose the method that will be least likely to overstate assets and income.

International Accounting Standards

17. (S.O. 7) World markets are becoming increasingly intertwined. Firms that conduct their operations in more than one country through subsidiaries, or branches in foreign countries are referred to as multinational corporations.

18. The International Accounting Standard Committee (IASC) exists to obtain uniformity in international accounting practices. To date, numerous International Accounting Standards have been issued for IASC members to introduce to their respective countries.

DEMONSTRATION PROBLEM (S.O. 5)

Sondgeroth Company is involved in a long-term construction contract to build a warehouse at a total estimated cost of $20 million. Additional information follows:

	Warehouse	
	Cash	Actual Costs
Year	**Collections**	**Incurred**
2001	$5,000,000	$3,000,000
2002	8,000,000	7,000,000
2003	6,500,000	6,000,000
2004	5,500,000	4,000,000

The project is completed in 2004 and all cash to be received from the project has been received.
In a separate transaction, Sondgeroth sold an office building it had constructed to Mendota Company for $40 million.   Sondgeroth's cost to construct the office building was $28 million. Sondgeroth appropriately used the installment method. Additional information follows:

	Cash
Year	**Collections**
2001	$ 8,000,000
2002	10,000,000
2003	12,500,000
2004	9,500,000

Instructions
(a)   Prepare a schedule to determine the gross profit for 2001, 2002, 2003, and 2004 for the long-term contract using the percentage-of-completion method.
(b)   Prepare a schedule to determine the gross profit for 2001, 2002, 2003, and 2004 from the installment sale.

SOLUTION TO DEMONSTRATION PROBLEM

(a)

Year	Costs Incurred (Current Period)	Ratio of Costs Incurred (Current Period) to Total Estimated Cost	=	Percent Complete (Current Period)	X	Total Revenue	=	Revenue Recognized (Current Period)
2001	$ 3,000,000	$3,000,000/$20,000,000		15%		$25,000,000		$ 3,750,000
2002	7,000,000	7,000,000/20,000,000		35%		25,000,000		8,750,000
2003	6,000,000	6,000,000/20,000,000		30%		25,000,000		7,500,000
2004	4,000,000	Balance to complete contract						5,000,000
Totals	$20,000,000							$25,000,000

	Revenue Recognized (Current Period)	–	Actual Cost Incurred (Current Period)	=	Gross Profit Recognized (Current Period)
2001	$ 3,750,000		$ 3,000,000		$ 750,000
2002	8,750,000		7,000,000		1,750,000
2003	7,500,000		6,000,000		1,500,000
2004	5,000,000		4,000,000		1,000,000
Totals	$25,000,000		$20,000,000		$5,000,000

(b)

	Cash Collections	Gross Profit Percentage	Gross Profit Recognized
2001	$ 8,000,000	30%*	$ 2,400,000
2002	10,000,000	30%	3,000,000
2003	12,500,000	30%	3,750,000
2004	9,500,000	30%	2,850,000
Totals	$40,000,000		$12,000,000

*Gross profit percentage is computed as follows:

Sales price	$40,000,000
Less: Construction	28,000,000
Gross profit	12,000,000
÷ Sales price	40,000,000
Gross profit %	30%

REVIEW QUESTIONS AND EXERCISES

TRUE—FALSE

Indicate whether each of the following is true (T) or false (F) in the space provided.

_____   1.   (S.O. 1)   To be considered part of generally accepted accounting principles, a principle should have substantial authoritative support.

_____   2.   (S.O. 1)   The conceptual framework consists of objectives, qualitative characteristics, elements, and operating guidelines.

_____   3.   (S.O. 2)   The information provided by financial reporting cannot be used in assessing future cash flows.

_____   4.   (S.O. 3)   If information is reliable, it has either predictive value or feedback value.

_____   5.   (S.O. 3)   Comparability means using the same accounting principles and methods from year to year within a company.

_____   6.   (S.O. 3)   It is not possible for a company to change to a new method of accounting because the information would not be consistent.

_____   7.   (S.O. 3)   Elements of financial statements include a set of definitions for such terms as assets, liabilities, equity, revenues, and expenses.

_____   8.   (S.O. 4)   The economic entity assumption states that the economic life of a business can be divided into artificial time periods.

_____   9.   (S.O. 4)   The going concern assumption has been proven invalid due to numerous business failures.

_____   10.   (S.O. 4)   The monetary unit assumption states that only transaction data capable of being expressed in terms of money should be included in the accounting records of the economic entity.

_____   11.   (S.O. 4)   The time period assumption states that companies will pay their debts within specified time periods.

_____   12.   (S.O. 5)   When the savings and loan industry recorded a large portion of its fees for granting a loan as revenue immediately, many thought this may have violated the revenue recognition principle.

_____   13.   (S.O. 5)   Under the percentage-of-completion method the formula to recognize revenue is cost incurred during the period divided by estimated total cost times total revenue.

_____   14.   (S.O. 5)   Under the installment method, all gross profit is recognized at the point of sale.

_____   15.   (S.O. 5)   Costs that will generate revenues only in the current accounting period are expensed immediately.

_____ 16. (S.O. 5) Costs carried as merchandise inventory are expensed in the period the goods are purchased by the merchandising company.

_____ 17. (S.O. 5) For most companies, the first note to the financial statements is the summary of significant accounting policies.

_____ 18. (S.O. 5) The cost principle is justified because it is considered both relevant and reliable.

_____ 19. (S.O. 6) An item is material if its inclusion or omission has no impact on a decision maker.

_____ 20. (S.O. 6) A common application of the conservatism constraint is the use of the lower of cost or market method for inventories.

MULTIPLE CHOICE

Circle the letter that best answers each of the following statements.

1. (S.O. 2) According to the FASB's study, which of the following is **not** amongst the items concluded to be an objective of financial reporting?
   a. Provide information that is helpful in assessing future cash flows.
   b. Provide information that identifies the economic resources (assets), the claims to those resources (liabilities), and the changes in those resources and claims.
   c. Provide economic and financial information for managers and other internal users.
   d. Provide information that is useful to those making investment and credit decisions.

2. (S.O. 3) The characteristic of relevance does **not** include:
   a. predictive value.
   b. feedback value.
   c. faithful representation.
   d. timeliness.

3. (S.O. 3) "Last year's report is useless because it lost its capacity to influence decisions." Grumpy said to Dopey. What characteristic of relevancy is Grumpy trying to explain to Dopey?
   a. Predictive value.
   b. Feedback value.
   c. Timeliness.
   d. Verifiable value.

4. (S.O. 3) The characteristic of reliability does **not** include:
   a. verifiability.
   b. comparability.
   c. faithful representation.
   d. neutrality.

5. (S.O. 3) Consistency means that:
   a. accounting information is always relevant.
   b. accounting information is always reliable.

c. different companies use the same accounting principles for similar transactions.

d. the same accounting methods are used from year to year within a company.

6. (S.O. 3) Doc was looking at the financial statements of Sneezy Company and Bashful Company. Which qualitative characteristic is most important to Doc?
    a. Comparability.
    b. Consistency.
    c. Feedback value.
    d. Neutrality.

7. (S.O. 4) The economic entity assumption states that:
    a. employees can intermingle their property with a business's property.
    b. the activities of the entity be kept separate and distinct from the activities of the owner and of all other economic entities.
    c. different economic entities can have the same claim to property.
    d. economic entities are assumed to carry on indefinitely.

8. (S.O. 4) The time period assumption recognizes that:
    a. revenue should be recognized in the accounting period in which it is earned.
    b. the economic life of a business can be divided into artificial time periods.
    c. expenses should be recognized in the period of their association with earned revenue.
    d. economic events can be identified with a particular unit of accountability.

9. (S.O. 4) The going concern assumption recognizes that:
    a. economic events can be identified with a particular unit of accountability.
    b. when a sale is involved, revenue is recognized at the point of sale.
    c. because of numerous business failures, enterprises should be accounted for based on a finite life.
    d. the enterprise will continue in operation long enough to carry out its existing objectives and commitments.

10. (S.O. 5) Under the revenue recognition principle, when a sale of inventory is involved, revenue is recognized:
    a. when cash is received.
    b. when a contract is signed.
    c. when the item is shipped to the customer.
    d. when the sales invoice is sent to the customer.

11. (S.O. 5) Otto Construction Company began a long-term construction contract on January 1, 2003. The contract is expected to be completed in 2004 at a total cost of $32,000,000. Otto's total revenue for the project is $37,000,000. Otto incurred contract costs of $12,000,000 in 2003. What gross profit should be recognized in 2003?
    a. $13,875,000.
    b. $1,875,000.
    c. $5,000,000.
    d. $1,621,622.

12. (S.O. 5) Bullock Construction Company began a long-term construction contract on January 1, 2003. The contract is expected to be completed in 2004 at a total cost of $20,000,000. Bullock's revenue for the project is $24,000,000. Bullock incurred contract costs of $8,000,000 in 2003. What gross profit should be recognized in 2003?
    a. $9,600,000.
    b. $6,666,667.
    c. $1,600,000.
    d. $1,333,333.

13. (S.O. 5) Sleepy Company had installment sales of $5,500,000 in its first year of operations. The cost of goods sold on installment was $3,025,000. Sleepy collected a total of $2,000,000 on the installment sales. Using the installment method, how much gross profit should be recognized in the first year?
    a. $900,000.
    b. $1,025,000.
    c. $1,100,000.
    d. $475,000.

14. (S.O. 5) Happy Company had installment sales of $8,000,000 in its first year of operations. The cost of goods sold on installment was $6,000,000. Happy collected a total of $4,000,000 on the installment sales. Using the installment method, how much gross profit should be recognized in the first year?
    a. $4,000,000.
    b. $3,000,000.
    c. $2,000,000.
    d. $1,000,000.

15. (S.O. 3) The full disclosure principle requires:
    a. that if something is disclosed, every detail possible is disclosed.
    b. that everything be fully disclosed.
    c. that only basic information be disclosed.
    d. that circumstances and events that make a difference to financial statement users be disclosed.

16. (S.O. 5) Which of the following is considered an unexpired cost?
    a. Prepaid Insurance.
    b. Advertising.
    c. Sales Salaries.
    d. Repairs.

17. (S.O. 5) Cost is criticized as irrelevant because:
    a. it represents the price paid at the date of acquisition.
    b. it is the amount for which someone should be accountable.
    c. it is objectively measurable.
    d. subsequent to acquisition, cost is not equivalent to market value.

18.   (S.O. 6) Zendejas Company purchased a ruler for $2.00. The ruler is expected to last for ten years. Leo, the accountant, expensed the cost of the ruler in the year of the purchase. Which constraint has Leo taken into account when making his accounting decision?
   a.   Conservatism.
   b.   Faithful Representation.
   c.   Neutrality.
   d.   Materiality.

19.   (S.O. 6) Which of the following is an example of conservatism?
   a.   Use of only the market method for inventories.
   b.   Use of the FIFO method when prices are rising.
   c.   Use of an accelerated depreciation method over a straight-line depreciation method.
   d.   Use of current cost accounting over constant dollar accounting.

20.   (S.O. 7)   Which of the following statements concerning international accounting is **incorrect?**
   a.   There is little uniformity in accounting standards from country to country.
   b.   There has been no effort to obtain uniformity in international accounting practices.
   c.   Firms that conduct their operations in more than one country through subsidiaries, divisions, or branches in foreign countries are referred to as multinational corporations.
   d.   World markets are becoming increasingly intertwined.

MATCHING

Match each term with its definition by writing the appropriate letter in the space provided.

Terms

_____ 1. Generally accepted accounting principles.

_____ 2. Conceptual framework.

_____ 3. Elements of financial statements.

_____ 4. Going concern assumption.

_____ 5. Percentage-of-completion method.

_____ 6. Installment method.

_____ 7. Full disclosure principle.

_____ 8. Comparability.

_____ 9. Reliability.

_____ 10. Consistency.

Definitions

a. Definitions of basic terms used in accounting.

b. A set of rules and practices that are recognized as a general guide for financial reporting purposes.

c. The assumption that the enterprise will continue in operation long enough to carry out its existing objectives and commitments.

d. Use of the same accounting principles and methods from year to year within a company.

e. A coherent system of interrelated objectives and fundamentals that can lead to consistent standards.

f. The quality of information that gives assurance that it is free of error and bias.

g. Recognition of revenue and income over time as cash installments are received.

h. Recognition of revenue and income on a construction project on the basis of costs incurred during the period.

i. Ability to compare accounting information of different companies because they use the same accounting principles.

j. Circumstances and events that make a difference to financial statement users that must be disclosed.

The Navigator

EXERCISES

EX. 12-1 (S.O. 5) Snow White Construction began work on a long-term construction contract in 2002. The contract called for Snow White to earn total revenues of $360,000,000. Snow White incurred contract costs, equal to the total estimated, of $93,000,000 in 2002, $126,000,000 in 2003, and $81,000,000 in 2004 when the contract was completed.

Instructions
Compute the amount of revenue and gross profit which should be recognized in 2002, 2003, and 2004 under the percentage-of-completion method.

_____

_____

_____

_____

_____

_____

_____

_____

_____

_____

_____

_____

_____

_____

_____

EX. 12-2 (S.O. 4, 5, and 6) Presented below are some business transactions that occurred during 2002 for Puck Company.

(a) Merchandise inventory purchased from Lysander Co. for $150,000 is reported at its market value of $170,000. The following entry was made:

Merchandise Inventory	20,000	
Gain		20,000

(b) The account receivable of $15,000 from Hermia Inc. was written off using the direct write-off method. The following entry was made:

Bad Debt Expense	15,000	
Accounts Receivable—Hermia		15,000

(c) A letter opener purchased from Helena, Co. costing $10 is being depreciated over 10 years. At year end the following entry was made:

Depreciation Expense—Letter Opener	1	
Accumulated Depreciation—Letter Opener		1

(d) The president of Puck Company, Demetrius, purchased a van for personal use and charged it to his expense account. The following entry was made:

Travel Expense	25,000	
Cash		25,000

Instructions

In each of the situations above, identify the assumption, principle, or constraint that has been violated, if any, and discuss the appropriateness of the journal entries. Give the correct journal entry, if necessary.

SOLUTIONS TO REVIEW QUESTIONS AND EXERCISES

TRUE-FALSE

1. (T)
2. (T)
3. (F)   One of the objectives of financial reporting is to provide information that is helpful in assessing future cash flows.
4. (F)   If information is reliable, it is verifiable, a faithful representation, and neutral.
5. (F)   Comparability means different companies use the same accounting principles to record similar transactions.
6. (F)   It is possible for a company to change to a new method of accounting if management can justify that the new method results in more meaningful financial information.
7. (T)
8. (F)   The economic entity assumption states that the activities of the entity be kept separate and distinct from the activities of the owner and of all other economic entities.
9. (F)   The going concern assumption is considered valid because experience indicates that, in spite of numerous business failures, companies have a fairly high continuance rate.
10. (T)
11. (F)   The time period assumption states that the economic life of a business can be divided into artificial time periods.
12. (T)
13. (T)
14. (F)   Under the installment method, revenue and gross profit are recognized in proportion to cash collected.
15. (T)
16. (F)   Costs carried as merchandise inventory are expensed as cost of goods sold in the period when the sale occurs.
17. (T)
18. (T)
19. (F)   An item is material when it is likely to influence the decision of a reasonably prudent investor or creditor.
20. (T)

MULTIPLE CHOICE

1. (c) Providing economic and financial information for managers and other internal users is the primary objective of managerial accounting. Answers (a), (b), and (d) were all the items concluded to be the objectives of financial reporting based on the FASB's study.

2. (c) Faithful representation pertains to the characteristic of reliability.

3. (c) For accounting information to be relevant it must be timely. That is, it must be available to decision makers before it loses its capacity to influence decisions.

4. (b) Comparability is one of the four qualitative characteristics.

5. (d) Choices (a) and (b) pertain to the characteristics of relevance and reliability, respectively. Choice (c) is a definition of comparability.

6. (a) Because Doc is looking at two different companies, he would like both companies to use the same accounting principles so he can compare one to the other.

7. (b) The economic entity assumption states that the activities of the entity be kept separate and distinct from the activities of the owner and of all other economic entities.

8. (b) Choice (a) is the revenue recognition principle, choice (c) is the matching principle, and choice (d) is the economic entity assumption.

9. (d) Answer (a) is the economic entity assumption and answer (b) is the revenue recognition principle. Answer (c) is the opposite viewpoint from the going concern assumption.

10. (c) Under the revenue recognition principle, revenue is recognized when the item is shipped to the customer.

11. (b) The formula for determining the revenue to be recognized is:

$$\frac{\$12,000,000}{\$32,000,000} \times \$37,000,000 = \$13,875,000$$

$13,875,000 - $12,000,000 = $1,875,000 gross profit.

12. (c) The formula for determining the revenue to be recognized is:

$$\frac{\$8,000,000}{\$20,000,000} \times \$24,000,000 = \$9,600,000$$

$9,600,000 - $8,000,000 = $1,600,000 gross profit.

13.   (a)   The gross profit rate for Sleepy is 45%:

$$\frac{\$5,500,000 \ - \ \$3,025,000}{\$5,500,000} = \underline{45\%}$$

The gross profit recognized is $900,000 ($2,000,000 X 45%).

14.   (d)   The gross profit rate for Happy is 25%:

$$\frac{\$8,000,000 \ - \ \$6,000,000}{\$8,000,000} = \underline{25\%}$$

The gross profit recognized is $1,000,000 ($4,000,000 X 25%).

15.   (d)   The full disclosure principle requires that circumstances and events that make a difference to financial statement users be disclosed.

16.   (a)   Examples of unexpired costs are Merchandise Inventory not sold yet, Supplies, Prepaid Insurance and Prepaid Rent. Answers (b), (c), and (d) are all examples of expired costs.

17.   (d)   Choices (a), (b), and (c) are all arguments in favor of the cost principle.

18.   (d)   Leo has taken "materiality" into account. Materiality relates to an item's impact on a firm's overall financial operations. Although the proper accounting would be to depreciate the ruler over a ten-year period, the cost and time to depreciate the item is far greater than the impact of $2.00 on the financial statements. Leo's ultimate decision to expense or capitalize would rest on whether the cost of the item would impact the decision of a reasonably prudent investor or creditor.

19.   (c)   Conservatism in accounting means that when in doubt the accountant should choose the method that will be least likely to overstate assets and income. Answer (a) is incorrect because the lower of cost of market would be conservative. Answer (b) is incorrect because using the LIFO method when prices are rising would be conservative. Answer (d) is incorrect because there is nothing that says current cost accounting will be least likely to overstate assets and income over the constant dollar accounting.

20.   (b)   Some efforts have been made to obtain uniformity in international accounting practices. In 1973 the International Accounting Standards Committee (IASC) was formed by agreement of accounting organizations from many countries.

MATCHING

1.	b	5.	h	8.	i
2.	e	6.	g	9.	f
3.	a	7.	j	10.	d
4.	c				

EXERCISES

EX. 12-1

Revenue recognized— percentage-of-completion method:

Year	Costs Incurred (Current Period)	Ratio of Costs Incurred (Current Period) to Total Estimated Cost	=	Percent Complete (Current Period)	X	Total Revenue	=	Revenue Recognized (Current Period)
2002	$ 93,000,000	$93,000,000/$300,000,000		31%		$360,000,000		$111,600,000
2003	126,000,000	$126,000,000/$300,000,000		42%		360,000,000		151,200,000
2004	81,000,000	Balance required to complete the contract						97,200,000
	$300,000,000							$360,000,000

Gross profit recognized—percentage-of-completion method:

	Revenue Recognized (Current Period)	−	Actual Cost Incurred (Current Period)	=	Gross Profit Recognized (Current Period)
2002	$111,600,000		$ 93,000,000		$18,600,000
2003	151,200,000		126,000,000		25,200,000
2004	97,200,000		81,000,000		16,200,000
	$360,000,000		$300,000,000		$60,000,000

EX. 12-2

(a)   Recognizing a gain on inventory because its market value is higher than the original cost violates the lower of cost or market method which was discussed in Chapter 9. The lower of cost or market method is an accounting principle which is based on the conservatism constraint. By using the lower of cost or market method, an accountant will least likely overstate assets and income on the financial statements. No entry should be made to recognize a gain on the inventory.

(b)   The matching principle requires that expenses be matched with revenues in the period in which the efforts are expended to generate revenues. The direct write-off method is not acceptable according to GAAP. Instead, the bad debt expenses are better matched with revenue if an estimate is made during each period and an allowance for doubtful accounts is used. If Puck Company had been estimating a bad debt expense each year, the following entry would have been made at the time it was determined the Hermia account receivable was uncollectible.

Allowance for Doubtful Accounts   15,000

    Accounts Receivable   15,000

(c) Although the proper matching would be achieved by depreciating the letter opener over a ten-year period, the cost and time to depreciate the item is far greater than the impact of $10.00 on the financial statements. Therefore, taking materiality into account, it would probably be acceptable to expense the whole $10.00 in the year of the purchase. To decide whether an item is material or not, an accountant should take into account whether the item is likely to influence the decision of a reasonably prudent investor or creditor. At the time of the purchase, the letter opener could have been expensed as follows:

Supplies Expense	10	
Cash		10

(d) By including personal assets within the company, the economic entity assumption has been violated. The economic entity assumption states that economic events can be identified with a particular unit of accountability. At the time of purchasing the van, the company should not have paid for the van and therefore no entry would have been needed.

1													1
2													2
3													3
4													4
5													5
6													6
7													7
8													8
9													9
10													10
11													11
12													12
13													13
14													14
15													15
16													16
17													17
18													18
19													19
20													20
21													21
22													22
23													23
24													24
25													25
26													26
27													27
28													28
29													29
30													30
31													31
32													32
33													33
34													34
35													35
36													36
37													37
38													38
39													39
40													40

1												1
2												2
3												3
4												4
5												5
6												6
7												7
8												8
9												9
10												10
11												11
12												12
13												13
14												14
15												15
16												16
17												17
18												18
19												19
20												20
21												21
22												22
23												23
24												24
25												25
26												26
27												27
28												28
29												29
30												30
31												31
32												32
33												33
34												34
35												35
36												36
37												37
38												38
39												39
40												40

Chapter **13**

ACCOUNTING FOR PARTNERSHIPS

The Navigator ✓
- ■ *Scan Study Objectives* ☐
- ■ *Read Preview* ☐
- ■ *Read Chapter Review* ☐
- ■ *Work Demonstration Problem* ☐
- ■ *Answer True-False Statements* ☐
- ■ *Answer Multiple-Choice Questions* ☐
- ■ *Match Terms and Definitions* ☐
- ■ *Solve Exercises* ☐

CHAPTER STUDY OBJECTIVES

After studying this chapter, you should be able to:
1. Identify the characteristics of the partnership form of business organization.
2. Explain the accounting entries for the formation of a partnership.
3. Identify the bases for dividing net income or net loss.
4. Describe the form and content of partnership financial statements.
5. Explain the effects of the entries when a new partner is admitted.
6. Describe the effect of the entries when a partner withdraws from the firm.
7. Explain the effects of the entries to record the liquidation of a partnership.

PREVIEW OF CHAPTER 13

In this chapter, we will discuss reasons why the partnership form of organization is often selected and explain the major issues in accounting for partnerships. The content and organization of this chapter are as follows:

CHAPTER REVIEW

Partnership Form of Organization

1. (S.O. 1) The Uniform Partnership Act provides the basic rules for the formation and operation of partnerships in more than 90% of the states. The Act defines a partnership as "an association of two or more persons to carry on as co-owners of a business for a profit."

Characteristics of Partnerships

2. The principal characteristics of the partnership form of business organization are (a) association of individuals, (b) mutual agency, (c) limited life, (d) unlimited liability, and (e) co-ownership of property.

3. The association of individuals in a partnership may be based on as simple an act as a handshake, however, it is preferable to state the agreement in writing.
   a. A partnership is a legal entity for certain purposes.
   b. A partnership is an accounting entity for financial reporting purposes.
   c. Net income of a partnership is not taxed as a separate entity.

4. Mutual agency means that each partner acts on behalf of the partnership when engaging in partnership business, and the act of any partner is binding on all other partners.

5. Partnerships have a limited life. Partnership dissolution occurs whenever a partner withdraws or a new partner is admitted.

6. Each partner has **unlimited liability.**
   a. Each partner is personally and individually liable for all partnership liabilities.
   b. Creditors' claims attach first to partnership assets and then to the personal resources of any partner, irrespective of that partner's capital equity in the company.
   c. Under **limited partnerships,** the liability of a limited partner is limited to the partners' capital equity. However, there must always be at least one partner with unlimited liability, often referred to as the general partner.

7. Partnership assets are **co-owned** by the partners. Once assets have been invested in the partnership they are owned jointly by all the partners.

Advantages and Disadvantages

8. Organizations with partnership characteristics include limited partnerships, limited liability partnerships, limited liability companies, and S corporations.

9. The **major advantages** of a partnership are:
   a. Combining skills and resources of two or more individuals.
   b. Ease of formation.
   c. Freedom from governmental regulations and restrictions.
   d. Ease of decision making.

10. The **major disadvantages** of a partnership are (a) mutual agency, (b) limited life, and (c) unlimited liability.

The Partnership Agreement

11. The **written contract** often referred to as the partnership agreement, contains such basic information as the name and principal location of the firm, the purpose of the business, and the date of inception.

Forming a Partnership

12. (S.O. 2) In the **formation of a partnership,** each partner's initial investment in a partnership should be recorded at the fair market value of the assets at the date of their transfer to the partnership.

Dividing Net Income or Net Loss

13. (S.O. 3) **Partnership net income or net loss** is shared equally unless the partnership contract specifically indicates otherwise.
     a. A partner's share of net income or net loss is recognized in the accounts through closing entries.
     b. Closing entries for a partnership are identical to the entries made for a proprietorship, except for the use of multiple capital and drawing accounts.

14. The various **income ratios** that may be used include:
     a. A fixed ratio, expressed as a proportion (6:4), a percentage (70% and 30%), or a fraction (2/3 and 1/3).
     b. A ratio based either on capital balances at the beginning of the year or on average capital balances during the year.
     c. Salaries to partners and the remainder on a fixed ratio.
     d. Interest on partners' capitals and the remainder on a fixed ratio.
     e. Salaries to partners, interest on partners' capitals, and the remainder on a fixed ratio.

     The objective is to reach agreement on a basis that will equitably reflect the differences among partners in terms of their capital investment and service to the partnership.

15. Provisions for salaries and interest must be applied before the remainder of net income or net loss is allocated on the specified fixed ratio. Detailed information concerning the division of net income or net loss should be shown at the bottom of the income statement.

Partnership Financial Statements

16. (S.O. 4) The **financial statements** of a partnership are similar to a proprietorship. The differences are generally related to the fact that a number of owners are involved in a partnership. The income statement for a partnership is identical to the income statement for a proprietorship except for the division of net income.

17. The owners' equity statement for a partnership is called the partners capital statement. It explains the changes in each partners' equity during an accounting period. Changes in capital may result from additional capital investment, drawings, and net income or net loss.

Admission of a Partner

18. (S.O. 5) A new partner may be **admitted** either by (1) purchasing the interest of one or more existing partners, or (2) investing assets in the partnership. The former affects only partners' capital accounts whereas the latter increases both net assets and total capital of the partnership.

19. When a net partner is admitted by **purchase of an interest,**
    a. The transaction is a personal one between one or more existing partners and the new partner.
    b. Any money or other consideration exchanged is the property of the participants and **not** the property of the partnership.
    c. Each partner's capital account is debited for the ownership claims that have been relinquished, and the new partner's capital account is credited with the capital equity purchased.
    d. Total assets, total liabilities, and total capital remain unchanged.

20. When a new partner is admitted by the **investment of assets,** both the total net assets and the total capital of the partnership increase. This is done by debiting Cash and crediting the new partner's capital account. When the capital credit does not equal the investment of assets in the partnership, the difference is considered a bonus either to the existing partners or the new partner.

21. A **bonus to old partners** results when the new partner's capital credit on the date of admittance is less than the new partner's investment in the firm. The procedure for determining the new partner's capital credit and the bonus to the old partners is as follows:
    a. Determine the total capital of the new partnership by adding the new partner's investment to the total capital of the old partnership.
    b. Determine the new partner's capital credit by multiplying the total capital of the new partnership by the new partner's ownership interest.
    c. Determine the amount of bonus by subtracting the new partner's capital credit from the new partner's investment.
    d. Allocate the bonus to the old partners on the basis of their income ratios.

22. A **bonus to a new partner** results when the new partner's capital credit is greater than the partner's investment of assets in the firm. The bonus results in a decrease in the capital balances of the old partners based on their income ratios before admission of the new partner.

Withdrawal of a Partner

23. (S.O. 6) As in the case of the admission of a partner, the **withdrawal of a partner** legally dissolves the partnership. The withdrawal of a partner may be accomplished by (a) payment from partners' personal assets or (b) payment from partnership assets. The former affects only the partners' capital accounts, whereas the latter decreases total net assets and total capital of the partnership.

24. The withdrawal of a partner when payment is made from partners' personal assets is the direct opposite of admitting a new partner who purchases a partner's interest.
    a. Payment from partners' personal assets is a personal transaction between the partners.
    b. Partnership assets are not involved and total capital does not change.
    c. The effect on the partnership is limited to a realignment of the partners' capital balances.

25. Using partnership assets to pay for a withdrawing partner's interest is the reverse of admitting a partner through the investment of assets in the partnership.
    a. Payment from partnership assets is a transaction that involves the partnership.
    b. Both partnership net assets and total capitals are decreased.
    c. Asset reevaluations should not be recorded.

26. When the partnership assets paid are in excess of the withdrawing partner's capital interest, **a bonus to the retiring partner** results. The bonus is deducted from the remaining partners' capital balances on the basis of their income ratios at the time of the withdrawal.

27. When the partnership assets paid are less than the withdrawing partner's capital interest, a **bonus to the remaining partners** results. The bonus is allocated to the capital accounts of the remaining partners on the basis of their income ratios.

Death of a Partner

28. The death of a partner dissolves the partnership, but provision generally is made for the surviving partners to continue operations. When a partner dies it is necessary to determine the partner's equity at the date of death.

Liquidation of a Partnership

29. (S.O. 7) The liquidation of a partnership terminates the business. In a **liquidation,** it is necessary to:
    a. Sell noncash assets for cash and recognize a gain or loss on realization.
    b. Allocate gain/loss on realization to the partners based on their income ratios.
    c. Pay partnership liabilities in cash.
    d. Distribute remaining cash to partners on the basis of their remaining capital balances.

Each of the steps must be performed in sequence.

30. The liquidation of a partnership may result in **no capital deficiency** (all partners have credit balances in their capital accounts) or in a **capital deficiency** (at least one partner's capital account has a debit balance.)

31. A **schedule of cash payments** may be used to determine the distribution of cash to each partner.

32. When there is a capital deficiency, the partners with the deficiency may pay the amount owed and the deficiency is eliminated.

33. If a partner with a capital deficiency is unable to pay the amount owed to the partnership, the partners with credit balances must absorb the loss as follows:
   a. The cash distributed to each partner is the difference between the partner's present capital balance and the loss that the partner may have to absorb if the capital deficiency is not paid.
   b. The allocation of the deficiency is made on the income ratios that exist between the partners with credit balances. The allocation is journalized and posted.

DEMONSTRATION PROBLEM (S.O. 5 and 6)

Montana and Fouts are partners who share income and losses in the ratio of 4:3, respectively. On October 31, their capital balances were: Montana, $145,000 and Fouts, $130,000. On that date they agreed to admit Elway as a partner with a 1/3 capital interest.   Elway invests $175,000 in the partnership. The income ratios for Montana, Fouts, and Elway are 4 : 3 : 2 respectively. On November 1, Fouts decides to retire from the partnership and the partnership pays Fouts $100,000 for his partnership interest. Assume there was no income on October 31, and November 1.

Instructions
(a) Make the journal entry on October 31 that admits Elway to the partnership.
(b) Make the journal entry on November 1 that retires Fouts from the partnership.

SOLUTION TO DEMONSTRATION PROBLEM

(a) Cash.. 175,000
           Montana, Capital [($175,000 - $150,000) X 4/7]................   14,286
           Fouts, Capital [($175,000 - $150,000) X 3/7].....................   10,714
           Elway, Capital [($145,000 + $130,000 + $175,000 ÷ 3].....   150,000

(b) Fouts, Capital ($130,000 + $10,714) 140,714
           Montana, Capital ($40,714 X 4/6)......................................   27,143
           Elway, Capital ($40,714 X 2/6)   13,571
           Cash   100,000
       (To record withdrawal of Fouts and bonus to
         remaining partners)

REVIEW QUESTIONS AND EXERCISES

TRUE—FALSE

Indicate whether each of the following is true (T) or false (F) in the space provided.

_____ 1. (S.O. 1) The Uniform Partnership Act provides the basic rules for the formation and operation of partnerships.

_____ 2. (S.O. 1) A partnership is an association of no more than two persons to carry on as co-owners of a business for profit.

_____ 3. (S.O. 1) In order for a partnership to be legally binding, a contract in writing is needed.

_____ 4. (S.O. 1) The purely personal assets, liabilities, and personal transactions of the partners are excluded from the accounting records of the partnership.

_____ 5. (S.O. 1) A partnership has a limited life.

_____ 6. (S.O. 1) Each partner is personally and individually liable for all partnership liabilities.

_____ 7. (S.O. 1) Under a limited partnership, at least half of the partners must be general partners.

_____ 8. (S.O. 1) Once assets have been invested in the partnership, they are owned jointly by all partners.

_____ 9. (S.O. 1) An advantage of a partnership is the mutual agency that exists.

_____ 10. (S.O. 1) A disadvantage of a partnership is the "red tape" that must be faced when forming the partnership due to government regulations and restrictions.

_____ 11. (S.O. 1) The articles of co-partnership are a written partnership agreement that contains such basic information as the name and principal location of the firm.

_____ 12. (S.O. 2) Each partner's initial investment in a partnership should be recorded at book value.

_____ 13. (S.O. 2) A partnership may start with an Allowance for Doubtful Accounts.

_____ 14. (S.O. 3) Partnership income is shared in proportion to each partner's capital equity interest unless the partnership contract specifically indicates the manner in which net income or net loss is to be divided.

_____ 15. (S.O. 3) When the partnership agreement specifically provides for salaries and interest, the provisions must be applied before the remainder of net income or net loss is divided.

_____ 16. (S.O. 5)   In an admission of a partner by investment of assets, the total net assets and total capital of the partnership do not change.

_____ 17. (S.O. 5)   A bonus to old partners results when the new partner's capital credit on the date of admittance is less than the new partner's investment of assets in the partnership.

_____ 18. (S.O. 6)   The withdrawal of a partner legally dissolves the partnership.

_____ 19. (S.O. 6)   A bonus to the remaining partners will result when the cash paid to the retiring partner is greater than the retiring partner's capital balance.

_____ 20. (S.O. 7)   In a liquidation, the final distribution of cash to partners should be on the basis of their income ratios.

MULTIPLE CHOICE

Circle the letter that best answers each of the following statements.

1. (S.O. 1) Which of the following would not be considered a characteristic of a partnership?
    a.   Mutual agency.
    b.   Unlimited life.
    c.   Unlimited liability.
    d.   Co-ownership of property.

2. (S.O. 1) Which of the following would **not** be considered an advantage of forming a partnership?
    a.   Skills and resources can be combined.
    b.   A partnership is easily formed.
    c.   A partnership has unlimited liability.
    d.   A partnership is relatively free from governmental regulations and restrictions.

3. (S.O. 1) The Unitas, Sayers, and Blanda partnership is terminated when the claims of company creditors exceed partnership assets by $50,000 The capital balances for Unitas, Sayers, and Blanda are $35,000, $5,000, and $0, respectively. The original claims of the creditors were negotiated by Sayers and Blanda. Which partner(s) is(are) personally and individually liable for all partnership liabilities?:
    a.   Unitas.
    b.   Sayers.
    c.   Sayers and Blanda.
    d.   Unitas, Sayers, and Blanda.

4. (S.O. 2) J. Nicklaus and S. Snead combine their individual sole proprietorships to start the Nicklaus-Snead partnership. J. Nicklaus and S. Snead invest in the partnership as follows:

	Book Value		Market Value	
	Nicklaus	**Snead**	**Nicklaus**	**Snead**
Cash	$7,000	$2,000	$7,000	$2,000
Accounts Receivable	3,000	1,000	3,000	1,000
Allowance for Doubtful				
Accounts	(500)	(200)	(700)	(300)
Equipment	5,000	8,000	4,500	3,000
Accumulated Depreciation	(1,000)	(3,000)		

The entries to record the investment will include a credit to:
a. Nicklaus, Capital of $13,500.
b. Snead, Capital of $5,700.
c. Nicklaus, Capital of $14,000.
d. Snead, Capital of $7,700.

5. (S.O. 3) The partnership agreement of Payton and Namath provides for salary allowances of $45,000 to Payton and $35,000 to Namath, with the remaining income or loss to be divided equally. During the year, Payton and Namath each withdraw cash equal to 80% of their salary allowances. If partnership net income is $100,000, Payton's equity in the partnership would:
a. increase more than Namath's.
b. decrease more than Namath's.
c. increase the same as Namath's.
d. decrease the same as Namath's.

The following information pertains to items 6 and 7.

The partnership agreement of Owens, Gehrig, and Nagurski provides for the following income ratio: (a) Owens, the managing partner, receives a salary allowance of $18,000, (b) each partner receives 15% interest on average capital investment, and (c) remaining net income or loss is divided equally. The average capital investments for the year were: Owens $100,000, Gehrig $200,000, and Nagurski $300,000.

6. (S.O. 3) If partnership net income is $120,000, the amount distributed to Gehrig should be:
a. $30,000.
b. $31,000.
c. $34,000.
d. $40,000.

7. (S.O. 3) If partnership net income is $90,000, the amount distributed to Owens should be:
a. $15,000.
b. $27,000.
c. $30,000.
d. $33,000.

8. (S.O. 5) H. Aaron joints the partnership of Kubek and Musial by paying $30,000 in cash. If the net assets of the partnership are still the same amount after Aaron has been admitted as a partner, then Aaron:
    a.   must have been admitted by investment of assets.
    b.   must have been admitted by purchase of a partner's interest.
    c.   must have received a bonus upon being admitted.
    d.   could have been admitted by an investment of assets or by a purchase of a partner's interest.

9. (S.O. 5) D. Butkus purchases a 25% interest for $10,000 when the Marchetti, Nomellini, Jones partnership has total capital of $90,000. Prior to the admission of Butkus, each partner has a capital balance of $30,000. Each partner relinquishes an equal amount of his capital balance to Butkus. The amount to be relinquished by Jones is:
    a. $5,000.
    b. $6,333.
    c. $7,500.
    d. $12,500.

10. (S.O. 5) S. Koufax invests $40,000 in cash in the DiMaggio and Mantle partnership for a one-third capital interest. If DiMaggio and Mantle each had $40,000 capital equity before the admission, what is Mantle's capital equity after the admission of Koufax?
    a. $26,667.
    b. $30,000.
    c. $40,000.
    d. $60,000.

11. (S.O. 5)   Jordon is admitted to a partnership with a 25% capital interest by a cash investment of $150,000. If total capital of the partnership is $650,000 before admitting Jordon, the bonus to Jordon is:
    a. $50,000.
    b. $25,000.
    c. $75,000.
    d. $100,000.

The following information pertains to items 12 and 13.

Ederle and Lenglen are partners who share income and losses in the ratio of 3 : 2, respectively. On August 31, their capital balances were: Ederle, $70,000 and Lenglen $60,000. On that date, they agree to admit Marble as a partner with a one-third capital interest.

12. (S.O. 5) If Marble invests $50,000 in the partnership, what is Ederle's capital balance after Marble's admittance?
    a. $60,000.
    b. $63,333.
    c. $64,000.
    d. $70,000.

13. (S.O. 5) If Marble invests $80,000 in the partnership, what is Lenglen's capital balance after Marble's admittance?
   a. $70,000.
   b. $64,000.
   c. $63,000.
   d. $60,000.

Items 14, 15, and 16 relate to the following information.

On November 30, capital balances are Holm $60,000, Berg $50,000 and Madison $50,000. The income ratios are 20%, 20% and 60% respectively. Holm decides to retire from the partnership.

14. (S.O. 6) The partnership pays Holm $70,000 cash for her partnership interest. After Holm's retirement, what is the balance of Berg's capital account?
   a. $47,500.
   b. $48,000.
   c. $50,000.
   d. $65,000.

15. (S.O. 6) The partnership pays Holm $50,000 cash for her partnership interest. After Holm's retirement, what is the balance of Madison's capital account?
   a. $44,000.
   b. $50,000.
   c. $56,000.
   d. $57,500.

16. (S.O. 6) In order for Berg and Madison to have equal capital interests after the retirement of Holm, how much partnership cash would have to be paid to Holm for her partnership interest?
   a. $0.
   b. $53,333.
   c. $60,000.
   d. Any amount paid to Holm will cause Berg and Madison to still have equal capital balances.

17. (S.O. 7) In the liquidation of a partnership, the gains and losses from assets sold are:
   a. divided equally among the partners.
   b. divided among the partners in the stated income ratio.
   c. divided among the partners in proportion to their capital equity interests.
   d. ignored.

18. (S.O. 7) In liquidation, balances prior to the distribution of cash to the partners are: Cash $240,000; Marciano, Capital $112,000; Tunney, Capital $104,000, and Jeffries, Capital $24,000. The income ratio is 6 : 2 : 2, respectively. How much cash should be distributed to Marciano?
   a. $100,000.
   b. $109,000.
   c. $112,000.
   d. $120,000.

19. (S.O. 7) Assume the same facts in question 18 above, except that there is only $204,000 in cash and Jeffries has a capital deficiency of $12,000. How much cash should be distributed to Tunney if Jeffries does not pay his deficiency?
    a. $98,000.
    b. $101,000.
    c. $95,000.
    d. $104,000.

20. (S.O. 7) An entry is not required in the liquidation of a partnership to record the:
    a. payment of cash to creditors.
    b. distribution of cash to the partners.
    c. sale of noncash assets.
    d. allocation of a capital deficiency to partners with credit balances when the deficient partners is expected to pay the deficiency.

MATCHING

Match each term with its definition by writing the appropriate letter in the space provided.

Terms

_____ 1. Uniform Partnership Act.

_____ 2. Unlimited liability.

_____ 3. Partnership agreement.

_____ 4. Partnership.

_____ 5. Schedule of cash payments.

_____ 6. Mutual agency.

_____ 7. Partners' capital statement.

_____ 8. Co-ownership of property.

_____ 9. Limited partnership.

_____ 10. Income ratio.

_____ 11. Capital deficiency.

Definitions

a. Each partner acts on behalf of the partnership when engaging in partnership business.

b. Provides the basic rules for the formation and operation of partnerships in over ninety percent of the states.

c. A partnership in which the liability of one or more partners is limited to the partner's capital equity.

d. The basis for dividing both net income and net loss in a partnership.

e. The owners' equity statement for a partnership.

f. Once assets have been invested in the partnership they are owned jointly by all the partners.

g. An association of two or more persons to carry on as co-owners of a business for profit.

h A contract expressing the voluntary agreement of two or more individuals in a partnership.

i. Each partner is personally and individually liable for all partnership liabilities.

j. A debit balance in a partner's capital account.

k. A schedule showing the distribution of cash to the partners in the liquidation of a partnership.

The Navigator

EXERCISES

EX. 13-1 (S.O. 3) A partnership agreement between W. Chamberlain and B. Russell provides for (1) salary allowances of $36,000 to Chamberlain and $35,500 to Russell, (2) interest allowances of 10% on beginning capital balances, and (3) remaining income or loss is to be divided equally. The beginning capital balances are Chamberlain $76,000 and Russell $54,000, and net income is $90,000.

Instructions
(a) Prepare a schedule for the division of net income.
(b) Record the closing entry to transfer the net income to the partners' capital accounts.

(a)
                                   Division of Net Income

	Chamberlain	Russell	Total
Salary allowance			
Interest allowance			
Chamberlain			
Russell			
Total interest			
Total salaries and interest			
Remaining income			
Chamberlain			
Russell			
Total remainder			
Total division			

(b)

	General Journal		J1
Date	Account Title	Debit	Credit

EX. 13-2 (S.O. 7) In the HOG Company, partners Hull, Orr, and Gretzky have income ratios of 3 : 2 : 1. At the time of liquidation the balance sheet shows: Cash $40,000; Noncash assets $204,000; Liabilities $160,000; Hull, Capital $52,000; Orr, Capital $24,000; and Gretzky, Capital $8,000. The noncash assets are sold for $168,000 in cash.

Instructions
(a) Prepare a schedule of cash payments.
(b) Journalize the transactions assuming creditors are paid in full and available cash is distributed to the partners.

(a)

HOG COMPANY
Schedule of Cash Payments

Item	Cash	+	Noncash Assets	=	Liabilities	+	Hull, Capital	+	Orr, Capital	+	Gretzky, Capital
Balances before liquidation											
Sale of noncash assets and allocation of loss											
New balances											
Pay liabilities											
New balances											
Cash distribution to partners											
Final balances											

(b)

	General Journal		J1
Date	Account Title	Debit	Credit

The
Navigator

SOLUTIONS TO REVIEW QUESTIONS AND EXERCISES

TRUE-FALSE

1. (T)
2. (F) A partnership is a voluntary association of two or more individuals to carry on as co-owners of a business for profit.
3. (F) A partnership may be based on as simple an act as a handshake.
4. (T)
5. (T)
6. (T)
7. (F) Under a limited partnership, there must be at least one partner with unlimited liability, often referred to as the general partner.
8. (T)
9. (F) Mutual agency is thought of as a disadvantage because one partner can legally bind all of the other partners without the other partners' approval.
10. (F) An advantage of a partnership is that it is relatively free from government regulations and restrictions.
11. (T)
12. (F) Each partner's initial investment in a partnership should be recorded at the fair market value of the assets at the date of their transfer to the partnership.
13. (T)
14. (F) Partnership income or loss is shared equally unless the partnership contract specifically indicates the manner in which net income or net loss is to be divided.
15. (T)
16. (F) In an admission by investment of assets, the new partner is investing an asset of value to the partnership which will increase the net assets and total capital of the partnership.
17. (T)
18. (T)
19. (F) A bonus to the remaining partners will result when the cash paid to the retiring partner is less than the retiring partner's capital balance.
20. (F) In liquidation, cash should be distributed to partners on the basis of their remaining capital balances.

MULTIPLE CHOICE

1. (b) A partnership does not have unlimited life. Any change in the number of partners, regardless of the cause, results in the dissolution of the partnership. The other answer choices are all considered characteristics of a partnership.

2. (c) Unlimited liability is a disadvantage of a partnership. The other choices are advantageous.

3. (d) Each partner is personally and individually liable for all partnership liabilities. Creditors' claims attach first to partnership assets and then extend to the personal resources of any partner, irrespective of that partner's capital equity in the company.

4. (b) Each partner's initial investment in a partnership should be recorded at the fair market value of the assets at the date of their transfer to the partnership. Thus, Nicklaus' capital interest would equal $13,800, and Snead's $5,700.

5. (a) Salaries to partners are not expenses of the partnership, rather, they increase a partner's capital. Payton and Namath increased their capital accounts through a salary allowance by $45,000 and $35,000, respectively. Each had withdrawals equal to 80% of their salary causing 20% of their salaries to remain in the business. Therefore, Payton and Namath had a net increase in their equity due to salaries and withdrawals of $9,000 and $7,000 respectively. By adding the equally divided remaining net income, Payton's equity in the partnership has increased $2,000 more than Namath's.

6. (c) The division of net income is:

	Owens	Gehrig	Nagurski
Salary allowance	$18,000	$ ---	$ --
15% interest on average capital	15,000	30,000	45,000
Remainder $12,000 divided equally	4,000	4,000	4,000
Total division	$37,000	$34,000	$49,000

7. (b) The division of net income is:

	Owens	Gehrig	Nagurski
Salary allowance	$18,000	$ ---	$ --
15% interest on average capital	15,000	30,000	45,000
Remainder ($18,000) divided equally	(6,000)	(6,000)	(6,000)
Total division	$27,000	$24,000	$39,000

8. (b) In a purchase of a partner's interest, the total net assets and total capital of the partnership do not change. In admission by investment of assets, both the total net assets and the total capital change. If Aaron received a bonus upon being admitted (c), then he was admitted by investment of assets and total assets and the total capital changed.

9. (a) Total capital of the new partnership is $100,000 ($90,000 + $100,000). Butkus receives a 25% interest or $25,000. Since Butkus invested $10,000 he receives a bonus of $15,000 ($25,000 - $10,000). The three partners relinquish an equal share of their capital for the bonus, or each relinquishes $5,000.

10. (c) Because Koufax is investing $40,000 in cash in the partnership, the total capital equity will equal $120,000. His investment is equal to 1/3 of $120,000. Therefore, no bonus is given and Mantle's capital equity after the admission of Koufax will remain at $40,000.

11. (a) The total capital of the partnership after admitting Jordon is $800,000 ($650,000 + $150,000). Jordon's equity is $200,000 ($800,000 X 25%). The excess of the capital credit over the assets invested is the bonus to Jordon ($200,000 - $150,000 = $50,000).

12.   (c)   The total capital of the new partnership is $180,000 ($130,000 + $50,000). Marble is to receive a 1/3 interest or $60,000. Thus, a bonus of $10,000 ($60,000 - $50,000) is given to Marble. The bonus is allocated to the old partners on the basis of their income ratios which are 3 : 2. As a result, Ederle's capital balance will decrease $6,000 ($10,000 X 3/5) to $64,000 ($70,000 - $6,000).

13.   (b)   The total capital of the new partnership is $210,000 ($130,000 + $80,000). Marble is receiving a capital interest of $70,000 ($210,000 X 1/3) that is less than her investment of $80,000. Thus, a bonus of $10,000 is given to the old partners on the basis of their income ratios which are 3 : 2. As a result, Lenglen's capital interest will increase by $4,000 ($10,000 X 2/5) to $64,000 ($60,000 + $4,000).

14.   (a)   A bonus of $10,000 is given to Holm because the $70,000 payment is greater than Holm's capital interest of $60,000. The bonus is allocated to Berg and Madison on the income ratio that exists between them which is 20 : 60. Therefore, Berg's share of the bonus is $2,500 ($10,000 X 20/80) and the new capital balance is $47,500 ($50,000 - $2,500).

15.   (d)   A bonus of $10,000 is given to the remaining partners because the payment of $50,000 is less than the retiring partner's $60,000 capital interest. The bonus is allocated to Berg and Madison based on the income ratio that exists between them which is 20 : 60. Therefore, Madison's share of the bonus is $7,500 ($10,000 X 60/80) and the new capital balance is $57,500 ($50,000 + $7,500).

16.   (c)   Before retirement of Holm, Berg and Madison have equal capital balances. Since Berg and Madison have unequal income sharing percentages, any bonus will cause an unequal distribution between them. Thus, Holm will have to receive an amount equal to her capital interest ($60,000) in order for Berg and Madison to remain with equal capital balances.

17.   (b)   In liquidation, it is necessary to convert all noncash assets into cash and to allocate all gains or losses on the basis of the partners' stated income ratio.

18.   (c)   All partners have credit balances because the sum of the capital balances equals the balance in cash. Since the cash is distributed on the basis of capital balances, Marciano will receive $112,000 in cash.

19.   (b)   Jeffries' capital deficiency must be allocated to the partners with credit balances on the basis of their income ratios which is 60 : 20. Thus, Tunney's share of the deficiency is $3,000 ($12,000 X 20/80) and the cash to be distributed to Tunney is $101,000 ($104,000 - $3,000).

20.   (d)   No entry is made to record the allocation of a capital deficiency when payment of the deficiency is expected. When payment occurs, an entry is made in which Cash is debited and the deficient partner's capital account is credited.

MATCHING

1.	b	7.	e	
2.	i	8.	f	
3.	h	9.	c	
4.	g	10.	d	
5.	k	11.	j	
6.	a			

EXERCISES

EX. 13-1

(a)   <u>**Division of Net Income**</u>

	Chamberlain	Russell	Total
Salary allowance	$36,000	$35,500	$71,500
Interest allowance			
Chamberlain ($76,000 X 10%)	7,600		
Russell ($54,000 X 10%)		5,400	
Total interest			13,000
Total salaries and interest	43,600	40,900	84,500
Remaining income, $5,500 ($90,000 – $84,500)			
Chamberlain ($5,500 X 50%)	2,750		
Russell ($5,500 X 50%)		2,750	
Total remainder			5,500
Total division	$46,350	$43,650	$90,000

(b)

General Journal			J1
Date	Account Title	Debit	Credit
Dec. 31	Income Summary	90,000	
	W. Chamberlain, Capital		46,350
	B. Russell, Capital		43,650
	(To close net income to partners'		
	capital accounts)		

EX. 13-2

(a)

HOG COMPANY
Schedule of Cash Payments

Item	Cash	+	Noncash Assets	=	Liabilities	+	Hull, Capital	+	Orr, Capital	+	Gretzky, Capital
Balances before liquidation	40,000	+	204,000	=	$160,000	+	52,000	+	24,000	+	8,000
Sale of noncash assets and allocation of loss	168,000	+	(204,000)	=			(18,000)*	+	(12,000)*	+	(6,000)*
New balances	208,000	+	-0-	=	160,000	+	34,000	+	12,000	+	2,000
Pay liabilities	(160,000)		-0-	=	(160,000)						
New balances	48,000	+	-0-	=	-0-	+	34,000	+	12,000	+	2,000
Cash distribution to partners	(48,000)						(34,000)	+	(12,000)	+	(2,000)
Final balances	-0-	+	-0-	=	-0-	+	-0-	+	-0-	+	-0-

*Loss on sale is $36,000 allocated 3/6 to Hull, 2/6 to Orr and 1/6 to Gretzky.

(b)

	General Journal		J1
Date	**Account Title**	**Debit**	**Credit**
	Cash	168,000	
	Loss on Realization	36,000	
	Noncash Assets		204,000
	(To record realization of noncash		
	assets)		
	Hull, Capital ($36,000 X 3/6)	18,000	
	Orr, Capital ($36,000 X 2/6)	12,000	
	Gretzky, Capital ($36,000 X 1/6)	6,000	
	Loss on Realization		36,000
	(To allocate loss on realization to		
	partners)		
	Liabilities	160,000	
	Cash		160,000
	(To record payment of partnership		
	liabilities)		
	Hull, Capital ($52,000 - $18,000)	34,000	
	Orr, Capital ($24,000 - $12,000)	12,000	
	Gretzky, Capital ($8,000 - $6,000)	2,000	
	Cash		48,000
	(To record distribution of cash to		
	partners)		

	1																	
1																		1
2																		2
3																		3
4																		4
5																		5
6																		6
7																		7
8																		8
9																		9
10																		10
11																		11
12																		12
13																		13
14																		14
15																		15
16																		16
17																		17
18																		18
19																		19
20																		20
21																		21
22																		22
23																		23
24																		24
25																		25
26																		26
27																		27
28																		28
29																		29
30																		30
31																		31
32																		32
33																		33
34																		34
35																		35
36																		36
37																		37
38																		38
39																		39
40																		40

	1	2	3	4	5	6	7	8	9	10	11	12	13	
1														1
2														2
3														3
4														4
5														5
6														6
7														7
8														8
9														9
10														10
11														11
12														12
13														13
14														14
15														15
16														16
17														17
18														18
19														19
20														20
21														21
22														22
23														23
24														24
25														25
26														26
27														27
28														28
29														29
30														30
31														31
32														32
33														33
34														34
35														35
36														36
37														37
38														38
39														39
40														40